THE END IS...?

Rev. Nemu

THE NEMU'S END SERIES:

BOOK I: SCIENCE REVEALED

BOOK II: NEURO-APOCALYPSE

BOOK III: APOCALYPSES PAST, PRESENT AND PERSONAL

NEMU'S END

The History, Psychology
& Poetry of the
Apocalypse

Volume II:

NEURO-
APOCALYPSE

Published by Psychedelic Press
Printed in Cornwall, UK

www.psychedelicpress.co.uk

ISBN: 9780992808822

For the Daughters of the Voice

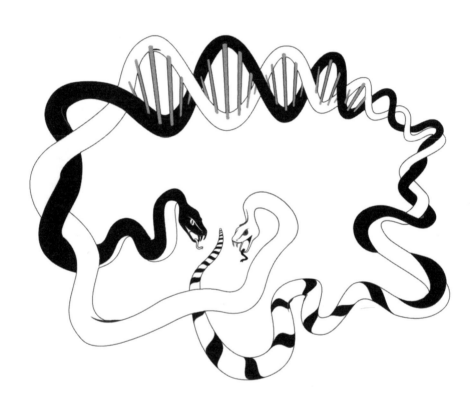

CONTENTS

JAPANESE WHISPERS

*If any man preach any other Gospel unto you than that
ye have received, let him be accursed.*

- Galatians 1:9

N THE BEGINNING, in the very first week of a four-year stay in Kyoto, a Japanese man in a dapper suit appeared at my door bearing books. I had been witnessed by the Jehovah's Witnesses, and a bilingual missionary had been dispatched. The apocalypse is never far from my doorstep, and there it was again, wearing a cravat.

Though I enjoy the company of rude apocalypticals, I had already read two histories of the Witnesses and stacks of their literature while researching their beliefs on medicine in comparison with other doomsday cults of history. They were academically interesting, to a point, but that point had been passed, and I had long ago forsworn the baiting of narrow-minded Christians for sport. When the witness at the door introduced himself as William (*née* Takeya), and told me in a slightly posh British accent that he had lived in York for ten years, I became intrigued by him as a cross-cultural, trans-global, post-modern instance of the religious impulse. I sent him away with my dissertation (which I kept on hand for this very occasion), and told him I would speak with him again once he had read it.

He returned the following week with his wife, and I invited them across the threshold. My funky skinhead girlfriend (whose threshold it was) and my curmudgeonly guests eyed each other with mutual disapproval before she bolted upstairs, and then William turned his attention to my work.

"You have quoted many books," he began, "but you have not quoted the Bible."

I argued that other books were more relevant to comparative history. Moreover, I continued, the Bible could make for treacherous reading, and had led the elders of his church to no less than seven failed doomsday predictions between 1873 and 1975.[1] He replied that said final (mis)judgements were not relevant to the modern Witnesses, who had ceased to set dates. This tit-for-tat nastiness wasn't going anywhere, so we moved on to scripture and touched briefly on Taoism, but William appeared to be in some discomfort. Eventually he explained that he had been sitting Western-style in chairs for so long that his knees were severely tested by sitting cross-legged on the floor in the usual Japanese fashion. There were no chairs in the house, so William decided he would stand.

His wife helped him to his feet. She was not as Westernized as his knees, her English was poor and thickly accented, and she barely entered the discussion. On one occasion, however, she piped up with a scriptural point, repeating a word several times for my benefit. As an English teacher I tend to be quite good at deciphering accents, but I couldn't make it out.

"Fruitage," said William, helpfully and with excellent diction.

"*Fruitage?*" I echoed, suppressing a giggle. It's a silly word, and it sounds like 'frottage'.

"Yes. Fruitage."

"That's not a word," I explained, with the calm authority of a professional.

"It's a biblical word," he replied, with the calm authority of a dedicated Bible-thumper. He flipped deftly through well-worn pages of the New World Translation, and smiled warmly as he pointed to the verse. There was no arguing with the book, but I wasn't happy – the word would have merited nothing less than an angry red line in any reasonable educational institution. His wife could barely string a sentence together, how could she possibly have beaten the teacher?

This accursed collective noun is found in the Epistle to the Galatians, St. Paul's grumbling missive about how churches were interpreting the Gospels a few Greek whispers away. Galatians and the rest of the New Testament date from generations after the stories they describe, and are written in Greek even though the language of Jerusalem was Aramaic. That, however, was just the beginning of the story's drift across different cultures. The first centuries of the Common Era saw an explosion of texts, as radical Jews and bi-curious pagans retold the story around the Mediterranean. In the 1st century there were at least twenty contemporary Gospels, written from various perspectives, including the Gospels of Judas and Mary Magdalene.[2] They record different details, and present radically divergent philosophies. All except the fab four (Matthew, Mark, Luke and John) were declared heretical in the 2nd century, and even these contradict each other. The writings of St. Paul set the standard for orthodoxy, exalting the virtues of a docile citizen with "the fruitage of the spirit is love, joy, peace, patience, kindness, goodness, faith, mildness, self-control".[3]

Translations of the censored canon multiplied in different languages over the next millennium and a half, and then this litter of bastards was hastily compiled into several versions of the Greek Textus Receptus, all heavy with typographical and translation errors. These became one source for our familiar King James Version (KJV) of 1611. The other source was the Vulgate, translated into Latin in the 4th century by St. Jerome, a passionate misogynist who described the Jewish prophets as "rude and repellent".[4] The KJV faithfully retains the errors and prejudices of both sources. Its translators were not Hebrew scholars, and didn't care to consult the rabbis who were, so they couldn't learn much directly from the Old Testament. King James demanded something simple and uncontroversial, and with few textual notes, so much of the philosophical complexity was lost. Political hard lines softened. Matthew's lines about the coming "end of the epoch" became an unthinkably distant "end of the world".[5] This is "the Apocalypse" dressed up for politics rather than its nemesis, a final event to wait for rather than a transformative possibility to seize.

The KJV is a politicized rendition of a compilation of translations of contradictory transcripts written in a language foreign to the characters who performed its rather far-fetched episodes. It makes for admirable poetry, if you like that kind of thing, and millions have taken it as gospel; but is it the Word of God? The Witnesses went further with their own translation, which is better in many ways, though it also introduces their own particular bias. There's more "Jehovah" to be witnessed, for one thing, even in the New Testament where the terrible name is not used at all in the Greek. There is also more "fruitage". The Witness Bible translates Matthew's line faithfully, as "the end of the age" rather than the end of the world. That end is the subject of book 3 of this series. The book in your hands is about an apocalypse far more personal, when the veil (*kaluptein*) is drawn away (*apo-*) in the human mind, and we will be crashing through veils of linguistics, psychology, psychedelics and politics to reveal it. We can learn something about all of these fields by exploring the literary tradition that began 3000 years ago in the Judean hills and has been doctored by generations of scribes ever since.

The Hebrew Torah is written without vowels or punctuation. The original scrolls, which were written in Paleo-Hebrew and are now lost, may not have had spaces between words either; other examples of that script from that time didn't.[67] According to the great sage Nachmanides, the Ramban of blessed memory, it was originally written in black fire on white fire without spaces, and it reveals different secrets according to how the words are broken up:[8]

AWORDSENDSWHEREYOUWISH

A WORD'S END'S WHERE YOU WISH

A WORD SENDS WHERE YOU WISH

Hebrew biblical verses are extremely poetically constructed, switching plural and singulars, placing in places ambiguous ambidextrous adjectives. Consonants harden or soften and vowels switch according to the letters around them, according to the preferences and habits of the reader. The Hebrew Bible is said to have 70 faces, with one for every angle on a verse.[9] Meaning shifts as understanding drifts on a tongue so flexible, where *yada* means 'to show', 'to distinguish', 'to know' and 'to have intercourse with'. "And Adam knew the woman Eve", but what can we really know about a woman who can be read so many ways?[10] She justified her famous indiscretion saying "the serpent beguiled me"; but the same letters pronounced differently say "the serpent elevated me".[11] Like people in their multifaceted complexity, like subatomic particles spinning spookily, the letters of the Hebrew Bible behave differently in different contexts, depending on the perspective of the person generating meaning from them.

Changing the vocalization of the vowels shifts the meaning around, which is hinted at by the fact that the Hebrew word for 'vowel' also means 'movement': *tenu'ah*.[12] Different vowellings can send a passage off in totally different directions, so flexible readers could read and reread, reconstructing meaning as they explored the text and the self, responding to the particular challenges facing them and their communities. The sense of a verse was up for grabs until the 7th century AD, when the Masoretes imposed a standardized pronunciation scheme, inventing a set of vowel points to accompany the letters. As one orthodox scholar puts it:

> The vowel points alone add whole conjugations to the language. This system is one of the most artificial, particular, and extensive comments ever written on the Word of God; for there is not one word in the Bible that is not the subject of a particular gloss through its influence.[13]

Even this standard didn't become standard everywhere; the Eastern churches still read a different translation of the Old Testament today, based on a variant vowelling of the Hebrew. In certain Jewish circles the word games continued even after standardization, though nothing was published until the 13th century, when the Zohar began with a different beginning:

> With a beginning, [it] created Elohim, the heavens and the earth.[14]

Put like this, something is there before Elohim, something nameless that created Elohim. This arrangement beautifully evokes, both in sentiment and detail, the first verse of another ancient classic with a twisty tongue, the *Tao Te Ching*:

> The Tao that can be told of is not the eternal Tao;
>> The name that can be named is not the eternal name.
> The nameless is the origin of Heaven and Earth;
>> The named is the mother of all things.[15]

Elohim says far more than the English 'God'. The grammar surrounding it points at a singular word, even though ~*im* is a plural ending. *El* means 'strength' or 'power', pluralised as *elim*, but *elohim* adds an extra letter *H*. *H* signifies the feminine, being a feminine singular noun ending. *Elohim* is sometimes feminine, described as "she" in the Zohar, and Moses as her "husband" elsewhere.[16][17] Capital G 'God' is a masculine singular proper noun, but *elohim* has masculine, feminine, singular and plural nuances. It is all of them, or beyond all of them. The same word denotes pagan gods and goddess. Ashtoreth appears three times in the Bible, twice as "the goddess [*elohim*] of the Zidonians" and once as "the abomination of the Zidonians".[18]

Tongues twist around words bitten off, but few tongues twist like Hebrew. The Ramban takes the first fourteen letters of the Bible as an example, breaking them up differently to reveal a completely different genesis:[19]

> In the head Elohim has been created.*

This rewording is rather more germane to our story of the neuro-apocalypse, and it was proposed by one of the most exalted Jewish scholars of all time. One might continue slicing up the following words in the same vein:

> You are heavens, and you are earth.†

Debate over text is central to Jewish tradition, and the more semantic and linguistic somersaults that are turned during the argument the better. Sometimes a conclusion remains elusive. In one Talmudic legend a delighted heavenly voice calls out, "Both these and those are words of the living God!" in support of two contradictory opinions, and even the voice can be interpreted in several ways.[20] It could also mean "Both these and those are the *living* words of God!"

Legend recalls that the earth was plunged into darkness for three days when the Torah was first translated into Greek.[21] Greek words have a much narrower spectrum of meanings, and Greek grammar carves out words more sharply than Hebrew does, canalizing thought more strictly and offering less freedom of interpretation. The new Greek scriptures were less ambiguous, and often incompatible with one another, leaving little space for constructive debate between sects and texts.

---

* Genesis 1:1: בראשיתבראאלהיםאתהשמימסואתהארץ

בראשית ברא אלהים - In the beginning, God created...

בראש יתברא אלהים - In the head, God was / the gods were created.

† את השמים ו את הארץ - ...the heavens and the earth

אתה שמים ו אתה ארץ - You are heavens, and you are earth.

Whereas Hebrew arguments revolved around interpretations of words and stories, classical philosophy sought to establish 'the truth' using rhetoric, grammar and logic – the tools left behind by Aristotle. A rabbi's proposition is an invitation for a friendly mental wrestling match amongst learned equals, whereas priests in the Hellenistic world read passages to the unlettered, giving sermons from the pulpit as statesmen or philosophers might address the public square. Hebrew magic was recast as Greek tragedy. Those who followed *hetero-doxa* (different doctrines), rather than *ortho-doxa* (correct/straight doctrines) were decried, as Paul chastised the Galatians. Heretics continued to be persecuted down the centuries, and even today groups are excommunicated for practices "irreconcilable with a coherent living of the Catholic Faith".[22]

"We are all Greeks," wrote Shelley, "our laws, our literature, our religion, our arts have their root in Greece."[23] Fortunately our sexual mores aren't rooted too deeply in Greece, else we'd all be pederasts as well, but our sciences certainly are. Science took over from religion the business of protecting people from teachings that are not the correct teachings. The true nature of things remains the principle object of inquiry, and Aristotle's three laws of thought are still almighty in public debate and the academy:

1) the law of identity: A is A

2) the law of non-contradiction: NOT (A and not A)

3) the law of the excluded middle: EITHER (A or not A)

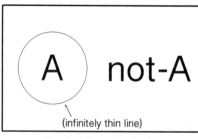
(infinitely thin line)

Fig. 1 Aristotelian logic

Put another way, something is what it is, it isn't what it isn't, and everything is either something or something else. These laws are the founding stones of Western philosophy,

18

and they rest squarely upon the solid, unambiguous bedrock of Greek grammar. If your thinking does not follow these laws then you aren't thinking straight, according to Aristotle. You are probably thinking bendy.

Centuries before Aristotle, pre-Socratic philosophers questioned the rigid edges of Greek syntax. If individual grains of sand fall one by one upon the ground, asked Eubulides of Miletus, at what exact point do 'grains' become 'a heap'? His grains were swept under the carpet when Aristotle's laws of thought became common sense, and ambiguity remains insufferable in the lab and the lawcourt. Even in humour, *double entendre* and puns are answered with painful groans. In Hebrew scripture, by contrast, puns are keys to mysteries, and ambiguity is abundant. Gender fluidity, for example, is not only evidenced in the name of Elohim, but also in biblical stories where Eve is described as "he" and Noah goes into "her" tent.[24] The categories were sharpened up in translation, and some of the men on the margin were absorbed into the Christian clergy, where they could wear all kinds of fabulous dresses as long as they remained "wedded to God" and outside of normal social and sexual relations. Such dichotemies have grown brittle over the ages, but only in the 1st century ADBC (After David Bowie Cometh) have Olympic judges had to decide whether an athelete should compete against men or women.[25]

With Aristotle's laws of logic everything either is or isn't, and every wall casts a shadow. The shadows flickered spectacularly with a series of paradoxical interference patterns observed in the physics of the very small at the turn of the 20th century. 'Both these waves and those particles are the living words of God!', cries the kabbalist cosmologist in delight. Once again learned experts are being called upon to interpret the meaning of signs and numbers on print-outs that evoke a reality that defies 'common sense'. Objectivity fails as the observer's spin is spun back into the spin of the smallest.

With spookiness in physics, paradox in psychology and doublespeak in politics, 'the truth' is becoming ever more multifaceted. Aristotle's veils were punctured by a series of revelations – Paracelsus poisoned his medicine, Descartes picked apart his maths, Galileo blurred his optics and Einstein time-stretched his continuum, and yet we are still stuck with his bloody-minded *well-is-it-or-isn't-it?* logic. Binary logic is still considered 'common sense', and we have forgotten that there used to be other ways to think. But we are beginning to remember.

Science Revealed, the first book of this trilogy, ambushed rationalism in the fields of science and roughed it up against the razor-wire fences. *Neuro-Apocalypse* besieges the fortress that keeps watch over the fields, beginning in the beginning:

> In the beginning was the Word [Logos], and the Word was with God, and the Word was God [...] [and] all things were made by him[26]

Now I dig the concept of the Logos, and this verse expresses it with beautifully poetic rhythm and recursive repetition. John the Evangelist and I have spent many happy hours alone together with our thoughts, but on the other hand – for there is only one other hand with so sharp a tongue – "In the beginning was the Logos" sounds like a rather exclusive proposition with which to begin a creation story. In the opening verse John is already rasping against the poetry of the *Tao Te Ching*, whereas the older, smoother tongue of Genesis kissed the Tao at its opening. The New Testament (NT) has some great bits, some crap bits, and some irresolvable contradictions – a truly dualistic text on many levels. What really sets it apart from the Old Testament (OT) is the language itself and the binary logic built into it. Though the Aristotelian exclusive proposition fails dismally at describing our multi-layered minds and universes, it is formidable in the senate, the academy and the lawcourt, as well as on the battlefield. Aristotle's star pupil Alexander rode out to conquer the known world as soon as he came of age, leaving mass graves and torched cities in his wake. Mighty indeed is the sword of the Logos, slicing the skin to peer within; but an unfathomably deep abyss yawns beneath the wound.

With the Greek NT and the Latin Vulgate, and later with the English KJV, the word was made flesh and crucified upon the unforgiving frame of Indo-European grammar. The Christian culture that grew in and out of expanding empires proved to have an amazing capacity for self-replication, and the Bible was its code loop, hijacking technologies to copy and distribute itself. The Good News spread in Latin letters down Roman roads, cutting through the chaos of Barbarian territories, setting the terms of a running commentary that would wander far and wide, from Jerusalem to Japan, via York and the end of days. Church fathers bleached out ambiguity with creeds and canons, burning texts and turning thumbscrews down through the centuries. The abuse of the innocent, the undecided and the heretical continues today, and significance is a matter of statistics. Perhaps Aristotelian frames of reference tend inevitably towards Alexandrian megalomania, or perhaps it is simply a function of empire, whose very nature corrupts the fruits of the mind.

This is a book about language, perception, cognition and revelation. It is not about the Bible per se, though we will return periodically to it, for as Carl Jung wrote, "our psychology, whole lives, our language and imagery are built upon the Bible."[27] Both the Bible and the world are transformed when the dust of convention and the slime of politics is wiped away, when you look at them from different angles and break them up into different chunks. Disabusing ourselves of the ludicrous notion that it is some kind of moral guide, we will find all sorts of good stuff in the Good Book, including a stash of good drugs and a functional map of the brain itself. We will witness Jehovah, but not from the doorstep with gammy knees. We will lithely scale the walls of thought and drop into labyrinths of language, to navigate the traps and blinds built into the architecture. There are chambers to breach, and within them treasures of cognition beyond recognition – psychedelic synaesthesia, autistic savantism, the spirits of epileptic fits, and genius awoken by a knock on the head. This is an apocalypse of veils, not cravats, and its fruitage is extra fruity.

In the head God was created, so let's draw Him out. You are heavens, and you are earth. It is time to get to know ourselves.

$$\Omega$$

Reverend's General Warning

Overdoses of the Bible, while rarely fatal these days, can cause torpor and impotence. Among other things this book is supposed to be fun – so if holy bibliophilia is not your thing, feel free to skim the detail and come back to it if and when the Holy Spirit moves you.

Those who are bi(ble)-curious should be aware that it is arguably the most lethal book in history. Read responsibly, and observe the following instructions in order to avoid accidents.

1. When a verse looks like it recommends something hateful or disempowering, familiarize yourself with the vocabulary used, including variant meanings and usage in other verses (blueletterbible.com is easy). This should go some way towards separating out the politics of translation from the poetry. Take Psalm 37, for example:

   "The meek shall inherit the earth."[28]

   Inherit: *yarash*, but more commonly translated as 'possess', and with a connotation of 'to seize'.

   Earth: *eretz*, usually 'land'.

   Meek: *anav*. Elsewhere "the man Moses was very meek (*anav*)", but Moses was no timid little mouse. He stood up to Pharaoh, and was wrathful when his soldiers carried out an insufficiently total massacre.[29] Humility to the will of God seems closer to the meaning of *anav* in this sentence. Most commonly it is 'poor', and even when it is translated as 'meek' in the KJV it often describes poverty, as in "*the meek shall eat and be satisfied.*"[30]

24

Another possible translation is therefore: "The poor shall seize the land", and this works much better with my politics. The popular translations (and mistranslations) of the Bible were made with specific agendas in mind, and sometimes played fast and loose with the original languages, but nobody has a monopoly on the interpretation of poetry. The Bible says all kinds of things at the same time, and it is often more illuminating to exclude things that it *doesn't* say rather than try to establish definitively what it does.

2. If the verse remains robustly offensive after step 1, research its history. "He that believeth not shall be damned," for example, seems out of place in *Mark*, and it is also the only time that the Gospel brings up the business of damnation. Sure enough, scholars believe that this line is an interpolation (a scrap of text inserted at a later date).[31] Jewish Scribes, Church Fathers and medieval translators were all guilty of interpolating where they felt that the Word of God needed tweaking.

3. Bear in mind that both the Old and New Testaments are collections of texts from different times and places. Some of them reacted against empire, others were written in support. Some verses laid down laws, whereas others glorified characters that broke them. The homophobia and lists of Thou-shalt-nots derive from radically different political milieus to the cosmology of Genesis and the poetry of Psalms, and individual chapters or even verses may be pieced together from texts originating in different centuries.[32] The Bible is not a pill to swallow but an attic to rummage through, and there are all kinds of disturbing relics hidden amongst the treasures. Be careful what you pick up.

4. Beware of St. Paul, and beware of the tricks of clerics.

5. Except reverends.

Ω

THE MONKEY NUT

"I'm just going outside to smoke a fag…"

- Nicotine-deprived Londoner

"…You're going to shoot a homosexual?!"

- Alarmed Californian

N THE BEGINNING, back in the mists of time where my memory first comes into focus, I'm watching in despair as urine spreads around the foot of my chair. I was one of a legion of four-year old children in a classroom like an aircraft hangar, with the letters of the alphabet stretched along the wall, their number beyond reckoning. The classroom shrank as I grew, and I remember events punctuating the continuum more regularly: learning to draw a joined-up Y; asking what brackets do; biting a tall boy on the chest at the height of my head when he was blocking my

way out of the room. Everything sped up as it started making sense, and it is still speeding up. Birthdays came by once an aeon, now they slip past with alarming regularity. Space and time change as we explore the world around us, the worlds within us. At first we hack through uncharted jungle, and later our minds run along well-worn paths. A fully socialized adult can taxi down familiar mental boulevards more or less unconsciously – until he crashes into something that has moved.

I have long enjoyed running my perceptive system off-road, though once in the mid-90s I took a most unpleasant drive through an illegal reggae party in a field. It was all nice and irie until a police helicopter passed overhead, cutting through the bass-line and illuminating hundreds of scowls and middle fingers with a spotlight. *Sound of da Police* came on the sound system and everyone started *whoop-whoop*-ing. The chopper soon chop chop chopped off on its way, but things were not as they had been. I shook a stone out from my boot and continued chatting to my new friend, but the stone returned. As I took off my boot for the second time, a thought flashed urgently into my mind – *these boots are ugly!*

I had bombed a large dose of speed – *my shirt is ugly too!* – and the games were beginning, but these were not the games I had been expecting – *why is this girl talking to me, with my silly haircut and my ugly shirt?* She turned out to be Mark Morrison's drug dealer, out on parole for some horrific act of violence involving a knife and a cross-dresser, so I wandered off in my stony boots to find someone less creepy. But people were looking at me askance. They were pointing at me and whispering my name, plotting against me. Within minutes I was cowering on the grass, surrounded by jeering strangers.

My friends thought it best to take me away, but they were not my friends anymore. I only trusted one of them enough to let him walk with me, while the others walked a tactful distance ahead. Meanwhile I could hear footsteps behind me, clear and distinct, and the rising sun cast sinister shadows among the trees at the edge of my vision, enemies who vanished when I looked straight at them. I went to Slough and tortured and killed a few hours in a cafe before going to my temp job at Yellow Pages, typing out pun-filled adverts all day: *Sheds you could just DIY for!* It was a bad job sober, speedy and sleepless it became hellish. At one point I looked up at my screen to see a bullet point list of my faults instead of the advert I had typed.

The twisted visions continued until the following day. The paranoia lasted for over a week, and then it passed, thank Mother Mary of Perpetual Succour and the angels of serotonin. I emerged with two valuable insights. Firstly, speed is not my friend. Secondly, the picture we see is modified by the stories in our heads. The nervous system finds what it expects to find. I was expecting treachery, and found it everywhere, but no brain is free of expectations. We call false interpretations of the visual scene 'hallucinations', even though everything we see is an interpretation. The world perceived is the visual equivalent of a theory as yet unfalsified.

Take a good look at the sign at the beginning of this chapter.

Read it carefully.

If you still haven't had your apocalypse, trace over each letter with your finger.

We read between the lines and reconstruct the lines themselves. Neurons fire constantly in their hundreds of millions, as messages from the retina are processed and mixed with echoes from memory. As I edit these words into a book, my brain is busy editing countless streams of information from within and without into a coherent picture. Sometimes a word twitches as the automatic spell-checker corrects it on my screen, though it had looked normal to me, a fully rendered set of letters not a vague gray smudge. In truth, however, the area was uncharted, a patch of assumption on a map. Other times I can sit considering my responsiblities for ages, trying to work out why the spell-checker has underlined 'responsiblities' in quizzical red.

The retina discerns fine detail in the region called the fovea. Though it maps onto over half of the visual cortex, it covers only 1% of the retina, corresponding to a circle about twice the width of your thumbnail at arm's length.[1] That is the extent of what you discern in detail at a given moment.[2] Normally your eyes flick around and the internal world is sustained by memory and guess and wishful thinking, but the illusion is easily broken. Flip to a random page, fix your gaze on a random word, and count how many words you can read around it without shifting your gaze. Then let your eyes wander, and fix your gaze on the same word again; you should be able to make out twice as many.

The mind navigates through educated guesses. We jump from conclusion to conclusion, constantly mistaking our firing neurons for our wives and our hats, and we are taken in by the illusion – until it collapses, and a tired driver swerves around something that isn't there into a ditch. "Transient hallucinatory experiences are common in individuals without mental disorder", according to the American Medical Association textbook.[3] We make it up all the time. It's not so obvious in the light, but normal subjects deprived of light begin hallucinating within hours.[4] Back at the Hellish Yellowish Pages of Slough, a tormented temp doing data entry in my brain pasted a "transient hallucinatory experience" onto the computer screen on my internal screen. Clearly a list of my short-comings seemed more appropriate to context than an advert for a Manchester removals company.

I gave up speed that very day, though I continued fiddling with my nervous system until I took the ultimate trip by taking my brain to Japan. My interest in that country had first been piqued in a guesthouse in Barcelona, where I ate dinner late at night with Spaniards and drank beer for breakfast with

Estonians, where a lover's tiff between Italians bloomed into an opera of around ten voices over three floors. The most intriguing customs were those of the Japanese guest, whose superlatively considerate behaviour, doing small things for people without being asked, struck me as completely effortless and singularly exotic. My curiosity grew back in the U.K. as I read manga and tried martial arts, and especially when I discovered that the Japanese had made a traditional art form of rope bondage. Then, in my final year at university, I bumped into a quirky friend crossing the road on a last minute errand to collect documents to apply for a teaching post in Japan. He asked about my plans for the following year. I remembered the guesthouse for a second, and thought about knots for another second. Then I turned about-face and marched into a six-year tangle amongst the manners, manacles and mind-frames of the Far East.

Ω

When I first moved to Japan the language sounded like an unbroken stream of *ki*'s, *ta*'s and *so*'s, except for "*nani*" and "*da-né*", which always jumped out at me. *Nani* means 'what', and *da-né* means 'isn't it', but more importantly both of them sound like 'Danny', which is my name. The noise gradually resolved into discrete syllables, then into recognisable chunks, and finally meaning – though the people were not so easy to tell apart. This may be because my brain is heavily weighted towards sound information; I hear an out-of-tune guitar string immediately, and often fail to register when my wife cuts her hair. Whatever the reason, I must confess that even after six years in the country my Japanese friends mostly looked alike, give or take the odd beard. At any rate, they were impossible to locate in a crowd.

The funny thing is, some Japanese think the same about Caucasians. Once, when I was relaxing with friends in a hot spring in pre-apocalyptic Fukushima, an old farmer waded over through the scalding water, and looked at the three of us in turn

– a well-built and well-fed Anglo-Saxon with a wisp of sandy hair on his balding head, a lanky Australian of Italian descent with thick eyebrows and dark curly hair, and a freckly Jewish skinhead with a handsome nose. He asked if we were brothers. We explained our diverse roots. "Aah," he said, shaking his generic head, "you foreigners all look the same!"

Apparently foreigners can all sound the same as well, as illustrated in a dramatic manner by a friend of mine who was trying to pick up theatre tickets. He greeted the receptionist, presumably with a "*konnichiwa!*" as camp as one might expect from the tap-dancing, drag-wearing trapeze artist he is. She took one look at his black face and said "sorry, no Engrish". His accent and grammar were nearly perfect after decades in the country, and he had booked the tickets without incident from the same woman over the phone earlier that day; but try as he might, he could not make himself understood. The scene before her eyes veiled her ears (and he wasn't even in drag that day). Eventually he left frustrated, and walked across the road to call from a phone box. Over the phone she immediately recognised him from earlier, and began chatting, so he asked her to look across the road at the foreigner waving at her. With the veil successfully torn where it had snagged, he was able to pick up his tickets.

Sense impressions are not snapshots of the world. They are more like lines in a dialogue between within and without, and each storyteller hears and narrates from their own perspective. Elderly or unfit people, for example, tend to overestimate the angle of a hill in the distance.[5] Healthy young observers usually underestimate it – unless they are carrying heavy bags, in which case they overestimate. The world seen is modified by our expectations of how we might interact with it – in this case the effort involved in climbing the hill. Whatever looms large in one's thoughts grows larger on the internal screen, so a pimple dominating a teenager's mind also dominates the mirror, and an anorexic too weak to walk sees flesh spilling out of her wheelchair. Victims of an armed robbery usually overestimate the calibre of the gun that had been pointed at them, and they remember nearby people as having been much further away.[6] Size and scale are stretched by our fears, our expectations and our desires, and the distorted impressions are stored faithfully in memory. In fact, it is precisely those memories associated with extremes of emotion, the most severely warped perceptual experiences, that imprint most deeply.

Our ideas distort our worlds, and so do the ideas of others. When subjects sitting alone answer easy questions on the lengths of lines on cards (see diagram), their error rate is less than 1%; but when sitting with actors who are pretending to be subjects and giving incorrect answers, it climbs to nearly 37%.[7] Hearing false answers causes activity in the subject's visual cortex, as seen in brain imaging studies.[8] The foveas cannot 'see' both cards at once. When the eyes are focused on one, internal processes fill in the other, and it seems that other people's opinions modify the image itself at a pre-conscious level.

If our attention is elsewhere, we completely miss what should be strikingly obvious, in a phenomenon called 'inattentional blindness'. Nearly half the subjects counting basketball passes in a minute-long video miss a nine-second cameo of a woman in a gorilla suit walking among the players.[9] Around half of the time, pedestrians being asked directions fail to notice if the person asking is replaced by someone else as actors pass between them carrying a door to screen the switch.[10] Subjects asked to concentrate on crosses

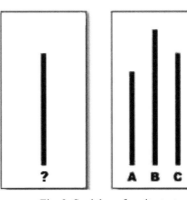

Fig. 2 Social conformity test

33

flashing up in the middle of a screen often miss an unexpected circle flashing up to one side.[11] A smiley face is noticed more often than a circle, but a moody face is not, so the editing must happen after some fairly complex pre-conscious processing has already taken place.[12] Subjects also spot their own names flashing up more frequently than if they are misspelled. In some way, forms that are more familiar or comfortable pass into the conscious mind easier. When it comes to smiley faces... you know the score.

It isn't your brain's job to accurately represent the world, rather to help you navigate it safely and exploit it fruitfully. The pre-conscious filter is a survival mechanism that functions at many levels of the nervous and hormonal systems to distort the senses. It enlarges mortal threats when we are scared. It makes the sense of smell 30% more acute when we are hungry.[13] It screens out moody faces, unlikely gorillas and arbitrary haircuts when our attention is elsewhere. It notices your name on a screen or in the noise of a crowd, and it picked out my name from streams of Japanese that had nothing to do with me. We like to think that our decisions are rational, based on the evidence before our eyes, but we fabricate evidence all the time – and seeing is believing. Between the light falling on the retina and the image perceived is a sea of unconscious processes, and it influences our decisions.

The worlds we behold are skewed and edited, veiled behind many veils and refracted through shards of memory, touched through the padded gloves of the nervous system; and our brains distort the past as much as the present. We modify our memories retrospectively, overestimating our past charitable donations, office attendance and salaries, underestimating the amount of alcohol we bought.[14] As neurobiologists put it, remembering is 'reconstructive', not 'reproductive', employing the same neural networks that are used in imagining the future.[15] We reconstruct episodes from the past as they fit into our narrative of the present, and sometimes details drift as stories are retold. Elderly people can incorporate elements from TV or their children's lives into their own biographies.[16] Witnesses can unwittingly adopt elements given by an interviewer into the recollection of a crime scene, including details such as broken glass that was originally absent. With the right priming, a false childhood memory about getting lost at the shopping mall can also be implanted into a person's autobiography.[17] Looking back on my years in Japan, I remember fondly the people who made my stay a pleasure, and I have to strain to remember the ambient racism implicit in many of my encounters. I remember it as funny, though it was definitely tedious at the time.

We are not just meat-suits and physiology; we are also stories of our selves that we tell ourselves and each other. Long-term memories are made under the influence of neurotransmitters released when we are happy or engaged, which is why I can still remember every lyric Bad Religion ever sang, and have forgotten almost everything I once knew about the periodic table. This survival adaptation allows apes to remember what they care about (such as which plants are edible and which are good for building nests), while discarding irrelevant details. All apes are interested in bedding and food, but the human ape's interests range wider. A guy at my school could rattle off the scores and scorers of every World Cup final and semi-final ever played. We each remember what is important to us, and information that is easily integrated passes into our maps of reality. That which threatens us or bores us is lost, as stress chemicals inhibit the formation of long-term memories.

Personally, I forget what colour England play in, and I rarely get excited about numbers. Appointment times go in one ear and out the other, and I know neither my sisters' birthdays nor my waist size. My spelling is dreadful, and I have given up trying to write the name Nietzsche unaided, for I am not that kind of ubermentzsche. I can, however, tell you about Tycho Brahe's contributions to astronomy, and the name of the clairvoyant dwarf who divined for his dinner guests from under the table. My father struggled to learn even the simplest

Japanese phrase when visiting me, probably because he would rather run a mile than communicate with a stranger. He is a die-hard accountant, and his brain soaks up population counts and GDPs like a sponge; but I had to shout at him for days to make him remember the word *itadakimasu*, without which one cannot accept even a biscuit without insulting one's host. Both father and son are extremely conceited, of course, but our conceits are different, marking the edges of our categories of thought according to the contours of our respective worlds.

Ω

My first week in Japan was spent lodged on the 23rd floor of the Tokyo Hilton, along with hundreds of other excitable twenty-somethings, going to orientation workshops and events, trying to decipher vending machines in the streets of Harajuku. At the first party, which was given by the Ministry of Education, I was delighted to discover that Japanese drinking culture is fundamentally different, with tiny glasses and a custom to fill your neighbours' glasses. Only an alcoholic or a barbarian would fill their own, which means that your attention is constantly being drawn towards the glasses and the people around you. This connection between the individual and the collective is the principle preoccupation of the Japanese psyche, according to the director of the Japanese National Institute of Mental Health.[18]

Beyond the sphere of human interactions, the relationship between an object and its context is generally much stronger in Japan, and this can be measured experimentally. If asked to spot the differences between computer-generated scenes of airports, for example, Americans notice more differences in items in the foreground, like the colour of the helicopter's rotor, whereas Japanese notice more relational differences such as the amount of space between aircraft.[19] When describing underwater scenes, American subjects usually begin with the movements of the biggest or fastest fish; Japanese more often start with the context ("it looks like a pond"), and go on to describe 60% more background features.[20] Afterwards, Japanese take longer than Americans to recognise a fish from the animation if it is displayed on a different background to the original, and they make more errors. The background makes no measurable difference for Americans. It seems they isolate the fish more distinctly, whereas the Japanese mind codes items along with their background.

The Japanese eye sees through a broader lens, and this aesthetic is embodied throughout Japanese culture. The rocks in rock gardens, for example, are typically contextualized by gravel raked into waves around them, and often by the 'borrowed scenery' (*shakkei*) of a mountain beyond the garden as well. In the written form, a letter usually begins with lines situating it in the cycle of the year, describing mounting winter snow or scorching summer sun, and one of the rules of *haiku* poetry is that it should include a word that evokes the season. In Basho's famous *haiku*, the frog plopping loudly into the old pond is a spring frog, and the ripples of the plop spread out across a long literary tradition of amphibians making a racket in spring. Charcoal landscape scrolls often depict something in high definition, a remote temple or a lonely traveller, with a chaos of roughly-sketched clouds and mountains around them. There is no tradition of still life painting in Japan, where things make less sense in isolation.

Fig. 3 Japanese rock garden

After my orientation in Tokyo I was sent off to teach in a rural district of Fukushima, where I found that the bond between the individual and the context was also tight in the workplace. My duties began with three weeks at City Hall. Though the other school teachers were on holiday, I was officially a City Hall employee, and that meant I had to sit there in a shirt at my desk even though I had absolutely nothing to do. This was excruciating, but Japanese workers are expected to make far more severe sacrifices. Many of my colleagues would arrive early and stay late, giving up their time without receiving overtime pay, and no one takes their full quota of annual paid leave if they want to retain any hope of promotion. Once, when I went in on a Sunday to pick up a key I had forgotten, I encountered several colleagues in their ties at their computers, playing solitaire.

I filled my time at City Hall learning Japanese, and discovered that among its many wonderful quirks the language has different verbs for the same action depending on the context. The appropriate version of 'to eat' changes according to the relationship between the speaker and the listener, and according to the surroundings:

Taberu (general polite):

- *Tabemasyou ka?*

'Shall we eat?'

Meshiagaru (offering politely):

- *Bu-chou wa sushi o meshiagemasen ka?*

'Wouldn't you like to eat some sushi, Mr. Section-chief?'

Itadakimasu (receiving politely):

- *Bu-chou ga kureta o-sembé o itadakimashita.*

'I ate the rice cake the section-chief gave me.'

Kuu (informal, at home or out drinking):

- *Ika kué yo!*

'Eat some of this squid mate!'

With these verbs, and with titles such as *bu-chou* (section-chief) and *sensei* (teacher) constantly slipped into sentences, and also in other ways, relational dynamics are built into the language.

I enjoyed the City Hall drinking parties. Some of my colleagues didn't, though they had to go anyway – the parties were optional in principle only. People went drinking in context, with the entire education section, for example, and spouses were not invited (not being part of the education section). The feast would begin with everyone sitting behind trays laden with tiny dishes of prawns heads, spicy octopus lumps and assorted slimy morsels. The Western equivalent would be a buffet, where each individual chooses according to preference, but in Japan everyone eats the same meal. If you can't stomach raw jellyfish salad, you might quietly recontextualize yours onto a colleague's tray.

Before the festivities begin everyone sits in absolute silence as formal speeches are made, invariably opening with autumn leaves or spring blossoms evoking the seasonal context. *Kyoiku-chou*, the head of education, praises his team, addressing the assembled using the form of the word 'I' that is normally reserved for public address: *watakushi*. Elsewhere 'I' is different. *Watashi* is used by men speaking to superiors or strangers, and by women in most situations – unless they are young amongst their peers, in which case they might say *atashi*. Forgoing that small amount of labial tension, softening *watashi* to *atashi*, a young woman modifies her person in that context, and so a chat with *atashi* is about a million times more exciting than a conversation with stuffy old *watashi*. *Oré* is an informal 'I', and *ora* is an angry or drunken *oré*. Old people might use *waré*, contextualizing themselves according to their age, and there are regional variations like *washi*. '*Washi wa oishii to omou*' means something like 'I [*from my perspective as an old man from the countryside of Kyushu island*] think it is tasty.' There were once many more 'I's, including *chin* used exclusively by the emperor (now it means

39

'penis'). Samurai used *sessha* (literally 'clumsy person'). Not so long ago, a farmer so impertinent as to address a samurai by using *sessha* for himself might have been cut down on the spot for insolence.

Even today etiquette remains a serious matter in Japan. Using the wrong version of 'you' can be extremely rude, as I discovered by offending a colleague with an overfamiliar pronoun. Japanese often sidestep the minefield entirely by using titles such as *bu-chou*, even when speaking directly to the section-chief in question, addressing the relationship rather than the person. One headmaster simply called me *gaijin-san*: 'Would the honourable foreigner like some honourable tea?' he would ask, and I'm still not sure if he was being insulting or respectful, or just avoiding calling me *dani-san* (honourable flea). Japanese linguistic devices put you in your place several times per sentence, and generally that is where you stay. This may be part of the reason why Japan is one of the very few countries with the same imperial family stretching back to legendary times, a place that has never endured a revolution despite centuries of power politics and intrigue amongst the samurai.

When *watakushi* finishes giving his formal address, others make their speeches, including the new recruits who demonstrate their enthusiasm to fit in. Then the drinking begins with a collective chorus of *kampai!* Within an hour nearly everyone is trashed, partly from the constant encouragement to drink from neighbours brandishing bottles, and partly because Japanese livers lack the alcohol dehydrogenase enzyme which breaks down alcohol. With red faces and ties around their heads like samurai warriors, *kyoiku-chou* is flinging soybeans high in the air for subordinates to catch in their mouths, *bu-chou* is jabbing the foreigner's bum with his fingers and shouting *kanchou!* (enema!). Everyone gets silly together. For poor *gaijin-san*, cursed with a full complement of *gaijin* enzymes, it can be a constant effort to direct people's attention towards

40

one's tiny, empty glass, in order to be at least a little tipsy by karaoke time. Someone will almost certainly sing *Oh Danny Boy* if that is your name, and if it is Christmas you can bet it will be a white Christmas. Honourifics slip and grammar slides. Would you believe it, I actually once heard a drunken secretary saying *oré* to *kyoiku-chou* towards the end of an evening, expressing extraordinary intimacy. His wife almost certainly speaks to him more formally at breakfast.

The party ends with a final collective ritual of synchronized clapping:

Clap-clap-clap…clap-clap-clap… clap-clap-clap… clap.

Clap-clap-clap…clap-clap-clap… clap-clap-clap… clap.

Clap-clap-clap…clap-clap-clap… clap-clap-clap…

CLAP!

The final clap is exquisitely timed, then the hardcore move on to a hostess bar, and who knows what seediness thereafter; but those who know stay quiet. Boundaries dissolve and the fixed is made volatile, all together in the alchemy of union. *Solve et coagula*; dissolving and crystallizing. Veils are dropped to reveal hidden dimensions of a person, but by the morning the re-vealed has been re-covered. *Oré* becomes an outright insult again. Last night may never be mentioned again, except obliquely: '*Bu-chou*, do you have a headache this morning?' Chit-chat in the elevator is as formal as ever. Indeed, leaving the elevator is as complicated as ever, being a common site for one of Japan's many etiquette stalemates. In the elevator position, two or more people attempt to let each other exit first until the doors close, and this can continue into a second round. Once I waited for the doors to close twice to see what would happen, and it was painfully clear that I was just screwing with the poor guy's head. At the third ding he might have felt obliged to formally disembowel himself.

Ω

Why is the Japanese mind-frame so sensitive to context?

What purpose does all this serve?

Part of the answer derives from geography. Life was and remains hard on an archipelago on the edge of the Middle Kingdom, with almost no natural resources or nearby trading partners, where snow piles high in winter and rivers of sweat run in summer. The workable land forms a thin strip between sharp mountains and raging seas, and paddy fields are irrigated by shared networks, so until recently a spat with a neighbour could have resulted in your water supply being cut off. With the samurai lord at the top of the slope controlling the pump, and everyone closely interdependent, understanding one's place in the greater scheme of things was a matter of survival. There were also earthquakes, typhoons and tsunamis to face, periodically wrecking villages and forcing inhabitants to work together in order to survive and rebuild their lives. No looting was reported after the 2011 tsunami, unlike New Orleans after Hurricane Katrina, for example.[21] The crime rate dropped in Japan, in fact, and people formed orderly lines for hours to buy modest amounts of groceries so that the short supplies would go around.

In Japan there is simply not enough space, physically or socially, for millions of individualists to carry on without considering the impact of their behaviour. Doors do not swing, they slide. Things are miniaturized to reduce friction, and Japanese arrange themselves and their possessions with exquisite economy. My friend Ito-san would scold his daughter for letting a leg stray from the cross-legged position on the mat at dinnertime, but he would laugh at her noisy burps. Japanese grow up acutely sensitive to matters of discretion, of paying attention and taking care, and all of these ideas are represented in Japanese by the phrase *ki o tsukau*. Literally it means 'to use energy/attention/*chi*'. This concept of *ki* is fundamental to Japanese culture, and it covers all kinds of situations regarding relationships:

42

	Somewhat literal translation	Meaning
Ki o tsukete	Apply *ki*	Take care!
Ki ga tzuita:	*Ki* arrived	I noticed
Ki ni sawaru:	Something touches *ki*	It's annoying
Ki ni naru:	To become *ki*	It's interesting
Ki ga awanai:	*Ki* doesn't meet	We don't get on
Gen ki ga aru:	There is root *ki*	I have an erection

We don't have an equivalent term for *ki*, unless we are going to incorporate a load of spiritual, religious or New Age baggage with terms like vibes, the Holy Ghost, spirit or *prana*; but there is nothing remotely spiritual about *ki* when it is uttered in most Japanese conversations.

The vocabulary available in a culture profoundly influences the way people read the world around them. It dictates, to a degree, what is concealed and what is revealed as information is filtered into consciousness. English speakers are more at liberty to say that they don't believe in invisible nonsense than Japanese are, and Stephen Fry can answer a statement like "there's very negative energy in here" by becoming petulant about the misuse of the language of thermodynamics.[22] It is not so easy to be pedantic about such things in Japanese, because *ki* is built into the very language. People would be hard pressed to express themselves without it.

As a child grows up she constructs a climbing frame in the image of the particular universe she inhabits, and that includes the grammatical space. Grammar governs how the struts of the scaffolding slot together, how verbs relate nouns to each other, and how far an adjective stretches over the nouns around it. It stipulates which nouns need to be articulated, and what can be inferred. At one level of order, the architecture of language establishes how the world fits together. It directs how ideas can be presented, maybe even how they can be thought about. In

English, for example, the pronouns (I, she, they) are loud and proud, often at the beginning of a sentence:

'I want to eat a curry.'

The Japanese equivalent does not demand a pronoun at all. Clauses usually introduce the matter in question (the curry) first, leaving out what an English person would consider to be the agent:

'*Karé o tabetai.*'

There is no 'I', and the verb (*tabetai*) comes right at the end. This means that the speaker need not disclose any intentions towards the curry until many syllables and many moments have passed. She can monitor the paralinguistic radar bouncing off other people as her utterance progresses, steering towards the safety of *ohh*'s and *ehh*'s, carefully navigating through silent gaps, veering away from sharp winds whistling through the teeth that warn of an etiquette impasse ahead – someone having to object to the curry their honourable friend had proposed, for example, or having to eat it despite their haemorrhoids.

In English, listeners have much less influence on the emerging sentence. An English sentence usually reveals its intention at about the second word, so by the time you learn what you are actually talking about (a curry), you already know 'who' wants to 'do what' to it:

'I want to eat a curry.'

A Japanese raising the idea of a curry has plenty of opportunity to abandon the verb before she gets to it – verb overboard! – and weigh anchor with a different one. Even if she follows the original course to 'eat', the verb's grammar is only established at the very last moment with the suffix. 'Eating' begins with *tabe-*, but '*I want to eat...*', '*I don't want to eat...*', '*How about eating...*' and '*Let's eat...*' all turn on a final few syllables. With a final *ka*, the inclusive imperative '*Let's eat...*' morphs into a question '*Shall we eat...?*', and the question intonation rises only on the very last syllable. If radar signals don't indicate a clear course, then the clause could be qualified with extra clauses, or the speaker could just coast along on the last syllable of the verb stem for a while – '*karé o tabéeeeeh…*' – and wait for someone else to take the helm, as Japanese commonly finish each other's sentences. It is much simpler in England, and the curry is better, but complaining about the honourable Suzuki-san's honourable choice of an honourable meal just isn't very honourable. The curry itself is less important than how it affects the network of relationships it is embedded into.

'I', 'you', 'we' and 'they' are either modified or omitted in Japanese, and consensus is generated collectively, guided by the hierarchies in play. By contrast, the Indo-European languages that dominate in Europe place agents directly into phrases, lending themselves to a process of point and counterpoint, my idea and your idea, a dialectic of thesis and antithesis resolving in synthesis. In Euro-American culture independence is a sign of maturity, but in Japan the exact opposite is true, and a mature person is an inter-dependent person who fits in and makes life easier for those around them. Aside from sumo matches I witnessed only three fights in my six years in Japan, and two of them were between Americans and Irishmen fighting man-to-man outside pubs. The other began quietly at 3am with the approach of a teenager, as my friends and I were sitting on park swings bemushroomed. Members of Japan's many subcultures conform to strict internal norms, whether rockabilly fiends in winkle pickers or Goths wrapped in bloody bandages, and this guy's bandana and giant trousers identified him as a motorbike gang member. He apologized with a bow and politely requested our honourable co-operation in vacating the honourable park, which was about to be used for something vague and honourable. It seemed like the honourable thing to do. Shortly afterwards two gangs appeared. Insults were exchanged, and then the reds and the blues piled in *en masse*, some wielding wooden swords or staffs. No one was seriously hurt (that not being the point), and the winners spent the rest of the night marching around Sendai city in formation displaying their bruises.

On the rare occasions when Japanese fight it tends to be a communal affair, and at its extreme the 'I' can be completely consumed by the collective. Kamikaze suicide-bombers were by no means exceptional in Japanese history. Aizu festival commemorates the teenage samurai who looked back from afar to see their castle burning, and all committed ritual suicide together in shame. As things turned out it was a granary that had caught fire, not an act of war, but these rather stupid romantics passed into folklore all the same. They are honoured every year with grilled squid on sticks and a parade of suicidal samurai, kamikaze pilots and other self-effacing, self-erasing heroes of Japanese history falling gloriously at the peak of their beauty, like cherry blossoms in spring.

Ω

Life was good in Japan and it got better, and as one's mood changes so does the world. I hooked up with a Japanese woman who was easy on the eye but not strikingly different from her compatriots, and watched her morph into a figure of unsurpassable beauty as I explored her charms. We married for love and documents, though as the cycles of cherry flowers blossomed afresh and fell, things soured between us, as rice wine turns to vinegar. Something suffocated slowly between bouts of tranquilizer abuse and flying crockery, and one day I awoke from another night on the sofa to find that other beauties had emerged from their hibernation. The world had started to come into focus differently.

One day, I answered the phone to a question:

"Okusan ga imasu ka?"

okusan:	noun - wife
imasu:	verb - exist
ka:	question suffix - ?

It was not the first time someone had asked after my marital status, though it was the first time an unfamiliar woman had phoned me up out of the blue to do so. Rather flattered, and not without regret, I replied "*hai, imasu*" (yes, [she] exists).

A long pause followed.

Eventually the caller asked if she could speak to said wife.

For a brief moment I had enjoyed a floating world, where easy-on-the-ear, probably sexually adventurous and morally questionable young women were given to tracking me down and asking if I was available. I had completely missed the context framing her inquiry (an unfamiliar woman phoning up a married stranger), and failed to distinguish between two possible interpretations:

'Does <u>a</u> wife exist in relation to <u>you</u>?'

or:

'Does <u>your </u>wife exist in relation to <u>the space around you</u>?'

Had I been an Arab I might have understood her question to mean 'do you have any wive<u>s</u>?', because plural suffixes (like ~s in English) are nearly always omitted. So are possessive pronouns (your/his etc.), and the language has no articles (a/ the), so a given statement can be either general or specific, and may imply both. In English, 'do you like dogs?', 'do you like the dogs?' and 'do you like the dog?' all sound different. In Japanese they are the same: '*inu ga suki desu ka?*' (*dog - likeable - exist* - question-suffix).

The technical term for the way a word changes to express number, specificity, ownership and other grammatical functions is 'inflection'. English, Greek, Latin and the other Indo-European languages have highly inflecting nouns packed with information. Japanese, Chinese, Vietnamese, Korean, Thai and many other Asian languages have nouns that barely inflect (and Chinese people give similar answers to Japanese in tests of perception despite a radically different history and environment).[23] Where Japanese nouns do inflect, it is usually with an honorific prefix or suffix, like *o-* or *-san*, or even both as in *o-tou-san* (father). Japanese verbs, however, unlike Chinese, Vietnamese and Thai verbs, are highly-inflecting, packed with information about the relationships between the nouns they bring together.

The Japanese and English languages direct the attention to different aspects of the world, and different cognitive strategies can be detected in native speakers before the age of two.[24] If American toddlers are shown a pyramid made of cork and told "look at this *dax*", they tend to assume that *dax* is the name of the shape (i.e. it's a *dax*, or more formally, it is an instance of the category of things named '*dax*').[25] Afterwards, when asked to pick the *dax* from a set of shapes of various materials, they tend to choose a plastic or wooden pyramid (because a *dax* is 'a pyramid' to them). Japanese kids assume more often that *dax* refers to the material rather than the category (i.e. it's some *dax*). They are more likely to select a sphere or cube made of cork.

It is not simple to untangle first causes here, because linguistics, culture, history, geography and cosmology are weaved together as spools of a giant tapestry worked down through the generations. American mothers name nouns ('the piggy', 'the car') for their children twice as often as Japanese mothers do, and Japanese mothers model social relationships twice as often, exchanging toys, greetings and thank-yous.[26] This bias towards the relationship continues into school, where Japanese history teachers typically begin with the context of the war or revolution being studied, asking 'how' questions twice as often as American teachers do, thereby encouraging students to think about how politicians and peasants felt about the situations they were embedded into.[27] American teachers tend to start with outcomes and then establish causation ("The Thirty Years War occurred for three major reasons..."). They ask 'why' questions twice as often, directing the mind toward the motives of statesmen and revolutionaries with large plans and famous names.

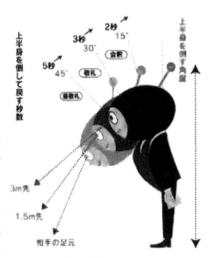

One day my co-teacher missed morning assembly. She arrived in good time for her first class, and yet the headmaster railed at her in front of her colleagues as she bowed and apologized. Later she apologized to me as well, and I asked what had happened. It turned out her father had died during the night, which

Fig. 4 How to bow

seemed reason enough to me; but Japanese almost never justify themselves in such situations, and the headmaster hadn't asked. The word excuse is *iiwaké* (literally 'a spoken reason'), and it has absolutely negative connotations. What matters is the situation here and now, to be addressed with gestures that reflect the gravity of the damage done to the relationships, such as a bow to the correct degree. Broken telephones, sick cats and dead fathers are not relevant. Those things pertain to Myuki-<u>san</u>, but it was Myuki-<u>sensei</u> who was expected at assembly.

With less serious problems the language helps to conceal individual agents. "*O-sara ga ochité-shimatta!*" means something like "the honourable plate fell, unfortunately!" The English equivalent would be "Dom dropped a plate" or "somebody dropped a plate", singling out a guilty party (even an unknown 'somebody'). Forcing Dom into the sentence is grammatically permissible. You can switch the verb and say, "<u>*Domu-san wa*</u> *o-sara ga otoshité-shimatta*", but this is far from honourable. It would sound spiteful.

Agents morph through mutable pronouns or are omitted entirely in Japanese, and agency seems more fluid. Surveys reveal that whereas Westerners tend to feel comfortable taking control, embodying the agency their tongues invoke so frequently, Japanese generally prefer not to be in control.[28] They also see life as more complex and unpredictable than Westerners do.[29] Objects and individuals blend into the background in cultural artefacts and in the psychology of perception. Blame spreads out and motives blur. The finality of a well-defined edge is so deeply abhorrent in Japanese culture that *shimatta!*, literally 'it is closed!', serves as a general curse word, when someone spills their noodles for example. Perhaps a similar sensibility is behind the fact that the most commonly heard word in Japanese is *sumimasen*, meaning 'it doesn't stop' and implying something that is about to be continued. It is used like 'excuse me' to catch someone's attention, to thank, to say hello or goodbye, and as a minor apology. Conversations nearly always begin and end with *sumimasen*, picking up the thread of a relationship that has been running along silently in the background. It is shouted out as loud as you like across a restaurant to call a waitress – "IT DOESN'T STOP!" It keeps flowing, like *ki*, where the language cuts channels for it.

Ω

In a noun-inflecting language such as English, a noun is plucked from the background like a Brussels sprout on a fork, where it can be analysed and categorized, compared and contrasted with other nouns. In a language where nouns inflect less, like Chinese or Japanese, they are torn messily from a sentence like a stir-fried noodle between chopsticks, together with bean sprouts and bits of egg. It makes less sense to seek specific agents, causes and qualities in the tangle. This may help explain why Japan produced only one Nobel laureate in the 1990s compared with 44 Americans, despite generous science funding.[30] The Japanese lens might be too broad for the narrow aperture of mainstream academia, although a wider frame has its advantages. It was Japanese primatologists, for example, who first recognised the complex social networks amongst chimpanzees, where Western researchers had focused exclusively on the mother-child bond.[31] Japan also leads the research into slime moulds, which are wonderful single-celled organisms that come together into multicellular slugs and mushroom-like structures when environmental pressures demand it. Only Japanese researchers thought to test their intelligence by testing if they could solve mazes (they can), or by periodically altering their chemical environment to see if they can measure time and preempt regular changes (they can).[32] [33] Such intelligence distributed across single-celled organisms is mind-blowing, to my mind at least – but my mind is accustomed to English patterns of thought. That particular apocalypse is easier in a language where individual agents vanish and leave space for *ki* to move.

Japan excels at streamlining, miniaturizing and perfecting technologies invented elsewhere, and leads the world in robotics. In many ways, however, the country has been dominated by China for most of its history. China bequeathed not only rice, tea and silk to Japan, but also the cosmology of the elements and most of its pictograms – though other letters were developed to express verb inflections and grammar particles. Chinese, which barely inflects at all, has very simple grammar. The way elements of a sentence come together is very much open to interpretation, especially in the classic texts, which is why there are so many radically different and mutually contradictory translations of the *Tao Te Ching*.[34] In China and among her neighbours, the philosopher's gaze was less concerned with items than relationships between them, including the flow between yin and yang and the interplay of the five elements. The same metaphors and essential principles can be applied across many domains of life, in agriculture and on the battlefield, in the boardroom or the bedroom.

Chinese medicine uses complex herbal mixtures and scattered acupuncture points, working via interacting organ systems with lines of influence dispersed around the body. The occidental academy has finally established the existence of these long-distance effects, measuring differences in saliva production and brain activity when a needle is put into an acupuncture point on the finger (unlike with a fake point); but Chinese medics have long understood that organs can affect distant body parts.[35] They were prescribing pituitary hormones isolated from urine at least 2,000 years ago, whereas Europeans didn't even have a word for hormones until 1905.[36][37] Until the birth of endocrinology a few years before they had no explanation for why a castrated teenager could continue hitting the high notes into adulthood, given that the vocal chords and the testicles are so widely separated.[38]

The surgical slice of English or Greek lends itself to analysis, to breaking things down into parts. European medics often prescribed 'specifics' for specific conditions, and continue to focus on killing the specific germs causing specific ills, transplanting malfunctioning organs and aiming 'magic bullets'. In treating symptoms this system does quite well, and the surgical techniques are amazing. In terms of preserving wellness, however, and tending to the mind and whatever else makes up a person, it leaves a lot to be desired, with over one in ten Americans on anti-depressants despite an advanced medical system.[39] China was millennia ahead in exploring the web of relationships in the human body, and millennia behind in other areas. Despite keeping accurate astronomical records for many centuries, Chinese astronomers believed that "earth takes its body from the yin, so it is flat and quiescent" until the 17th century, when Jesuit missionaries told them it was round.[40] Pythagoras had already posited that the earth was a sphere in the 6th century BC. Greek astronomers had accurately deduced its circumference from the movements of the heavens, and placed the sun at the centre of the solar system.[41]

What is the nature of something? What is the cause of something? These are some of the questions which Indo-European languages are well-equipped to discuss; and Socrates would have us discuss things. Verbal reasoning was for him the key to unlocking one's innate knowledge, and that is quite different to the oriental aesthetic where silence indicates wisdom.[42] In the course of their discussions, Greek philosophers proposed both atom and wave theories of matter, and discerned the function of both sensory and motor neurons.[43]

Our mental climbing frames are connected up into different configurations, and this influences our perceptions, our memories and our decisions; but the bars of the climbing frame can be bent. Japanese respond to tests of perception more like Americans after spending time in the US, and vice-versa for Americans living in Japan.[44] Bilingual minds can be primed towards one or other configuration. Chinese Americans shown pictures of the US House of Representatives before watching an animation of fish in an aquarium are more likely to describe the fish's motivation. Their peers shown dragons and temples describe more contextual factors.[45] Cultural cognitive styles also persist across generations, even in the absence of the associated language. Second-generation Chinese Americans (whose first language was English) scored poorly in tests when they were asked to vocalize their reasoning, as their native Chinese parents did, whereas European Americans were unaffected. Conversely, European Americans scored worse if they had to recite the ABC, while Asian Americans were not affected. Psychologist Dr. Heejung Kim comments:

> Although accepting the idea that language has a powerful influence on human thoughts and probably plays some role in the cultural differences demonstrated, the findings cannot be explained by the cross-linguistic difference only.[46]

So, are differences in cognition rooted in culture or in language? The question itself derives from an object-focused gaze, and we can learn a lot from that perspective, but from another perspective these cultural and linguistic streams swirl together in the consciousness of a people, and cannot be decisively drawn apart. They are written down together into the letters of scriptures that stabilize culture across generations and fix expressions and the thoughts embedded in them "till Kingdom come". In some ways, the Chinese classical canon and the Hebrew OT address similar concerns. Ritual norms and duties are collected in Leviticus and the *Classic of Rites*, genealogies in Numbers and the *Hundred Family Surnames*, the wisdom of hierophants in the Proverbs of Solomon and the *Analects of Confucius*. Both canons also contain core texts a good deal older and more mysterious, and here the differences are intriguing.[47] The *Book of Changes (I Ching)* is concerned with the shifting processes at play in the universe, whereas Genesis and Exodus are action-packed narratives driven by great men and great powers striving amongst themselves. Sometimes the powers contradict each other, as when El Shadday demands the sacrifice of Abraham's son and the angel of YHWH steps in to stop him.[48] Sometimes a prophet dissuades YHWH from "the evil which he thought to do unto his people".[49]

Hebrew scripture presents about 60 different agents of power, and each godname brings something into the story: *Ruach Elohim* (the Spirit of God); *El Roi* (God the Seer); *El Olam* (God the Eternal/Revealed); *Shaphat* (the Judge) and so on. The Hebrew language, by virtue of its grammar, generates many agents in the course of a conversation. In talking about coldness, for example, the agent is the person feeling the cold: *kar li* (cold *according-to-*me). Japanese is different: *samui desu* (coldness exists). It could apply to the room, or the speaker, or even the listener if she wanted to knit herself into the coldness with a few syllables.

In English *something* has to be cold, either '*I*'m cold' or '*it*'s cold'; but what is the '*it*' that is cold when *it*'s cold? East Asian languages don't require an *it*. A chilly Chinese might say *hen leng* (very cold), without naming the cause. The first cause in the *Tao Te Ching* is also nameless:

> The Tao that can be told of is not the eternal Tao;
>
> The name that can be named is not the eternal name.

What rains when *it* rains? The Hebrew *yored geshem* (falling rain) attributes agency to the rain itself. Japanese usually say *amé desu* (rain exists). English, however, evokes an Almighty agent beyond context every time It rains. The Greek equivalent is *vrehei* (it rains), the agent in the ~*ei* inflection indicating the third person singular (he/she/it). When it's cold in Greek, *kanei krio* (it does cold).

Greek is grammatically similar to English, and more straightforward than Hebrew, and it requires a different sort of poetry to evoke the paradox of human experience and the mystery of the Almighty cause:

> In the beginning was the Word, and the Word was with God, and the Word was God [...] All things were made by him; and without him was not any thing made.

Like the OT, the NT is an action-packed story, but its names of power tend to be titles of respect for either father or son, rather than distinct personalities (with the exception of Satan). The distinction between prophet and deity is also blurred. In the OT, YHWH sends the flood; and though "Moses stretched out his hand over the sea [...] YHWH caused the sea to go back."[50] Jesus is different, working the water himself, walking on it and turning it to wine. God Almighty and Christ Almighty are in many ways the same agent, as the man-god says:

> I and the Father are One.[51]

The Hebrews never called the deity Father, and they threw stones at Jesus for his bold words. Words are serious things in Hebrew, things of mystery and danger. The letters create and sustain the universe in old Jewish books, and magic words give power over things.[52] Words *are* things in a sense, as the same Hebrew word means both 'word' and 'thing'. Spelled *DBR*, *dabar* also means 'utterance', 'matter', 'concept' and so on. *DBR* can mean language itself. It can be a 'sentence' – both in the sense of a coherent collection of words in order and a punishment handed down.[53] Pronounced in various ways, *DBR* is 'to arrange', 'to plot against', 'to subdue' and 'to destroy', and both 'pestilence' and 'pasture'.[54] In all these things, it has a sense of order. The primitive root of *DBR* is the power 'to set in a row, to range in order'.[55]

Words are powerful in Hebrew tradition, and they are also ambiguous. Rabbinical debates over interpretation can last all day and end in a draw.[56] Japanese Zen Buddhism is more succinct, and embodies a fundamental distrust of words. Zen riddles pull a wedgie on the word, seeking to cleave apart clefts that will not readily part company:

> "'Words reach from edge to edge' – how about it?"
> [asks the Zen master].
>
> "Shut up!" the pupil says and slaps his master's face.[57]

Zen flowered on a tree with roots in the Indo-European soil of the Indus valley and branches growing across China basking in Taoist sunbeams. Perhaps this linguistic journey – from highly-inflected and precise conceptualization to vague clouds of ideation – leads naturally to the *koan* riddle, juxtaposing the logical framework of analytical thought against the interpenetrating streams of stuff in the universe. The Western scriptural tradition took a different route, laying Indo-European edges over ambiguous Hebraic smudges. Our lines define clearly, but beyond the lines there is another agent hiding in the shadow of the syntax.

In Japanese: rain exists.

In English or Greek: *It*'s raining.

It's been raining all day.

Isn't *it* just infernal?

Ω

56

GE(NE)MUSIS

I N THE BEGINNING, "In the beginning" was in Hebrew, but as the story was whispered away from Jerusalem in new languages it wandered in different directions, and inevitably things were left behind. Once upon a time Genesis could also have begun "In the head", or "With wisdom", and if it was "beginning", it could have been "In", "With" or "From the beginning", as well as "In a beginning", or just "In beginning". Though there is no article in the Hebrew phrase, English translations unanimously inject one "in the beginning", inoculating against a certain timeless line of enquiry. This raises a problem before "the first day [sic]" is out:

And there was evening and there was morning, day one [SIC].

All of the English translations put "the first day" here rather than "day one", but *yowm echad* doesn't mean 'the first day'. *Echad* means 'one'. 'The first day' would be *yowm ha-rishown*, as it is elsewhere in the Bible.[1] The remaining days of Genesis 1 all take ordinal numbers, which are faithfully translated as "second day", "third day" and so on. "Day one" is different. It is cardinally different, and this translation is a cardinal sin against poetry. It is not a translation, and nor is it an interpretation. It is an error, and even the Latin Vulgate is not so vulgar as to make it, reading "*dies unus*" (not "*dies primus*"). That chapter also begins without an article "*in principio*" (not "*in el principio*").

If "day one" wasn't the first day, what about the others?

Could they be happening all the time?

And there was evening
and there was morning,
the second day...
And there was evening
and there was morning,
the third day.
And God said,
"Let there be lights in the
firmament of the heaven
to divide the day
from the night"...

What were evenings on the days before the sun brought the dawn? And what kind of days begin in the evening and end in the morning? What THE DEVIL can it all mean?

Enigmas like these satisfy a certain class of literal-minded (but literally illiterate) atheist that the Bible is full of outlandish notions and logical contradictions. It is indeed, and it is also full of letters and words; its meaning depends on how you arrange them. The 'oral Torah' is the ancient tradition of commentary and debate over details of the 'written Torah', and it was also left behind when the Bible travelled beyond the tribe, despite being considered an integral part of the Torah by the Jews. It was written down after the destruction of Jerusalem in 70 AD. In its pages, esteemed rabbis interrogated the enigma of the night before the day and the day before the sun. To cut a long beard short, the Ramban noted that the root of the word 'evening' (*erev*) means 'disorder', and the root of 'morning' (*boker*) means 'to discern'.[2] And there was evening and there was morning, and there was chaos and there was order to be discerned arising from it at the end of each cycle, from day one to the sixth day.

AND ELOHIM SAW THAT IT WAS GOOD...

...and so did Pythagoras the Greek, "who first called heaven *kosmos*, because it is perfect and 'adorned' with infinite beauty."[3] When *kosmos* appears in the NT it is usually translated as 'world', but it means 'order'. It is also 'a jewel', which is a brilliantly orderly object growing out of the drab disorder of the surrounding rock. From *kaos* to *kosmos*, the emergence of order is good to behold, as a lotus arising from muddy waters, its beauty in the harmony of its colours, the symmetry of its petals, the architecture of its proteins. Order is good, and order is beautiful, generally. It freezes up, however, if it's not shaken up now and again.

Chaos was there before day one. Chaos awaits beyond the horizon, brewing up novelties and belching out catastrophes that reorder the cosmos, as inevitable as the night that follows the day that follows the night. Chaos is the wild and screaming sea from which code, concept and cosmos arise, and into which everything crumbles. Between them the powers created "every living creature that moveth" from chaos, and on the sixth day Elohim said:

"LET US MAKE MAN IN OUR IMAGE, AFTER OUR LIKENESS."

To whom was He talking?

Why the plurality in the powers?

And why does the deity have more than one name?

Ω

Notes on quotes

Generally the *KJV* is quoted because I enjoy the pomposity of the language. Occasionally I will substitute words or quote other Bibles, as noted in the endnotes.

My interpretations deviate from rabbinical and church traditions in some respects, and defenders of the faith have objected on that account, but I think they are faithful to the language and the spirit of the society at the time of composition. My conjectures in linguistics and grammar have been checked with experts in Greek, Hebrew and Arabic, sometimes through introductions and later by posing disingenuous questions on 'Ask the rabbi' websites. I sought the critique of a minister of apologetics by posing as a Christian concerned about what the church youngsters were smoking, denouncing Nemu as a corrupter of the youth. He submitted my chapter on drugs in the Bible to the question, with neither the clear thinking of the Jesuit nor the charity of the Franciscan (archived at www.nemusend.co.uk).

The interpretative tradition underwent massive shifts over the centuries, and there is no reason to think that the vowel scheme of the Masoretes in the 7th century AD, or the rabbinical rulings during the Babylon exile of the 6th century BC, represent an 'authentic' interpretation of a text that is centuries older. Anyway, there is no copyright on the Bible, so I will do with it as I please within the bounds of good grammar.

I also asked some neuroscientists and psycho-pharmacologists to check chapters, which was less complicated.

BEHIND THE WORD

The limits of my language mean
the limits of my world.

- Ludwig Wittgenstein[1]

N THE BEGINNING of each day at my childhood school, a boy we'll call Fred would go tumbling through the corridors with a huge stack of books, with pens and papers sticking out of every pocket, chaos incarnate. He was a strange and solitary chap who would disappear off to the computer room at lunchtime, and he had some impressive talents. He had memorized the entire school register, and could tell you the birthday of any of its 800 pupils, most of whom he didn't know. He could also calculate in seconds what day of the week you were born on.

Fortune brings us together now and again in London, and I have bumped into Fred at an acrobatics show, at the Anarchist Bookfair, and on a history walk around Southwark, for his interests are broad. Most recently I recognised his enigmatic gait and mop of curly hair coming over Waterloo Bridge as I sat outside a cafe. He asked what I was doing there.

"My wife is singing round the corner at King's College tonight," I replied.

"What are you doing sitting here then?" he asked.

Combinations of phonemes make words (*DBR* in Hebrew) that refer to things (*DBR*). Combinations of words make sentences (*DBR*) that describe matters (*DBR*) and concepts (*DBR*) and reasons (*DBRH*, the feminine form of *DBR*).[2] Ideally the reasoning should be as clear to the listener as it is to the speaker, as the meanings of words are more or less defined in the languages we share, more for a pedant and less for a poet. In practice, however, frames of reference don't match up perfectly, and our minds decode words into meaning differently. Fred's question was perfectly logical, given that it was already 'tonight' and 'my wife is singing' is in the present continuous tense, which generally refers to things continuing in the present. In my head, I was referring to an unspecified future (i.e. she is singing *later on* tonight). That should have been obvious from the context – me, in a café, near but not at King's College. But people read context differently. And some don't read it at all.

In certain fields it is necessary to decontextualize language and formally mark out the basics of what means what, and perhaps that is why Ludwig Wittgenstein's 1922 work *Tractatus Logico-Philosophicus* has become a central text in philosophy and linguistics departments. It begins with:

1   The world is everything that is the case.

1.1   The world is the totality of facts, not of things.

1.11   The world is determined by the facts,
        and by these being all the facts.[3]

This slim volume attempts to articulate the scope and limits of language in a series of bullet points, with words deployed without quarter for context, subtext or imagination. It is a brutal read, but at least the professors of the academy can agree upon its terms. The final chapter is a short, almost vulgar gesture towards metaphysics and Aristotle, comprising only one sentence:

> 7   Whereof one cannot speak, thereof one must be silent.

The *Tractatus* was immediately influential, and partly responsible for the formation of the Vienna Circle of logical positivists. They courted a visit from its author for years, but he had abandoned academia for lowly posts in rural elementary schools, where he caused scandals by shouting "rubbish!" as the priest answered youngsters' questions, and by pulling little girls' hair for their poor mathematics.[4] Corporal punishment was considered appropriate for boys, not for girls. They could not seriously be expected to understand algebra in the first place.[5]

Schoolmaster Wittgenstein's career ended abruptly when one of his beatings rendered a boy unconscious. He then spent a few years directing his singularly obsessive mind to redesigning a house down to the minutest detail, before finally returning to the academy after an absence of a decade, unannounced and unenrolled, sitting in on lectures at Cambridge. His mood was not much improved. Some of his arguments with Bertrand Russell have become legendary, such as that which reveals his hardline approach to what can be known. Russell proposed that "there is no rhinoceros in the room", and Wittgenstein refused to admit that the statement was true, even after the august don had conducted a thorough search under the tables.[6] "There is a table in the room" is not a problematic statement, as 'table' refers to a thing you can see and an image you can imagine. The table in the room is a 'fact', and Wittgenstein's world was "the totality of facts".[7] You can point to a 'table'. You can't point to 'no-rhinoceros'. The 'fact' of such a thing would be a horrific hybrid of everything in the universe except rhinoceroses (including earwax and the moons of Jupiter and the night bus from Trafalgar Square). If "the world is everything that is the case", then how can assertions about the world be meaningful when made in terms of nothings and infinities?[8]

Now this is a thorny, rhino-horny problem in the study of the nature of existence (which philosophers call ontology). Russell walked away from the exchange convinced that "the German engineer" was a fool; but within a few months he had changed his mind, as he confided to his mistress:[9]

> When he left me I was strangely excited by him. I love
> him and feel he will solve the problems I am too old to
> solve.[10]

Wittgenstein reciprocated in his own way, snapping at the professor during his doctoral interview examination, telling him he would never be capable of understanding his philosophy.

Far be it from me to feign comprehension of Wittgenstein's mighty postulates, though I have pulled at my own hair trying. From my lay and lowly perspective, language is at least partly about communication, and he failed dismally at that; for Wittgenstein may have been the only person ever to have understood Wittgenstein. When he finally condescended to accept the invitation of the Vienna Circle, he took to reading poetry aloud to the wall so as not to endure the meagre understanding of the assembled.[11] At one meeting he replied to Karl Popper's charge by throwing down a red hot poker and storming out of the room.[12]

"Nothing we could ever think or say should be the thing," said Wittgenstein, but such a *koan* would be difficult to pose in Hebrew, difficult to think even, as the word *is* the thing. They are both *DBR*, and this goes some way towards resolving the problem of ontology. The existence of a 'thing' in the world is something one can never really be sure of; it might be a "transient hallucinatory experience", for example. The 'thing' in your mind is easier – it exists in your mind from the moment you thingify it. The table in the room is a table in your mind, regardless of the world outside. 'No-rhinoceros' is more complex.

In later life Wittgenstein saw the limits of his conception of language, after a period of soul-searching that began when someone made a rude gesture at him and asked, "What is the logical form of that?"[13] For a time, though, his world of words was a castle unassailable. "The limits of my language mean the limits of my world", said young Ludwig, and that holds true for most minds, most of the time, as the monkey bars of the mind are a cage as much as a frame.[14] But is there something more to the world behind the ambiguous present continuous?

Ω

Sometimes cognition is not limited by linguistics. For most people calculation involves the mental manipulation of shared symbols such as '6' and '+', but for Daniel Tammet it is a visual affair. '1' is a flashing light to him, '5' is a clap of thunder, '89' looks like falling snow.[15] This is an example of synaesthesia, where sense modalities run together. A synaesthete might see someone else being tapped on the shoulder and feel it on their own, or they might taste names (like 'Hannah' with the flavour of rhubarb).[16] The most common form is when sounds are seen. Concepts visualized in the internal cinema are a similar species of experience, and so are the personality 'auras' seen around people. Tammet sees numbers, and when he multiplies two together, the images create a third between them which he can decode instantly to a hundred decimal places.

Synaesthesia is common just before epileptic fits.[17] As a toddler Tammet was diagnosed with epilepsy and severe autism, which often go together.[18] His screaming bouts could last all day, and he was almost totally disengaged from the outside world, but happily his more extreme symptoms passed after a series of severe epileptic seizures. Today he is almost unique, combining the prodigious talent of autistic savantism with an outgoing and relatively normal personality, though he can't tell left from right.

The word autism derives from the Greek *autos* meaning 'self', as autists are typically seriously impeded in relating to others; my friend's autistic nephew Marcelo, for example, has never even registered my existence.[19] More fundamentally, though, autists struggle with abstract concepts. Other people's feelings are abstract concepts. Tammet describes how he once kept asking a recently bereaved woman about her thoughts on death, unaware of the impact his curiosity might have had upon her.[20] While people's fingers are concrete concepts, their moods, their desires and personalities and whatever is inside them apart from ooze and tripe are abstract concepts. They can't be directly apprehended through the senses, only inferred.

Words are fundamentally abstract concepts; the combination of phonemes that sounds like *'tābəl* is the name of the thing you eat your dinner at in a locally agreed-upon abstract system of representation called English. Some autists never learn to speak, but there are different levels of abstraction, and most have at least some spoken language. Autists often have poor reading comprehension.[21] Text is a different abstract system of representation, where the thing you eat at is signified by the combination of 't', 'a', 'b', 'l', 'e'.

'Left' is another chamber of abstraction, a categorical set consisting of 'that side of things', and it lies outside of Tammet's skill set. Many autists struggle to generalize an abstract set from a series of concrete examples.[22] One carer describes finally succeeding to teach her charge to butter his toast, only to discover that he couldn't extend that skill to the general category of 'things that are spread on toast'.[23] She had to teach him how to spread peanut butter all over again. Dr. Temple Grandin, a high-functioning autistic academic, describes how she lacks "true abstract thinking", and how for her "concept is sensory based, not word based". She took a systematic approach, establishing categories by force of will:

> On everything in life, I was overwhelmed with a mass of details and I realized that I had to group them together and try to figure out unifying principles for masses of data [...] To form a concept from the many specific photo-realistic pictures I have stored in my memory, I sort them into categories. I categorized dogs from cats by sorting the animals by size [...] until our neighbors got a Dachshund [...] I had to create a new category in my mind to differentiate. All dogs, no matter how big or small, have the same nose shape.[24]

The autistic mind does not readily isolate 'things' out of the whole, whether concepts in the mind or objects in the visual field, and all that unsystematized detail can be "a confusing jumble of events, people, places, sounds and sights, without clear boundaries."[25] It can, therefore, be extremely challenging for autists to establish a sense of order in the relationships between things, and most learn routines to navigate through the chaos. Understandably, they can be touchy over maintaining these routines, and an unexpected visit or new cutlery can send an autist into a panic.[26]

Autists struggle to see the wood for the trees, struggle to see the trees for the leaves and the branches. As autistic writer Naoki Higashida describes it:

> When you see an object, it seems that you see it as an entire thing first, and only afterwards do its details follow on. But for people with autism, the details jump straight out at us first of all, and then only gradually, detail by detail, does the whole image sort of float into focus.[27]

Non-autists (hereafter 'nautists') can't help but attend to an abstract world of category and inference, of context and subtext. That world is obscure for autists, and metaphors tend to be lost on them. "George Bush is not exactly a rocket scientist" is a

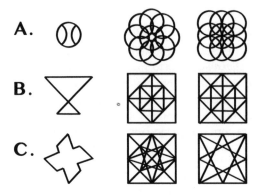

A.

B.

C.

Fig. 5 Embedded figures test

simple statement about a man's profession unless you can imagine the abstract category of jobs that very clever people have.[28] In some situations, though, the abstractions put nautists at a disadvantage.

When asked to recall words from a list read out, for example, nautists naturally group them by category.[29] For example, the sequence 'sour', 'cake', 'chocolate', 'salty', 'doughnut', 'bitter', 'spicy', 'cookie' and so on is usually recalled in sets, with subjects first listing '*things that are sweet*' and then '*tastes*', or vice versa. When asked a trick question, if 'sweet' was on the list, 98% reply incorrectly that it was. 'Sweet' fits into both sets, and makes perfect sense in the context. By rights it should be there – but it isn't. Autists are almost never fooled. They are not compelled to categorize the words in the first place. The detail doesn't get lost in the category. For the same reason, autists find embedded figures in designs faster than nautists.[30]

Autists are also less likely to be fooled by images that become distorted in our heads like the Shepard illusion, where two identically proportioned tabletops appear to be different sizes because of contextual cues.[31] The superb artistic skills of some autistic savants are partly due to the fact that most people translate the shades and lines falling on their retinas into 'eyes' and 'legs' and whatnot, and then draw eyes and legs and whatnot on the page. Autistic savants don't have the conceptual filter; they simply recreate the lines on the page.

Typically the visual cortex is also hyperconnected in autists, with many more local connections than nautists have, and some autists perceive visual detail with incredible acuity. Stephen Wiltshire, for example, sketched a perfect facsimile of the London skyline after flying over it once in a helicopter.[32] Another savant was solving detailed blank jigsaws at the age of three.[33] Though he never learned language, he spends his time happily weaving superlatively complex patterns into textiles.

The autistic visual field may be more flexible than in nautists. When one autist was allowed to play the last few minutes of a basketball game, he discovered to everyone's surprise that he could easily land three-pointers from around the court, and this partly involved visual distortion. He described seeing the basket as "a big old huge bucket that was huge."[34] Superb visual processing at the micro level may also help explain savant counting skills, like Dustin Hoffman's character in *Rain Man* counting spilt toothpicks in a split second. Most of us can't do this, because visual acuity declined sharply at the human

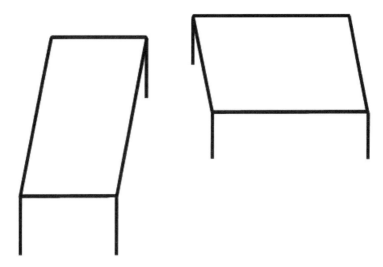

Fig. 6 The Shepard illusion

twig of the evolutionary tree. Ayamu the chimp can remember where nine digits have been displayed on a screen, touching the correct points afterwards to win a reward, completely thrashing nautists who have been training for months (though she hasn't been tested against autists).[35] She retains that level of accuracy when shown the pattern for only two tenths of a second, which is faster than you can blink.

Tammet's mathematical landscapes suggest an extremely refined visual cortex. Grandin seems to have outsourced much of her language processing to the visual cortex; she reads by "convert[ing] text to images as if watching a movie", and imagines the future by visualizing things on the other side of an imaginary door.[36] Along with the visual cortex, the temporal lobes also tend to be hyperconnected in autists. The temporal lobes play a central role in associating sensory input with known concepts, in recognising faces and objects for example.[37][38]

The autistic world is incredibly rich, even overwhelmingly so compared to a world chopped up and jammed into categories. A typical autistic trait is a fascination with parts of objects, as exhibited by one autist I had the honour of teaching. For me a desk is just a desk, whereas for my student Mari-chan the desk was a landscape to become engrossed in to the exclusion of everything else in the room. Her Japanese was basic, and she didn't learn any English from me at all. She was a prodigious pianist though. A line of keys that make noises is a concrete matter, and some autists apply a degree of concentration to it that aspiring Buddhists can only dream of, with their abstractions and their attendant distractions, their social dramas to worry about. This focus can lead to some spectacular musicianship. Blind Tom could play *Yankee Doodle* with one hand and *Fisher's Hornpipe* with the other while singing *Dixie*.[39] He knew 7,000 tunes and less than a hundred words. Derek Paravicini was born three and a half months premature, and he struggles to count to ten, but he was playing with fingers, fists, elbows and forehead by the age of two.[40] While exceptionally talented nautists can listen to a chord and name all three notes, Paravicini can play back on his keyboard every single note of a 50-piece orchestra blast. He can play any piece perfectly after one hearing, like Mozart could, according to legend.[41]

Prodigious musicality is a form of savantism that tends to manifest in autists born blind, perhaps because they are spared a great deal of information overload. The brain is immensely plastic, and blind people (both autists and nautists) outsource sound and touch information processing to their 'visual' centres. Some learn to find their way around by echolocation, as bats do.[42] Whether they 'see' shapes indicated by the sounds bouncing back at them, and whether Paravicini 'sees' sound as Tammet sees number, is another question. However it works, Paravicini's brainwaves spike at a wrong note in a tune.[43] Tammet's galvanic skin response spiked when he was shown an incorrect version of π, and he described how "parts of my numerical landscapes were broken up as though they had been vandalised."[44] Though he describes all irrational numbers as beautiful, he particularly enjoys π. He once publicly recited it to 22,500 decimal places for five hours straight, clearly enjoying the stream of digits, breaking rhythm only to go to the loo or eat a banana.[45] For Higashida,

> numbers are fixed, unchanging things [...] That simplicity, that clearness, it's so comforting to us [...] And when it comes to our favourite things, we can memorise these as easily as if they were jumping straight into our heads.[46]

I saw a guy at the bus stop reeling off bus routes to any passenger looking quizzically at the route map. People were baffled by his erudition, and his breach of London bus stop etiquette, but he was oblivious and content. He stayed there for as long as I observed him, as passengers came and went, and I don't think he was there to take a bus. Fred enjoyed the calendar as an object of beauty in itself. Calendar calculation is one of the most common savant skills, and is based on the perception

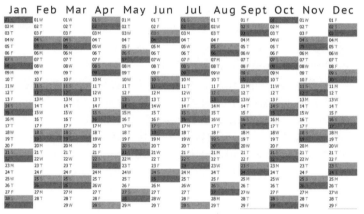

Fig. 7 Regular patterns in the calendar

of patterns in the days, data points that are as concrete as the tiles in geometric mosaics (which are objects of beauty for anyone with eyes to see them).[47][48]

Fig. 8 An autistic child

"Sometimes I actually pity you," writes Higashida, "for not being able to see the beauty of the world in the same way we do."[49] A keen love of beauty and order is common in autism, perhaps because order is so difficult to establish. Autistic toddlers often line up stones or stack tins.[50] As a toddler, Jake Barnett arranged matchsticks into street plans of towns he had visited, and he once laid out hundreds of coloured crayons in the order of the rainbow, having learned the sequence by watching light refract through splashing water.[51] He spoke in monosyllables, and his parents were told he would never communicate normally, but he enjoyed stargazing so his mother took him to the Planetarium. They attended a lecture, where the three-year-old broke his silence to answer the lecturer's question on why the moons of Mars were not spherical like our moon is, referring to their relatively small size and high speed of rotation, and the resulting effects on the force of gravity. At 13 he published his first academic paper, on condensed matter theory.[52]

Einstein barely spoke until he was three, and spent most of his time as a child playing the violin.[53][54] His mechanism of thought was synaesthetic:[55]

> words or language, as they are written or spoken, do not seem to play any role in my mechanism of thought. The psychical entities which seem to serve as elements in thought are certain signs and more or less clear images which can be 'voluntarily' reproduced and combined. The above mentioned elements are, in my case, of visual and some of muscular type. Conventional words or other signs have to be sought for laboriously only in a secondary stage, when the mentioned associative play is sufficiently established and can be reproduced at will.[56]

The normal ear hears a tune, but Paravicini hears every note. Wiltshire sees every window of every building, and Tammet sees number-shapes. Barnett visualizes equations in five dimensions. He loves to share the joy of maths with others, but when he gets going about wormholes and Hamiltonian equations he leaves people behind, like me with my muddy two and a half dimensions on a good day. There are bound to be communication problems across the gulf between dimensions, and between minds that struggle to form categories and those that are compelled to. We are all looking at very different worlds.

$$\Omega$$

Though savantism is rare, around one in ten autists shows some heightened skill, ranging from linguistic skills to exceptional balance, motor skills or prodigious strength.[57] Perhaps many more talents would be unleashed if nautists made more space for their marvellous worlds.[58] We tend to pathologise different modes of cognition rather than celebrate them, and this tells us more about the shortcomings of post-Enlightenment thinking than the minds of our autistic brothers and sisters. Autistic skills are completely under-valued by our economy, as they were when Blind Tom was given away for free along with his mother at a slave auction. He was not only good at retaining music, he also made his own compositions. So does Paravicini, who plays fantastic ragtime though his overwhelming urge to improvise makes for bizarre classical renditions. Many autists are highly innovative, even compulsively so. Inventing new words is another creative trait common in autism; technically it is called 'neologism'. Autists tend to generate more ideas than nautists under test conditions, and their ideas are more unusual.[59] Autists may not be the American Dream of rugged individualism and free enterprise; but then Ronald Reagan never made anything as cool as a robotic dog that barks, wags its tail and urinates, like one autist who can't count did.[60] Even those destined to do nothing that we can easily categorize and capitalize upon can be fascinating and inspirational, like Marcelo, who spends two or three enchanted hours every single day splashing in a water tank and shouting with joy at what he finds there. Maybe it is the thousands of exploding spectrums as the bubbles rise, or the fractals plunging down to infinite depths in the swoosh of his hand? No wonder he doesn't bother looking at boring old me.

Like many things, autism is more of a spectrum than a dualism, from severe autistic disorder through Asperger Syndrome, obsessive compulsive disorder (OCD) and attention deficit hyperactive disorder (ADHD). ADHD minds follow their fancy, and can be bored or repelled by the beige tones of the office cubicle or school curriculum. Personally I can forget to get the pot from the stove or the kids from school if

I'm engrossed in something to do with the apocalypse, while application forms and letters from the council fill me with irrational panic and almost physical discomfort. ADHD is over-represented among artists and CEOs, and also in prisons because such quirks can be difficult to integrate into normal society. The War on ADHD costs over $9 billion per year, supplying amphetamines to one in ten high school boys in the US.[61] Again this points to shortcomings in a society that labels as 'disorders' that which it cannot order. Grouping people by subcategories in the larger category of disorder would make little sense to an autist, along with the various categories of anxiety that schematize the human condition.

Medics have developed techniques for dealing with autism, including prenatal screens for prospective parents who would rather abort their growing disorder in the womb than run the risk of it messing up their plans. To be sure, severe autism can be terrible for a parent to deal with, not to mention the autist themselves, but surely eugenics is not the answer. Fortunately, while the search for a 'cure' continues, understanding about autism seems to be progressing. The neurodiversity movement is gaining traction with its critique of neurotypical cognition as the single correct mode of being.[62] The shift in the narrative is partly due to better media about the subject, including the *Rain Man* film. Its fictional character is based on Kim Peek, and strictly speaking Peek's savantism was related to a developmental condition called FG syndrome, but his cognition displayed many typical autistic characteristics. He was not fooled by the 'sweet things/tastes' memory test, for example.[63] His brain was also structurally similar to autistic brains. In autists the main bridge between hemispheres (the corpus callosum) tends to be reduced in size, and Peek's was entirely absent.[64][65] Autistic brains also have fewer long distance connections generally, and many more interconnections at the local level.[66][67]* This hyperconnectivity seems to be because the normal process of synaptic pruning, that eliminates superfluous

---

* The corpus callosum is generally larger in women than men, and autistic spectrum traits such as tunnel vision and antisocial behaviour also seem to be less common in women. It has been argued (Hall, J et al, PLoS One 2012;7(12)) that autists are 'extra-male', given that they develop physically faster than neurotypicals, and produce more testosterone. Testosterone stimulates local dendrite growth.

connections in the network, is reduced in autistic brains.[68] There is also less myelin insulation around the neurons, which again means that the networks are less streamlined.[69]

The corpus callosum generally inhibits activity on the opposite side of the brain, and without the connection and the inhibition between them the two hemispheres of Peek's brain learned to process information independently.[70] He could read two pages at once, one with each eye, turning the page every ten seconds. Reading before his second birthday, he read a good portion of the Salt Lake City Library in his 58 years, and would retain 98% of the information to answer obscure questions on it years later. Sometimes he would correct actors at the theatre who had performed their lines incorrectly.[71] My grandfather, for his part, used to announce to his family how many mistakes the musicians had made after attending piano recitals. He played the piano beautifully all day long, and needed help buttoning up his shirt correctly.

The manner in which Peek systematized data sheds some light on how hyperconnectivity can influence cognitive function. When asked about Beethoven's fifth symphony, for example, he immediately sang the opening '*Da Da Da Daaaah*'. That called to his mind the *dot-dot-dot-dash* of the letter V in Morse Code, which relates back to the number five of the fifth symphony via the Roman numeral V. These items are not related via causality, nor by logic or symbolism; they are related by implicit likeness. *Da Da Da Daaah* does not cause or symbolize or mean *dot-dot-dot-dash*. *Da Da Da Daaah* is *dot-dot-dot-dash*, which is also V, and V is also 5. The detail is instantly embedded into a broader network of corresponding things.

The language of correspondence is different to the rational language of the conscious mind. In dreams and visions, causality and logic are abandoned for implicit likenesses between symbols, and correspondence is also the signature of synchronicity (Jung's term for when we repeatedly encounter significant symbols that reveal something behind the surface of causal reactions). The golden beetle that flew into Jung's treatment room was not causally or symbolically related to the golden scarab his patient was describing from her dream at that very moment. It was related by implicit likeness:

> I handed the beetle to my patient with the words, "Here is your scarab." This experience punctured the desired hole in her rationalism and broke the ice of her intellectual resistance. The treatment could now be continued with satisfactory results.[72]

In ritual, high priests and low magicians work beneath the schematics of causality, using the language of incenses, incantations, gestures, numbers and colours – a broad palette of sense impressions familiar to ritualists from their meditations. Different subsystems of the central nervous system are affected and line up beyond the conscious mind, to turn the powerhouse of the unconscious on the object of conscious attention.

Ω

Savant skills, like much in the brain, are a matter of organization, and brains can be reorganized. When nerve cells degenerate and die with frontotemporal dementia, some patients rapidly develop prodigious musical and mathematical skills.[73][74] It happens exactly at the stage when they lose their ability to form grammatically meaningful sentences, when the normal networks of relationships begin to unravel. Prodigious skills can also be triggered by strokes, epileptic fits, violent muggings and other shocks to the temporal lobe – even lightning strikes, by Jove! Orlando Serrell's calendar calculation skills were bestowed upon him in 1979 by a speeding baseball to the left temple.[75] Knocked flat by a Shakti-pat from a baseball bat, he has been able to recall minute details of every single day since, including the weather and the clothes people were wearing. Dereck Amato dove into the shallow end of a swimming pool in foolishness and emerged a genius. Though he had never played piano before, he felt an urge to sit at the keys a few days later, and he discovered his musical imagination had become synaesthetic:

> I've always kind of explained it as black and white
> blocks that move left to right in almost kind of like
> a wave pattern if you will [...] The imagery of these
> blocks pushes me to play. It almost insists that I play.[76]

Compulsive urges are common at all points along the autistic spectrum, and also with acquired savantism. Alonzo Clemons, who fell on his head as a child and hasn't spoken much since, spends most of his time cheerfully making perfectly proportioned horses out of clay. When staff at a residential facility took his clay away, to encourage him to learn other skills like tying his shoelaces, he would lie in wait whenever a window was broken, knowing that the repairman would soon bring fresh putty for him to work with. Alonzo really wants to make horses, and moreover, it just so happens that the world is perilously undersupplied with accurately carved likenesses of horses. Every school should have one, along with other sources of wonder. Simple details like this are easily missed by sufferers of Non-Autistic Disorder Syndrome (NADS).[77] Of course, people who can't tie their shoelaces can be a bit of a drain on the patience and the economy, but supporting their quirks could make the world a happier place for neurotypical and neurodivergent people alike. Barnett's difficult symptoms diminish to almost nothing if he is allowed to do what he wants, which is physics. Naoki Higashida is happy as long as he can flap and run about where he likes.[78] He is tormented when he can't:

> My brain is always sending me off on little missions,
> whether or not I want to do them. And if I don't obey,
> then I have to fight a feeling of horror. Really it's like
> I'm being pushed over the brink into a kind of Hell.[79]

Many of the inspired artists described in *Science Revealed* were driven by overwhelming compulsions, such as Nietzsche, who wrote without "any choice in the matter".[80] Compulsions have fallen into the net of psychiatry, along with many other traits of the creative genius including obsession, perfectionism, anxiety and voices in the head. Cultures more clued up about creativity recognised its relationship with madness. As Plato put it,

> He who without divine madness comes to the doors of the Muses, confident that he will be a good poet by art, meets with no success, and the poetry of the sane man vanishes into nothingness before that of the inspired madmen.[81]

Even though full-blown schizophrenics are less likely to have children than neurotypicals, it appears that the genes associated with schizophrenia have spread successfully and levelled out to strikingly stable frequencies across different populations.[82] It seems that the link with inspiration means that there is an optimum degree of crazy, both in a person and in a population, and those in whom the force is strong make desirable partners as long as they manage to keep to the charming side of loopy. Some of the most brilliant minds of history have undoubtedly been some of the strangest, including that of Nikola Tesla, whose synaesthetic apocalypses gave birth to the modern technological age. His obsessions included hygiene and the number 3; he would also only stay in a hotel room divisible by 3, and he bathed with 18 towels (maybe because $1 + 8 = 3$ x 3, and $18 = 3$ x 3 x 2, and $3 + 3 + 2 = 1$ x 8).[83] He always ate the same meal at the same time at the same table of the Waldorf hotel, after cleaning his cutlery with 18 napkins and calculating the cubic volume of his food.[84] Tammet weighs his cereal. Some people are compelled to quantify and mathematize. They can be rather clever.

Tesla would probably have been diagnosed with OCD today. So would Newton, who worked almost solidly, sleeping when his concentration failed him, eating and washing when his servant reminded him.[85] His primary obsession was the apocalypse, and his interests in astronomy and chronology stemmed from his attempt to decipher heavenly omens and date events in scripture. He wrote 4,500 unpublished pages calculating when the world was going to end, leaving an intriguing "2060" scrawled in a margin that may or may not be his final date (it is also the date that London will sink under the sea, according to some ecologists).[86] [87] OCD traits are overrepresented amongst religious people generally, but Newton took it to another level.[88] According to his biographer:

> To force everything in the heavens and on earth into a rigid, tight frame, from which the most minuscule detail would not be allowed to escape free and random, was an underlying need of this anxiety-ridden man.[89]

Stranger still, Newton felt that this Great Work had been given to him personally by YHWH, who also left a clue in the anagram of his name: *Isaacus Neuutonus = Ieova sanctus unus* (the One Sanctified by Jehovah – or some such auto-messianic indiscretion).[90] In partnership with the Lord, the virgin Newton birthed the world's first universal physical formula, a concrete and perfectly-formed number relationship uniting planets, apples and tiny particles. Whether pathological or divine, the power that compelled Newton to work revealed macro-order over a scale never previously spanned by the human mind. It put a series of things in order – the force between two objects (F), the masses of the objects (m_1 and m_2), the distance between them (d), and the gravitational constant (G):

$$F_g = \frac{Gm_1m_2}{r^2}$$

Savant skills include microfine perception, superb motor control, perfect recall, incredible feats of calculation, and powerful creative urges blazing a trail of innovation. These are qualities that pertain to the demigods of mythology. Higashida's descriptions recall mystical texts, with heavenly bliss on one side and hellish terror on the other, his ecstasies turning on his freedom to indulge his urges. In times past, and today in territories beyond the frontiers of polite society, heavenly sensations and revelations were and are attributed to spiritual forces. When the Holy Spirit busts a move in the Pentecostal church, the congregation jitters and jives and speaks in tongues. The penitent at prayer or the sinner at sin may be visited by angels or devils, may hear the heavenly choir or smell the stink of sulphur. One neurologist described Joan of Arc's "dream-like state, [and] visions of angels and voices with a messianic message [as] quite typical of complex partial seizures."[91] The prophet Daniel's vision is accompanied by many features of a tonic-clonic (grand mal) epileptic fit, including loss of muscle tone and collapse, convulsions, inability to breathe or speak, hearing voices and finally losing consciousness.[92] Psalm 137 also describes something like a lateralized seizure:

> If I forget you, Jerusalem, Let my right hand forget its skill.
>
> Let my tongue stick to the roof of my mouth.

Less violent epileptic seizures are suggested by other biblical accounts:

> A deep sleep/unconsciousness fell upon Abram; and, lo, an horror of great darkness fell upon him. And [YHWH] said unto Abram…[93]

Terror and elation, premonition and déjà vu, dizziness, kundalini tingles and synaesthesia are all common in the throes of spiritual visitation, and also at the onset of epileptic convulsion. If the focal centre of an epileptic fit is in the visual cortex, the patient tends to see moving lights.[94] If it is in the auditory cortex, they likely hear a tone. If the focus also encompasses neighbouring regions of the temporal lobes then tones may become voices or pieces of music, and lights and shapes become people or scenes. Again there are parallels with biblical apocalypses, where entities may appear as sounds to one person and as visions to another.[95] The types of demonic, angelic and ancestral entities haunting the online epilepsy forums also recall the personalities encountered in mythology:

I would see ghosts on my street and things float across the room. Is anybody else here taking Zonogram? The voices would sometimes confuse me and say I'm godlike an angel [...] sometimes I wonder if I have ESP.

The last two nights she has come in to us saying that there is a shadow in her room that whispers to her, whispers her name and then said that she had her feet on his dead father's head.[96]

Newton's messianic messenger also visits the forums:

I only heard a voice once which said "you're the one" which left me rather puzzled at the time, I mean I'm the one what?[97]

A self-identifying voice-hearer I met in a cafe was accompanied by a mostly friendly voice that passed on insights and brilliant puns that he shared with me, about words in the Bible among other things. He was fascinating and very witty – or the voice was. He simply called it 'God', and unless he "fell into sin", as he put it, God didn't trouble him. While it is tempting to pathologise him, he certainly felt that the voice was beneficial and kept him from sin, whatever that means to him. We tend to think of voices as malevolent, and the nasty ones get more media attention, but plenty of people have heard voices – 13% of the population according to one estimate.[98] Those who maintain good relationships with their voices generally keep their dissociated selves to themselves, once they learn what is appropriate. The young Swedenborg had imaginary friends so full of cleverness that even his parents believed in them.[99] He called them angels, and they accompanied him until adulthood and helped the great polymath write his books.

Higashida's language about Hell notwithstanding, autists rarely couch their experience in religious terms; in fact, they are about ten times less likely than their peers to profess a belief in God (this makes sense, as God is the ultimate abstract concept, the way we do Him these days, and they are generally oblivious to the abstract).[100] Compulsion and ecstasy may be more ubiquitous and concrete elements of experience to autists, like water is to a fish. Temporal lobe epileptics are more amphibian, so to speak, slipping in and out of waves of unconventional brain function. They are generally more religious than average, and the galvanic response of their skin tends to be stronger for religious words than sexual words.[101] [102]

Tourette's Syndrome is also sometimes linked with hyper-religiosity, as well as OCD and compulsive ideation. This was the case for Dr. Samuel Johnson, with his whistles, his "tics and gesticulations", his routines at the doorway.[103] [104] He diligently said his prayer "to drive from me all such unquiet and perplexing thoughts […] to withdraw my mind from unprofitable and dangerous inquiries, from difficulties vainly curious, and doubts impossible to be solved".[105] On the flip side, his racing mind made him one of the greatest wits of the 18th century. Compulsive ideation is both informative and relentless as it runs through the permutations making Johnson almost uniquely equipped to write the first comprehensive dictionary with multiple descriptions of words (completed in eight years with six assistants, where *Le Dictionnaire* took 40 French scholars 55 years).[106]

Like invasive thoughts, vocal tics sometimes respond to context, echoing accents for example. Compared to the urge to blink or sneeze, a tic can be suppressed in many cases by force of will, or perhaps a silent limerick when the urge to swear arises – but it isn't pleasant.[107] If a vocal tic is interrupted halfway out, the individual may never discover what would have been said.[108] At full throttle they can erupt into poetry:

> Sky, I'm not even sure you exist right now.
>
> I'm painting a rainbow on your forehead, Sky.
>
> I'm writing a love-letter to the lamp-post in your gaps, Sky.
>
> I'm dancing with a carrier-bag across your blank back, Sky.
>
> I'm parking some ideas in your space, Sky.[109]

Context specific, responsive and rhythmical, there is wit in these words – but whose, if the speaker is as surprised as the listener? Poetics also feature in the case of a tonic-clonic epileptic, whose convulsion left him experiencing words as "continuously rhyming in his head" for the next five years, along with an overwhelming compulsion to write poetry and show it to others.[110] Is this on the same spectrum as Nietzsche's rogue writing hand, or Blake writing "without premeditation and even against my will", or Robert Anton Wilson who said of his words "you just let them run rampant and they come out of your fingers and onto the paper".[111]

Compulsive writing is sometimes present with epilepsy, and one patient started compulsively writing poetry when her dose of medication was reduced.[112][113] Did she hit the sweet point between order and disorder that triggers compulsion without convulsion, not too hot and not too cold for Goldi-lobes? We tend to think of epilepsy as irregular but it is orderly, involving the synchronization of a large pool of neurons over widely separated regions of the brain. Convulsing muscles tense and relax in a rhythmic and orderly fashion, more regularly than muscles making an omelette, for example. With new hi-tech devices for scanning the brain and manipulating its magnetic field, many things are being explained in terms of brain activity these days – more activity, less activity, irregular activity – but epileptic brain activity is only 'irregular' in the sense that it is unlike the disorder that is regularly observed.

Autonomous things are said, heard, felt and thought at some point between control and release, with glorious diversity in the manifesting of urge and compulsion. We notice something extraordinary happening in the brain when it is accompanied by foaming at the mouth, but a seizure may manifest outwardly as a fluttering eyelid or nothing at all.[114] What is going on when invisible voices speak in the swirl of a brainwave, pouring forth ideation in rhythm and rhyme through the pens of poets and the mouths of mediums? Is there something present in the absence, when the individual steps out of day-to-day existence for a moment?

> And Enoch walked with Elohim: and he was not; for Elohim took him.[115]

Come, let us learn the secrets of the Hebrews, while reading selectively from the classier books, beginning "in the head" where the powers balance the competing urges and interacting lobes of the human brain. While this may seem like a strange way to approach scripture, it is surely less strange than trying to understand the story of jealous, wrathful and mass-murdering deities and patriarchs as some kind of moral compass.

Let us begin, as is our custom, in the beginning.

Ω

00:19 it's not going to be a bad one. It's come up fast.The slow burn is the worst.

00:21 it was the smell that told me. I smell things like burning herbs. Then they go, and when it's over they're gone.

00:29 I can feel fragments of identity speaking to me. It gets harder to describe I taste salt and something else. I exult in these moments. it's the payoff for the bad times, the weary times. In these moments I kiss God.

00:31 I can see all the colours now, under your skin! Look at your hand. Do you doubt that you contain an infinity of shades? tone and chroma, chapter and verse. you are the book of madder-rose and indigo. my hands will be taken soon, for a while. but how lovely that i can speak colour with my hands, while the time lasts!

00:33 its coming. i break open like achrysalis, i split. cant say much more. but you are the divine! look at your hands, draw breth, and do not doubt that you taste eternity.

00:37 over soon. i would be a river if i could. i would bleed eternal/divine. wont see it when i wake up. see it NOW. all colours. when you see all the colours. all the colours, in any one colour. that is to taste the divine. over soon. I want to remember! the keys look like bone, like brick. pyramids and saints toes. all colours. all the colours. they all saw all the colours.

00:40 keys like bone, but containign all colours. the colours never leave us. God is spectrum, infinite spectrum. sound, colour touch all a spectrum

00:54 It's over. I had the fit, I'm fine except I think I hit my elbow on something and I bit muy tongue.

> - Description of a complex partial seizure moving to full convulsion, typed out as it happened[116]

IN THE /b/GINNING

AUM!
This syllable is this whole world…
The past, the present, the future…
And whatever else…

- Mandukya Upanishads

IN THE BEGINNING…

…is *b'reishiyt* in Hebrew, and that begins with /b/. Tradition has it that the Hebrew letters "depict the soul of all that was formed and all that will be formed"; so why, by the holy generative organs of God, would the book of beginnings begin with the second letter?[1]

> The *alef* complained before the Holy One, blessed be He, pleading before Him: "Sovereign of the Universe! I am the first of the letters, yet Thou didst not create Thy world with me […] Why was the world created with a *beyt*?"[2]

Is /b/ simply the phoneme of choice with which to begin cosmic revelations, a bilabial big bang in the beginning, even in other beginnings, with _Bismillah_ at the beginning of the Quran, and _Biblos_ in the NT? _Buh_ certainly projects better than _El_. Try shouting 'Barry' and 'Elliot' to see which sounds more articulate.

...CREATED ELOHIM...

B'RAiShYT BaRA ALoHYM: "In the beginning created Elohim", whose name begins with _alef_. It would have been grammatically sound to put Elohim second, before the creating rather than after it; or it could have gone first as _alef_ would have preferred, beginning the Word of God with the word for God, and simultaneously beginning the Bible with the first letter. But the beginning and the creating are written out before Elohim. Elohim is introduced with a booming double gong-bash bonging in the beginning: /b/ followed by a rolled /r/ reverberating and extended with an /a/, twice over. _B'RAiShYT BaRA ALoHYM_, and the echo carried across the territories and down the centuries.

In commentaries and commentaries upon commentaries, the letters of the holy scroll have been examined in bewildering detail, put through all manner of permutations, their cosmological and moral implications drawn out. The rabbis drew the line, however, at inquiring into the _alef_ before the _beyt_ which begins 'in the beginning':

> Just as the _beyt_ is closed at the sides but open in front,
> so you are not permitted to investigate what is above
> and what is below, what is before and what is behind.[3]

Hebrew letters are also words, and words have meanings that change with the vowelling. _Alef_ (pronounced _elef_) means 'ox', and an ox is both powerful and indefinite, neither raging bull nor docile cow. Oxen are also dangerous animals in the OT, whereas _beyt_ is safe as houses; _BaYiT_ means a 'house' or 'building', the archetype of solidity.[4 5] The letters of the Bible march out of the building from its open side, from right to left in the way of the Hebrews, the way Greek letters used to march before they switched sides 27 centuries ago.[6] The letters go in the way of the hemispheres, from diffuse and locally busy networks on the right to more clearly focused networks on the left, where the Broca's area and Wernicke's area work together with the rest of the brain and body to produce language.[7][8] We make things up as we go along with our words and letters, organizing the swirl of…

…THE HEAVEN AND THE EARTH…

…into order, representing it to consciousness and to each other. Our letters and our thoughts make sense of the world, casting light into the darkness, throwing shadows.

…AND THE EARTH WAS WITHOUT FORM, AND VOID; AND DARKNESS WAS UPON THE FACE OF THE DEEP…

Peering beyond the back wall of the house of *beyt* into the infinite and undivided no man's land of *alef* breaks the rabbi's taboo and throws caution to the wind; for *alef* is the mother letter of air, and it is very windy indeed.[9] In the *Commentary on Alef*:

> Great winds were around the *Shekinah* at every moment. These are: a hovering wind, a strong wind, an earthquake wind and a storm-wind […] A tempest was his chariot, the storm-wind was his seat […] And out of the sound of the praise of many waters, the Holy One, blessed be He, gave his consent to create the world.[10]

…AND THE WIND OF ELOHIM MOVED…[11]

'Vowel' is 'movement' in Hebrew; the same word indicates both.[12] Nearly all alphabets begin with the vowel 'a', from

Japanese to Greek to Sanskrit to Yoruba. *Alef* is the primal utterance, the *aah-aah* and *ooh-ooh* of the simians. It is *aaah!* and *ohh!* and *iaaaaaeeeeaaaaaaah!*, wide-eyed, wide-mouthed ejaculations of inarticulate wonder or terror or orgasm at the void. A mother screams *alef* as her baby emerges from the deep dark void, and *alef* is all the noise the newborn can make at the blinding chaos in the beginning. *Alef* is pronounced with the throat fully open and the tongue, teeth and lips out of the way. Its potential is directed in sound according to conditions around it – the consonants beside it supplying its edges, and the intention behind it supplying the vowels and making pronouncements. By convention the first *alef* of Genesis is read '*ei*', but changing the way air moves through the folds of the throat and the passage of consonants changes the story. Changing *ei* to *oh*, from *reish* to *rosh*, moves the beginning to the 'head'. "In the head was created Elohim".

The voice is the original biofeedback machine, and as *alefs* are fed back through the ears into the head the newborn learns to modulate them, shaping sound from within to reflect and affect the aural environment. By the third day of life, French babies and German babies can already be distinguished by their intonation.[13]

...UPON THE FACE OF THE WATERS...

'Waters' is *MaYiM* in Hebrew, beginning and ending with /m/. *Mem* is the mother letter of water, the second mother letter after *alef* the mother letter of air, and it falls exactly half-way through the alphabet.[14] The baby's *aaa* becomes *mmm* when the mouth is clamped on a breast, or vice versa: *AM*. *AM* is the name of his mummy in Hebrew (in Portuguese it is *mãe*, in Italian *mama*, in Latin *mater*, in Sanskrit *mata*). At around the third month, when his mouth closes on its own, he can pronounce it all by himself.[15] Though besotted mums might disagree, '*mamamama*' won't be associated with anyone in particular until the baby is a year old or so.[16]

...AND GOD SAID...

'To say' is also *AM*, this time pronounced '*om*'. *Alef* to *mem* spans the universe, from a fully-open to a fully-closed mouth, and much can be communicated by combining these two mother letters: satisfaction or displeasure; confusion or curiosity; agreement or disagreement. Things go either way according to intonation. *AM* (pronounced *im*) also means 'if' and 'when', words that close down the options from many to one, defining something specific out of numerous possibilities – if and when you make your choice. The letters reversed as *MA* suggest the opposite, not the possibility of definition but a defined possibility, a thing with something unclear about it. *Ma* means 'what', as in 'what's that crawling on your shoulder?' It is definitely something, but it could be anything. *M'oomah* (*MAWMH*) is a large but indeterminate amount, and *m'od* (*MAD*) is 'exceeding abundance'.[17] Again it evokes the idea of one specific thing, and an unfathomably large amount of it.

Mem binds infinity between the lips, bringing the infinite into a manageable mouthful as a baby <u>mi</u>lking <u>ma</u>-<u>ma</u>'s <u>mamma</u>ries, bringing endless potential into a sweet and satisfying trickle. *Mmmmmm* is the sound of satisfaction. It is voiced during sex as the void draws us in towards the climax of the open vowel, and again during labour as the void prepares to reveal new life. *Mmm* is the noise usually sounded in sleep, and *mmm* may be all the noise someone on their death bed can make as they approach their final breath and the void beyond. *Mmm* rises and falls smoothly between states of consciousness, like the waxing and waning of the <u>Mo</u>on. The flow between mother and newborn is continuous, with nutrients, antibodies and hormones passing in the milk, warmth shared skin to skin, bliss and stress reciprocated between their nervous systems. Occasionally other entities drop into the continuum, including a bristly face belonging to the father, whose Hebrew name is *AB*. *AB* bursts into and interrupts the current in various ways in its meanings: 'brandishing a sword'; 'coiling upward'; 'a young ear of grain'; 'desire'; 'hatred'.[18] Reversed as *BA* it is the opposite process opening up space in hardness: 'to dig'; 'to engrave'; 'an entrance'; 'a well'; a 'pit'.[19]

As the mother letters draw apart, a range of phonemes carve out possibilities between them, between *ALoHYM* and *ADaM* and big daddy *AB-RaHaM. AM* flows, but /b/ fractures at the primordial place of revelation, in the head of a baby in the beginning. The bilabial /b/ and the sharper bilabial /p/ are commonly the earliest sounds babbled in pattern.[20][21] Bit by bit, form rises into space and space plunges into form. Now we're talkin', and what sense are we making? We're talking boobies and babies and many things close to the baby, *bambino* in Italian (baby), and in Japanese *ba* (auntie), *baa* (granny) and *baba* (poo). At the booby is where baby finds the other, and in doing so it becomes conscious of itself, the *ba-ba* between the immmmensity of *ma-ma* and the pointed power of *pa-pa*, of *pater* in Latin or *pitara* in Sanskrit.

The nascent mind expands, associating the internal and external in sound, which is in both. As the muscles gradually come under control, cooing and goo-gooing at the back of the throat gives way to murmuring, then mumbling and then babbling as the front of the mouth is conquered.[22] Between utterance and eloquence, the first plosives /b/ and /p/ catch and release the breath on the lips, splitting up the passage of air into sections, unlike the mother letters *aaa* and *mmm* which extend the airflow uninterrupted.

... *"Let there be light."* ...

Until the muscles that aim and focus the eyes come under control, the newborn's eyes may wander independently; and if learning to see is anything like learning other muscular skills it is acquired actively, through feedback and force of will. The first visual response is when the baby glances towards a light source.[23]

...AND THERE WAS LIGHT...

Consciousness expands in the head, filling the mouth and spilling out through eyes. The baby strains at patches of contrast to establish edges, creating and sustaining the world re-presented to consciousness within.[24] By around the third month, the eyes can focus to about 20cm to discern an array of grins and breasts out of the chaos. The movements of the powers beyond are still a blur, and even what can be discerned dissolves as soon as it is out of view. Young babies do not exhibit an understanding of 'object permanence'; they seem to think that something hidden (under a hat, for example) could be absolutely anywhere (rather than where it was before the hat covered it over).[25] Peek-a-boo is an endlessly surprising apocalypse until object permanence develops and spoils the fun, by fixing objects where they are on the map.

A baby's perception of shade and depth improves from around the fourth month, as eyes and neurological pathways develop. Hands begin to sense hard and soft and everything in between, and soon creamy lukewarm gooey milk will be supplemented with liquids and chunks that are colder and warmer. Lips and tongue generate and perfect new sounds to add further shades to the voice, laying the foundations for a wide spectrum of meaning. In the Hebrew alphabet, the bilabial /b/ at the outer edge of the voice instrument is followed by the guttural /g/ at the inner edge. Next is /d/, back towards the front on the tip of the tongue, and then /h/ in the middle. The letter *heh* is a phoneme we share with monkeys, 'the king of speech' according to the kabbalists, and it begins a sequence of letters that modulate rather than break the flow of noise and air.[26]

...AND...

...is the letter *waw* in Hebrew. *Waw* was pronounced /w/ in ancient times (though it is sometimes /v/ in modern Hebrew).[27] The first semi-vowel, it focuses the flow between the lips, but it does not interrupt the flow. *Waw* glides out of one word or clause and into the next, and its meaning of 'and' brings two things either side of it together in terms of meaning. Genesis 1:1 begins with /b/, but every other verse begins with /w/, as one episode flows into the next in sound. Prefixed to a verb, /w/ brings together that which went before and that which comes after in another way. Biblical Hebrew verbs don't have tenses, only a completed or perfect form ('she remembered', 'we are all lost'), and a progressive or imperfect form that isn't finished yet ('he will walk', 'she dwells'). Past and future are interpreted from contextual cues, and when *waw* is prefixed to a verb it switches the track from past to future or vice versa. The phoneme /w/ joins up meaning across time, as well as space and sound.

The letters that follow /w/ in the alphabet are fricatives that turn the flow to friction. The next is /z/ buzzing behind the teeth, then the very Middle Eastern /kh/ rasped from the throat, then /th/ (though the letter *tet* is voiced differently in modern pronunciation).[28] After that comes the other semi-vowel /y/.

...*Elohim saw the light, that it was good...*

In the light the eyes delight in things and their qualities. There is no 'bad' for another few chapters, but its germ is born here with 'good', and a world of dualism is established immediately afterwards,

...*And Elohim divided the light from the darkness...*

Right from the double gong-bash in the beginning, sound and meaning are exquisitely intertwined in Hebrew, bringing together within and without, before and after. The world around the baby is broken up into things, the breath is broken up into sounds, and the two are linked in significance as the utterances begin to make sense.

...And Elohim called...

'Call' is *KaRaA*, an onomatopoeia evoking the voice of a baby or an animal; theEnglish onomatopoeia 'cry' uses the same phonemes. Babies cry out at the objects of their attention, usually pointing at them as they do so, and their mothers bring them close or push them away. Babies babble various phonemes in patterns without any obvious meaning; but cries are different, uttered meaningfully with clear intent, and often combining the vowels and the semi-vowels: *waaii?*, *ayayayaiiii!*, *waaa!* and so on. Those combinations retain their meaning into adulthood, as cries of wonder (*wow!*, *uau!* in Portuguese, *ua!* in Japanese), and cries of pain (*ow!* and *owch!*, *ai!* in Latin countries, *itai!* in Japanese).

...[AT] THE LIGHT, "DAY"...

Or perhaps "Elohim called '*yowm*' at the light". Young babies see things and vocalize at them, and from around the fourth month those things are becoming familiar as object permanence develops, as their neck muscles can support their heads and they can look where they wish. Naming things with fixed names is different to vocalizing at them. Names don't appear until after the six days of creation, and it is neither Elohim nor any other power who chooses them. It is Adam.[29]

'Day' is *YoWM*, the first utterance in the Bible. It is the word *AM* modified by replacing the *alef* with both semi-vowels /w/ and /y/. Where *alef* extends indefinitely, semi-vowels cannot be sustained (try holding 'light-year' on the /y/ – it becomes a different sound). The semi-vowels contract into time like consonants, focusing sound to a finite point while keeping the flow unobstructed like a vowel. *Yowd* squeezes the flow at the back of the mouth. It is the smallest character, drawn as a point with a flick and called "the little that contains much" – for *yowd* aches to expand .[30] *Yad* is 'a place' or 'to point', its meaning focusing attention in space. It is also 'the hand', the point through which babies and adults engage the world outside, pointing things out, pointing out things, manipulating them. When YHWH Elohim 'forms' it is *yatzar*, gliding in with /y/, unlike *bara* cutting out with /b/. *Yatzar* derives from a root meaning 'to squeeze' or "to mould into a form; especially as a potter".[31] YHWH is another god that begins with *yowd*, who applies pressure in space and time "with a strong hand [*yad*]."[32]

Elohim, the god that begins with *alef*, is different. He is there creating in the beginning, but when the work of creation is done He retreats behind the scenes into the cycles of nature. "He changeth the times and the seasons", but He is too aloof (too *alef*) to squeeze and squelch in the mud directly.[33] He remains unmanifest, the Absolute. Emanations of power are different, focused into space with agency and purpose, usually manifesting as a god that begins with *yowd*. Others include Yah, YHWH Elohim, YHWH Rafa (the Lord who heals), and a host of other lords, even the Lord of Hosts YHWH Tz'vaot. *Yowd* emerges from infinite potential into a finite world. Flanked with *heh*, a letter of physical manifestation often forming the feminine noun-ending, it makes the verb 'to be': *HYH*. Y and H also form the first half of YHWH, who later reveals Himself as 'I AM THAT I AM' (*AHYH ASR AHYH*). The second half of YH:WH pairs and earths the other semi-vowel *waw* with *heh*.

The first word '*yowm*' glides across the possibilities of the palate, squeezing /y/ at the back, opening to full flow and then squeezing /w/ between the lips as they close on the /m/. It emerges like the light of day, beginning gradually, increasing its intensity, then fading to nothing.

...*AND* [AT] *THE DARKNESS HE CALLED, "NIGHT"...*

...which is *LaYLa*, a *yowd* flanked by *lamed*s (pronounced "lamb 'ead"). The phoneme /l/ is formed by nearly blocking the airflow, diverting it sideways at the back of the mouth. It is the letter immediately before *mem*, the final adjustment on the journey from the first mother letter in the beginning to the second mother letter in the middle. Pronouncing /l/ is more difficult, not usually mastered until the third year. In Hebrew its meaning would be learned quickly, however, because combined with *alef* it is *LA*, pronounced *lo* and meaning 'no'. *LA* diverts flow with /l/ and the energy of *alef* behind it. This is the sound fed back to the baby from outside when things go in a direction they shouldn't.[34] As babies explore they learn, which is *LiMuD*, another vowelling of *LaMeD*. The baby learns about good and naughty, establishing edges in his social world as sharp as the edges his eyes discern in the physical world around him.

Lamed means 'ox-goad', the stick used to poke and hit an ox. The ox-goad tames and directs the primal and indefinite energy of *alef* the ox, driving it down furrows and around wheels, focusing potential into the ends of civilization. The other permutation of the energetic *alef* and the directed *lamed* is *AL*, which means 'power'. *AL* pluralised and with a feminine *heh* is *ALoHYM*, all the powers in one. As a preposition, *AL* means 'to' or 'for', again focusing movement and intention towards a destination.

…AND THERE WAS EVENING AND THERE WAS MORNING…

…and there was chaos and there was order…

…DAY ONE.

A child's vocabulary expands exponentially over their second and third years, and with it their range of expression; and yet the phonemes themselves take longer to develop. The sibilant /s/ is the most challenging of all the Hebrew sounds, and usually mastered from around five or six years old as the milk teeth are being replaced, though 10% still haven't managed it by eight years old and some take a lisp into adulthood.[35] The penultimate letter of the Hebrew alphabet is *shin*, pronounced either /s/ or /sh/. It is the third and final mother letter, the mother letter of fire that hisses like fire, bringing things towards a close with the final letter /t/. The *shin* phonemes are the most abrasive, the *pssst!* that interrupts, the *ssh!* that silences, the *hisssss!* that protests, the sound that makes a cat's head turn. It is the sound of resistance against the teeth, and *shin* also means tooth, both the fang that kills and the molar that grinds down chunks. *Shin* is both the fire of digestion and destruction.

Things in the world are fixed in the first seven years, including the sense of self, which may not be fully defined in toddlers; they often refer to themselves in the third person ("Johnny want..."), rather than "I want...".[36] Once a child learns who they are and what the Tooth Fairy is, they know forever, though the associations tend to change radically at around six or seven as the fantasy world and the real world draw apart, as the sibilants first emerge from the mouth.[37] The average well-adjusted five-year-old is physically incapable of keeping a secret, his thoughts spill out incontinent like wee down a chair-leg. After spending an afternoon decorating daddy's surprise birthday cake, a five-year-old will most likely blurt out the secret the moment daddy comes home. A seven-year-old is different, learning to control the flow enough to hiss and piss (and later diss) appropriately. His frontal lobes are developing, and will continue to do so well into adolescence. Gradually he gains more influence over his urges, modulating the free flow between inside and outside, between private thoughts and public actions.[38] A toddler draws on the living room walls without malice and without considering the consequences, but things change as they become more sensitive to what is going on in other people's heads. Children begin to play mummy off against daddy, to get a biscuit when they have already brushed their teeth, for example. A biscuit can be either good or bad depending on perspective, depending on the memories collected and ideas generated as the Tree of the Knowledge of Good and Evil branches out through the networks of an individual's brain.

The power that begins with *shin* is *El ShaDaY*, usually translated as 'Almighty'. The name is related to the verb *ShaDaD* (to destroy), and also to *ShaD* (a breast).[30] The breast sacrifices its living cells as milk to be broken down by the baby, and when the teeth grow the child can enjoy destroying independently. Destruction and preservation are the two sides of *EL ShaDaY*, two sides of the same process; and all the more so when people are competing for resources.

Shin means 'sharp', and *shin* begins *SaTaN*, who challenges with suffering and enlightens with tests.[41] Hissing in the Garden of Eden is the sharpest tongue in the Bible, the serpent *nachaSh*, whose name means 'the whisssperer'.[42] He ruptures the steady state of the garden and begins the story, making his entry by resisting the excesses of YHWH. *Shin* is a snaky sibilant indeed, destructive, divisive, transformative like a tooth. The power of resistance that is brought into the head and into the world at this final stage of phonetic and cerebral development is the most dangerous to wield. It is also the most human, and the source of our humanity, as it is by resisting the push of the powers that we are able to bring them in line with our ideals.

Where the water of *mem* brings things together, the fire of *shin* breaks them apart. The final mother letter burns to the ground the house that began at *beyt*, releasing the energy that bound it together, releasing ashes to the winds of *alef*. Fire makes volatile the fixed, and it also fixes the volatile, as a kiln hardens clay into ceramic. Together *shin* and *mem* and *yowd* make *ShaMaYiM*, the heavens, which are everything fluid in the universe.

...AND GOD SAID...

In Genesis 1, every act of creation and division except the first is preceded by *w'yomer Elohim*: "And God said...". In the head is created and sustained a world within. In the mouth, ideation is clothed with word and structure to be sent out into the swirl. "With the letters he created," says a marvellous old book, for the creative act is the act of speech, and words are magical. *ABaRA K'DaBaRa*, says the Hebrew magician: 'I will create (*BaRA*) as I speak (*DaBaR*)'.[43] The world solidifies where the attention is directed.

> *… "Let the waters under the heavens be gathered together unto one place, and let the dry appear"…*

The KJV ad-libs 'dry <u>land</u>' here, though there is only 'dry' in the original. The volatile is fixed in one place, coming into focus where the powers set their attention, as the fovea in the eye discerns something solid in a sea of possibilities, as a distributed wave packet condenses into p p p p particles.

> *…And it was so.*

Ω

NUMB3RS

All parts of the cortex, when electrically excited, produce alterations both of respiration and circulation. The blood-pressure rises, as a rule, all over the body, no matter where the cortical irritation is applied [...] Mosso, using his ingenious 'plethysmo-graph' as an indicator, discovered that the blood-supply to the arms diminished during intellectual activity, and found furthermore that the arterial tension (as shown by the sphygmo-graph) was increased in these members.

So slight an emotion as that produced by the entrance of Professor Ludwig into the laboratory was instantly followed by a shrinkage of the arms. The brain itself is an excessively vascular organ, a sponge full of blood, in fact; and another of Mosso's inventions showed that when less blood went to the arms, more went to the head. The subject to be observed lay on a delicately balanced table which could tip downward either at the head or at the foot if the weight of either end were increased. The moment emotional or intellectual activity began in the subject, down went the balance at the head-end, in consequence of the redistribution of blood in his system.

- William James, 1890[1]

 N THE BEGINNING I was seated in something like a giant perm machine, with electrodes on my scalp, a needle in my arm, and a tennis ball jammed against my chin to keep my brain still. My sanity had been established by means of multiple choice questions (it's official!), and I was enduring a rather dull 50 minutes looking at slides of scrambled chaos, tapping buttons when something looked like an object.

And there was chaos, and there was order; test one.

The control phase over, I braced myself for a 2mg dose of Home Office-sourced psilocybin in 10ml of saline – and then the doctor beside me started waving his hands. "There's a clot!" he exclaimed, and I felt a twinge of fear. Technicians fiddled as I began to regret my appetite for strange drug adventures. Nervous disturbances in my brain at the order of femtoteslas were recorded every 10 milliseconds. Time passed, as billions of neurons fired through trillions of synapses. Soon I was reassured that the clot was in the needle, not in my arm. Eventually a button was pressed somewhere, and an uncomfortable wave of decontextualized *wub* washed over me in the name of science.

When empirics first turned their attention towards the brain there were plenty of war wounds and lunatics to examine, and not much in the way of medical ethics to worry about, but they were limited by their equipment. In the 1990s technologies like the MRI scanner opened up a new frontier, but as we begin scoping out the territory, through a scanner darkly, let us not get too carried away. While the tools produce beautiful graphics from the surface of the brain, data from deeper regions is much less clear. There are technological and methodological limitations which may generate artefacts and distortions at all levels, and there are also untested philosophical assumptions embedded into the culture of neuroscience. As one of the champions of transcranial magnetic stimulation (TMS) puts it:

> From the perspective of modern neuroscience all behaviors and all experiences are created by the dynamic matrix of chemical and electromagnetic events within the human brain.[2]

To that kind of sweeping humbug I can only reply that these machines are younger than I am, and at 39 I'm not too old to check with my mum before coming to conclusions on important matters. We can learn something by plotting fluctuations in blood flow and voltage in a few millimetres of a motionless brain as it performs tasks in a magnetically-sealed room. We can't yet fathom the intelligence coursing through an estimated 100 billion neurons stretching from foot to forebrain, with more connections than there are atoms in the universe.[3][4] Its parts are not like offices in a city, chapters in an encyclopaedia, bits in a hard drive or anything else we can imagine. Every cognitive act involves widely distributed networks, and the silent areas may be as important as those which are noisy, perhaps even more so, because in many things the more skilled we are at something the less effort is required. People with higher IQ scores show less brain activity when solving puzzles than others, not more, so we should be cautious about inferring too much about parts of the brain from an absence of activity.[5]

There is also no way of knowing, from inside the brain, how much of our thinking is generated by the brain.[6] Someone hearing a phone speak for the first time might deduce, by analogy with a barking dog, that the communication originates in the device itself; but something entirely different is happening. The phone is translating invisible information from electromagnetic waves into sound waves, and electromagnetic waves were only discovered by science in 1820. There may be powers as yet unmeasured and unnamed, forces nebulous and vexatious for noisy public atheists and clergymen of dubious credentials to get worked up about.[7] Those who work with brain imaging tend to be more cautious in their conclusions than evangelicals with agendas. Rumours circulate about some of their number burning sage in the clinic before the day's experiments or praying to the virgin for favour on their researches.[8]

Ω

With these caveats on the nature of our lens out of the way, let us return to neurobiology to see what it can tell us about the webs of cognition and the apocalypses beyond them. Scans reveal that the brainwave profiles of praying nuns and meditating monks resemble each other in many ways, with reduced activity in the parietal lobes behind the crown of the head, for example.[9][10] The parietal lobes (PLs) seem to be heavily involved in integrating partially-processed information from the world outside into whole objects and whole scenes. When dots are grouped into shapes in the mind's eye, there is a burst of PL activity.[11] Damage can interfere with the process of defining items of the visual field out of the background, and in generating a single, defined and organised impression of the whole scene (gestalt).[12]

Definition (*de* + *finis*, meaning 'end') establishes the edges of a thing, making a set of impressions into a percept that is perceived. Higashida, whose autism reduces the flow of input from the PLs as well as other lobes, experiences definition in slow motion; a 'thing' comes into focus "only gradually, detail by detail".[13] PL lesions interfere

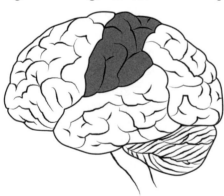

Fig. 9 Parietal lobe

with definition across the sense modalities, causing difficulties in identifying 3D shapes by touch, or numbers traced on the hand.[14] Patients may have difficulties drawing simple items, or assembling objects from their parts.[15] They may struggle to locate

Fig. 10 Drawings by patients with parietal lobe damage

sounds in the environment, because the PLs are also involved in breaking noise into sounds, including those sounds we perceive as words.[16]

The Hebrews, who knew a few things about a few things and a few words about a few words, used the word *DBR* for both 'word' and 'thing'. *DBR* is a chunk of the world defined out of its context. It isn't named yet, in the order of cognitive processes, but when it is it could be a tree (or a branch (or a leaf (or a cell..(.)))), depending on the scale we focus in to. It could be the sound of a tree falling, if there is a brain there to make a sound. A *DBR* can be something bound in time rather than space, a 'matter', 'deed' or 'affair'.* The process of definition joins up the dots between separate acts of perception, making objects in space, events in time, and a dynamic internal map of the world. The fluidity of that map is also compromised with PL damage, so some patients see things jumping from one place to another, or moving in a series of frames.[17]

One of the 'things' pulled together from a collection of points in space is the mental representation of the self itself: 'I AM'. It may be the first thing defined, the principle thing in the human head in the beginning. PL processes locate this thing in space, and with PL damage a self with an ill-defined edge can move clumsily through the world and reach for objects inaccurately.[18]

---

* "And David said unto him, 'How went the matter [*DBR*]?'" (2 Samuel 3:15)

Drivers extend the self beyond the skin, piloting their cars with the same unconscious skill as they manoeuvre their bodies, and the same PL substructures are activated when they do.[19] Perhaps this expanding I AM explains why some men react to you touching their wing mirrors as if you had touched their nipples. As well as through position in space, I AM is related to the rest of the world via events in time, as the principle actor in an epic narrative of the self. Shifts in PL activity are measured as subjects judge how well adjectives describe themselves.[20]

The term *ego* (meaning 'I') was used by that nasty coke-fiend Sigmund Freud to evoke something similar to this I AM, though others have used it differently. To him, it was the organ of mind that develops at the edge of the unconscious and conscious worlds, managing and directing survival urges and pleasure drives arising from the "dark, inaccessible part of our personality" (the *id*), turning them towards things in the external world that will satisfy them.[21]

Monks and nuns language their experience of PL inhibition respectively as merging into the process of meditation or becoming at one with God. A meditation popular amongst Spiritists, done as they prepare to traffic with another world, deliberately targets the edge of I AM by visualizing roots growing from the feet into the earth (and with practice it can get pretty trippy). As the boundaries blur, I AM comes into focus in a different way. In Higashida's words,

> I get the sensation that my body's now a speck, a speck from long before I was born, a speck that is melting into nature herself. This sensation is so amazing that I forget that I'm a human being.[22]

His awareness slipping back before history as the edges dissolve recalls one of the most grammatically intriguing lines in the NT:

Before Abraham was, *I am*.[23]

Ω

Categorizing a defined thing (*DBR*) is a different cognitive process to the initial act of definition. The thing with udders falls into an established set, and becomes an instance of a known item named 'cow', in a process that involves the temporal lobes,

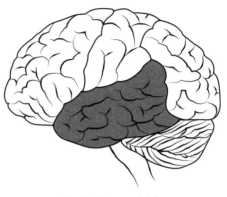

Fig. 11 Temporal lobe

which are situated next to the PLs on the back half of the side of the head. The temporal lobes (TLs) contain substructures "to do with the processing of signs, tokens, representations of things," as psychiatrist Iain McGilchrist puts it, and they are inhibited during prayer and meditation along with the PLs.[24] With TL damage the fixed can become unhooked across the senses. Familiar faces and objects may become unrecognisable, common sounds like a cat's *miaow* may not be recognised, and organizing pictures into sets can become difficult.[25][26][27][28] Damage to the left TL can cause Wernicke's aphasia, where people forget or confuse their nouns, calling a 'bunny' a 'baguette' for example.[29] Though it affects the speech is fundamentally a signification problem, not a speech problem. Deaf people with the same condition mix up their sign language signs.[30]

'Noun' comes from *nomen* in Latin, which means 'name'. 'Name' is *shem* (*SM*) in Hebrew, which also means 'fame', 'report' and 'monument' – "a mark or memorial of individuality", as one biblical authority puts it.[31] * Derived from a root meaning 'to fix' or 'to establish', *SM* describes something fixed, something known to be what it is. *SM*s are mental constructs that only exist in the mind, abstracted away from the immense sea of change at the other end of the pinhole of the fovea behind a series of filters. As Seneca pointed out when paraphrasing the

---

* "This is my memorial (*shem*) unto all generations." (Exodus 3:15)
"His fame (*shem*) was in all nations round about." (1 Kings 4:31)

mysterious Heraclitus, "into the same river we step and do not step twice; for the name of the river remains the same, but the water has flowed past."[32] And the I AM that steps in the river is also fluid, an infinitesimal point of awareness between I WAS and I WILL BE.

Without a name, things are perceived differently or even not at all. Himba tribespeople, who have no word for 'blue', struggle to identify a single blue square in a circle of green squares.[33] On the other hand, they have two different words for what I would call 'green', and can easily distinguish between two shades which look the same to me. Russians, with an extra blue in their lexicon, distinguish two blue hues better than you do.[34] We slice up the rainbow differently in different languages. Wavelengths hitting the retina and vibrations hitting the eardrum are filtered through familiar categories as they become elements of thought represented (i.e. re-presented) to the internal world. Certain lucky people like Marcelo and Jake Barnett may see the full brilliance of the spectrum in a splash of water, but for most of us, most of the time, the word conceals as it reveals.

Names (*SM*) fix the things (*DBR*) that can be conceived of and communicated, including intangible concepts like 'botany', 'judo' and 'the Dutch East India Company'. The categories one knows are determined, to some degree, by an individual's history and culture. If, for example, I ask you to imagine a 'cow'...

(go on, imagine a cow)

...the image evoked will depend on your experiences. My cow prototype is a black and white British Friesian, which is a different beast to the brown Girs my neighbour in Brazil used to keep. The mega-set of 'cow' contains British Friesians, Brazilian Girs, Indian Brahmans and so on. It also contains each and every one of my neighbour's cows – Katarina, Morena, Bella and so on. And it contains one just like Katarina with one more hair, and one just like Morena with one less white blood cell. The herd is infinite, its infinities multiplying as you scale in.

TL processes are implicated in assigning adjectives as well as nouns; choosing adjectives to describe a known thing (a famous political figure) is associated with activity in the left TL.[35] A cow is a noun, and basically the same thing to more or less everyone, but adjectival sets vary more between people, so a cow may be 'kosher' to a Jew and holy to a Hindu, 'lucrative' to a cowboy and 'disastrous' to an Amazonian ecologist. 'Cow' can be 'good' or 'evil', depending on your emotional history with it, and that involves the limbic system. The limbic system feeds emotions into the mix, waves of anger washing through the junction of the amygdalas into the TLs, ripples of pleasure and sadness roughing up and smoothing down the textures of the categories, steeping sets in love and bleaching them with trauma. This is all beyond our direct control, like tears and laughter, like the hormones and gastric juices; they are all stimulated by the limbic system via the autonomic nervous system. Conditioned emotional memories laid down mean that when a 'thing with udders' is categorized as an instance of the 'cow' set, it is already guilty by association of anything learned in previous interactions with that set.

TL processes and limbic system processes associate things (*DBR*) with names (*SM*), and names with emotional memories. To give another example, whenever I hear my Russian student speaking on the phone in his mother-tongue I have to force myself to entertain the possibility that he might not be organizing an assassination. Like most Englishers of

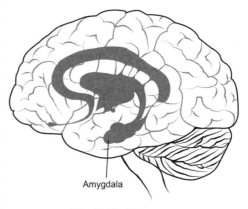

Amygdala

Fig. 12 Limbic system

111

my age, my formative experiences of Russians speaking into phones were all mega-villains causing international mischief while explosions and Bond girls assailed my boiling pubescent amygdalas. All this rubbing my trigger has left a (frankly prejudiced) trace in my habits of association regarding the set named 'Russians'. The media does the same when it presents 'news' pickled in old biases, flashing with sensation and high definition mega-drama. First impressions last, and reason has very little to do with it.

*SM*s exert forces in the internal world before reason comes into the story. Seeing an image of the thing named 'hammer' potentiates motor cortex networks that are engaged when a subject performs a power grip.[36] An image of a grape primes different networks that pertain to a precision grip. It happens automatically, regardless of whether or not the action is going to be performed (one cannot reasonably hope to strike a nail with an image of a hammer). It happens all the time as we unconsciously categorize things around us.

Ω

Familiar protocols are primed to be carried out in the motor cortex, which is situated beneath the crown of the head at the back of the frontal lobes. Before impulses emerge from the motor cortex, on the way to the muscles to translate into action, they are first modified by input from the rest of the frontal lobes beneath the forehead. The frontal lobes (FLs) inhibit impulses, both at the level of the neuron and in terms of behaviour, vetoing actions primed in the motor cortex before they begin. Patients with damaged FLs can develop 'environmental dependency syndrome', and may be triggered into responding impulsively to things around them – grabbing a stranger's spectacles from the table and putting them on, picking up pens and scribbling, or compulsively copying what other people do.[37] [38] [39] My mum once saw a car crash victim groping obscenely at the nurses in the emergency ward trying to save his life. He was completely at the mercy of his primal drives and the visual triggers around him after the blood vessels supplying his FLs had been destroyed.

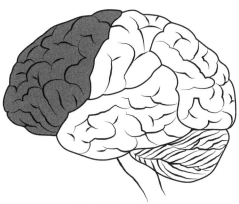

The FLs suppress immediate gratification of desires for long-term benefits,

Fig. 13 Frontal lobe

and with damage a person might snatch food from someone else's plate, for example.[40][41] A rhesus monkey with her FLs in working order, however, will refrain from eating if taking food causes a troop-mate in an adjoining cage to receive an electric shock.[42] Even rats do this, and the process of inhibition again seems to be functionally related to their tiny forebrains.[43][44] In rhesus monkeys their sympathies are influenced by learning, as individuals that had already been victims refrained for longer, fasting for as long as 12 days. Human ethical choices involve more complex reasoning – comparing and contrasting, inquiring into a broader story. The FLs, which are considerably expanded in man compared to other apes, allow us to relate things into a scheme, and so damage can cause problems for subjects finding ways to arrange matchsticks.[45][46] The FLs also structure events in time, factoring in memories and predicting trajectories, linking I AM to I WAS and I WILL BE.

Uncovering themes and considering consequences, making goals and adapting behaviour to realise them, the FLs explore connections between events on the surface to model what might lie beneath, looking through someone's behaviour into their mind. Damage can cause patients to be less empathic, less astute about the motives of others, easier to trick, and more swayed by false claims in advertising.[47][48][49] We make up our minds by de-scribing, writing stories and formulas to make sense of what we encounter. We assemble new complexes of ideas, and we also build names for them from parts of other words, adding 'mega' to 'phone' and 'neuro' to 'apocalypse'. This is a FL process technically called 'neologism' (which is itself a neologism).

With FL damage people can let their habits of self-care slip.[50] They may also read situations poorly and take inappropriate courses of action, overstepping boundaries between themselves and other selves.[51] If the FLs are compromised by psychoactives that suppress their function (like tequila), a person can compare pros and cons differently, and make less inhibited choices.[52] They might try riding a unicycle, for example, or a kickboxer's girlfriend. FL damage is often implicated in addiction and pathological gambling.[53]

Consciousness, including social consciousness, expresses itself in degrees of inhibition. Some ancient parts of the brain will consistently demand that all the sweeties be devoured at once, as they have done since at least the Triassic Period; if the context is wrong, however, then the younger FLs spring into action, reminding you of your place in the cosmos and the sweet shop, aborting a pig-out before it begins.[54] Blood flow is generally greater in the FLs of introverted people, who tend to think a little deeper and behave in a more measured way.[55] It increases when nuns pray and monks meditate.[56] Meditation can also offer relief from Tourette's syndrome, a disturbance that "seems to lie in the very highest parts of the 'old brain'", according to Dr. Oliver Sacks, "the thalamus, hypothalamus, limbic system and amygdala".[57][58] The constant act of inhibition leads to more extensive networks developing in the FLs, which may explain why people with Tourette's perform motor tasks more quickly and more skillfully than neurotypicals.[59][60] One of Singapore's top cage fighters has Tourette's, and Tim Howard plays goalkeeper in the English Premier League despite suffering from Tourette's and being an American.[61] [62] [63] He believes that his Tourette's improves his reactions.[64]

The FLs stop some of us fidgeting some of the time, and usually keep us from running around as our impulses would have us. There is an autistic boy who watches stock car racing videos in my local library, flapping and bouncing in his chair and squealing with joy. My daughters are as fascinated by him as I am, and when they talk to him he straightens up to answer their questions with perfect composure and a surprisingly solemn tone. Then he returns his attention to the screen and goes wild again.

Before the conscious processes associated with the FLs begin, things have already been defined, named and coloured with emotion. Among the collections put together are coherent sentences, and in 95% of brains this involves much more activity on the left side. That is to say that the left FL generally plays an essential role in generating grammatical structure (though understanding of the meaning of a whole sentence may have more to do with the right side).[65]Left FL damage reduces fluency, and may result in Broca's aphasia, where the grammar relating words together is compromised:

> Thursday... ten o'clock, ah doctors... two... an'
> doctors... and er... teeth... yah[66]

Wernicke's aphasia, with left TL rather than left FL injury, is different. The nouns are lost, but grammatical structures are preserved.

It is oversimplistic to divide the brain into verbal and non-verbal or rational and intuitive sides; the networks are unthinkably complex, and thinking involves both hemispheres (except in rare cases like Peek's). The behaviours specific to lesions on one side or the other is intriguing, though, and so is the anatomy at the level of the neuron. On the right, networks are more extensively interconnected, with more dendrites between neurons and also more connections between regions.[67]

On the left, connections are a little more clearly focused, with better-established paths of impulse flow.[68][69]

Birds focus on the object of their attention with the right eye (and the left hemisphere). They scan the wider world with their left eye (and right hemisphere), the side that in humans seems geared towards context and detecting anomalies.[70][71] Like each eye, each hemisphere contributes something slightly different from its own angle, giving depth to the world.[72] Though it might be misleading to talk about which side is in charge, neuroanatomist Jill Bolte Taylor's almost unique perspective is thought-provoking:

> It's that little voice that says to me, "I am. I am." And as soon as my left hemisphere says to me "I am," I become separate. I become a single solid individual, separate from the energy flow around me and separate from you. And this was the portion of my brain that I lost on the morning of my stroke […] And I look down at my arm and I realize that I can no longer define the boundaries of my body. I can't define where I begin and where I end, because the atoms and the molecules of my arm blended with the atoms and molecules of the wall. And all I could detect was this energy. Energy! And I'm asking myself, "What is wrong with me? What is going on?" And in that moment, my left hemisphere brain chatter went totally silent […] I felt enormous and expansive […] Then all of a sudden my left hemisphere comes back online and it says to me, "Hey! We've got a problem! We've got to get some help."[73]

It is tempting to speculate – for the FLs are functionally obliged to speculate – as to what is happening on each side of our brains, and how that relates to other conditions where highly branched, diffuse networks are in play, such as autism and the psilocybin state. But can a brain understand a brain, from inside a brain?

Ω

One way to think about thinking is to divide it into 'divergent' and 'convergent' processes, according to the scheme devised by psychologist J. P. Guilford.[74] Divergent thinking is an open-ended enterprise that creatively manipulates elements of thought, mentally putting them through steps and into various configurations (how many things can you do with a stick or an F-sharp?) It multiplies options, creating novel solutions and making predictions about how things will go. The FLs are heavily involved in divergent thinking, which is why FL damage barely alters performance in IQ tests.[75] These tests, and most school exams, don't measure divergent thinking. They measure convergent thinking, where items are categorized and known rules are applied to them, a process with a limited and predetermined number of options. Determining whether a painting is by Picasso or Monet, or if a piece of music is classical or blues, requires convergent thinking. The former distinction has been mastered by pigeons, the latter by carp.[76] [77]

The Categorizer thinks convergently, and is disrupted by TL injury. The Manipulator thinks divergently, and is disrupted by FL injury (and maybe some forms of schooling). The FLs give us the capacity to develop better judgement and nurture ideals, and are critical in making moral and social choices.[78] That crazed sex maniac Freud coined the term *superego* to describe the complex of processes involved, made up of scruples adopted from family and society, as well as the moral codes that individuals construct as they reflect upon their choices and experiences. Regardless of how an individual decides, once their TLs become habituated to a principle they tend to remain obedient to it. The highest circuits of cognition maintain a veto, but if veils sit in place unshaken they grow thick with mental dust, and habits tend to take over.

Even activities that initially require a great deal of focus soon become habitual, so you need not mentalize every twitch of the thighs once you have learned how to cycle, and you hit the brakes without a thought when someone steps into the road.

Scripts run along unchecked at the edge of consciousness, twiddling our hair and biting our nails, slipping other people's lighters into our pockets, running through habits of physical and mental activity. Sequences become fixed and familiar. Addiction and all the sub-programs it involves can run along as a series of routines in the background until the addict consciously brings it into the foreground. "My name is Oliver and I am an alcoholic."[79] I AM THAT I AM.

Meditation can help break cycles of destructive behaviour, and is a useful support for addiction therapy.[80] Most meditations begin by suppressing the gross movements of the body and mind, and then focusing on an object that slips between conscious and unconscious control. A pattern of breathing, a rosary, or the spin of a dervish becomes second nature with practice, moving the mind at the edge of worlds. The boundary between willed and unwilled becomes blurred, or perhaps the blur that is always there becomes more obvious. The will extends gradually through the veil to control processes that are usually unconscious, slowing the heartbeat and even raising the temperature of the fingers by as much as 17 degrees.[81 82 83] Biofeedback subjects looking at displays of their own blood pressure and muscle tone soon learn to control those parameters directly, and to focus in and fire a single neuron at will. The major part of this is inhibition, like learning to raise one eyebrow while looking in the mirror (you already know how to raise an eyebrow, and must practice to inhibit the other from rising with it).[84] Conscious reflection can reverse the normal state of affairs where behaviour is determined by unconscious impulses.

Meditation suppresses PL activity, smudging lines and blurring edges. It suppresses TL activity, loosening categorical conceptions are unhooking habits of classification. FL activity, however, is increased, opening up space for new constellations of ideas under the influence of whatever is kept in mind. For the nuns and monks, that should be the prayer of St. Francis or a visualization of one of the forms of the Buddha, but concentration can take anything as an object. I once attained a remarkably deep trance contemplating my anger after an ex-girlfriend made me miss two trains in a row. It wasn't a tantric exercise or anything like that, I was simply livid and incapable of thinking about anything else. After about 40 minutes of fuming single-mindedly at the station while she went to get her forgotten ticket, I quite suddenly melted into a transcendent state of bliss.

Silence is pregnant with possibility, especially with potentiated FLs and inhibited TLs. 'That thing I married' might escape the set of 'awful things I have to endure', and be reframed as 'beloved thing', or maybe 'ex-beloved thing'. Meditation causes "very permanent changes in the way in which the brain works", which may equip people to put their apocalypses into action, to make the word flesh by behaving in accordance with the new order imagined.[85] They might listen to the 'beloved thing', rather than ignoring the 'awful thing'. The fact that meditators are less easily pressurised into acting against their ideals raises utopian possibilities, including the promise that mindful communities might jam the cogs of habitual obedience that perpetuate Milgram's nightmare.* [86]

Meditation and various techniques of ecstasy have long posed a threat to the status quo and the state, which prefers the names just as they are, with their established associations. For most of us, 'taxes' are thought to be 'an unavoidable circumstance'; but freed from the tyranny of habit, 'taxes' might become 'a gross imposition on the fruits of my labour', or 'fuel for the machine of oppression'. Perhaps this explains why Quakers emerged from their worshipful silences to pioneer some of history's greatest campaigns of tax resistance, along with non-violent and even naked acts of civil disobedience.[87] They were carrying on a tradition that goes back through the radical tracts of the gospels to the prophetic books of the Hebrews, an uncompromising critique of monarchy and

---

* See *Science Revealed* page 93 for Milgram's nightmare.

empire that continued to flare up as the centuries rolled on, despite agents in the pay of Caesar and the CIA occasionally martyring liberation theologists.[88] William of Ockham, a monk and nominalist much quoted by rationalists, fled into exile after challenging the Pope on property rights.[89] Martin Luther was a devout man of prayer, as was Martin Luther King and Malcolm X. Gandhi, who lived as a renunciant, suppressed his natural urges and fasted for the political goals he had articulated. When Buddhist monk Thich Quang Duc self-immolated in South Vietnam in 1963, his powers of inhibition maintained awesome composure as he began to burn – motionless, soundless and photogenic in lotus for over ten minutes until he toppled over. One of the most powerful photos of the century landed on President Kennedy's desk the following morning, and within months the government he was protesting against had fallen.[90]

William Godwin, dubbed "the founder of philosophical anarchism", believed that "truth dwells in contemplation" and "can scarcely be acquired in crowded halls and amidst noisy debates."[91] [92] His description of the ideal man suggests the qualities of a well-conditioned PL, for he has,

> a certain confidence in the unseen hand that sustains
> the whole. He is glad that there is something greater
> than himself, in the presence of which he feels his soul
> penetrated with a sacred awe.[93]

That confidence makes people both charismatic and difficult to control. States have long militated against rivals in the battle for the hearts and minds of the population, persecuting Gnostics in the 3rd century, Quakers in the early Modern period, and Falun Dafa and Santo Daime today. Wandering mendicants with fine-tuned neuro-technologies and apocalyptic stories can cause headaches for heads of state, and in Christian lands the God-struck were often whisked away to monasteries up mountains, out of sight and out of mind, far away from any right-thinking folk they might corrupt with their heavenly infinities. They swore solemn vows before the Eternal Father to remain at the monastery in poverty, to be obedient and well-mannered, and in some traditions they took a vow of silence.[94] A merchant looking for something sublime might climb the mountain to pray before the Lord and His serene and taciturn friars, before heading back down to town to salute the Crown and the officers of the watch.

At the Abbey near where I grew up, the monks dwindled until only two remained; then my mum crashed into one of them in her car. She's no great friend of contemplation, my mum, and described a silent Vipassana meditation weekend retreat as the most boring experience of her life, but other people seem interested. Mindfulness courses and retreats are more popular than ever, as seekers and CEOs procure self-knowledge and stress management. Whether this brings compassion into the boardroom or simply makes the machinery of corporatism more efficient is something that Buddhists are meditating upon.[95]

The brains of monks and nuns practicing are similar in terms of inhibited PLs, inhibited TLs, and excited FLs. The main difference is that Franciscan prayers activate language areas, and Buddhist visualizations activate the visual cortex.[96] The Pentecostal brain speaking in tongues, however, has the opposite profile, with PLs and TLs unaffected and activity in the FLs inhibited. According to chief researcher Andrew Newberg, this "would give them the sensation that someone else was 'running the show'", and indeed Pentecostalists do not describe losing their sense of self.[97] They describe the Holy Spirit taking control of their bodies while they are still there. The FL inhibitory powers are themselves inhibited, unleashing movements that would usually be suppressed, and they include those producing mouth shapes and sound, making for a hopping, howling ho-down for Jesus. In the rite of initiation, the minister speaks in tongues into the ear of the initiate while grasping their forehead above the FLs. If all goes to plan, if the Spirit is strong and the synapses willing, the initiate begins to speak in tongues as well. It shows extraordinary command of the brain, but maybe the FL inhibition and lack of any serious assault on the 'names' fixed in the TLs has something to do with the political conservatism and creationist science so popular amongst the Pentecostal brotherhood.

There are many ways up the mountain, and it seems there are many mountains, each with its own vistas. FL inhibition can also be induced with low intensity magnetic fields, and focusing on the prefrontal cortex enhances routine mathematical skills, making people better at following rules.[98] Conversely, inhibiting the left frontotemporal area makes subjects more attentive to the detail in the world rather than the letter of the law, giving them what researchers called "savant-like skills".[99] Subjects became more likely to notice repeated words in proverbs (like the sign on page 26). They were less vulnerable to the usual trap of encountering a 'thing' (DBR), and immediately assuming a 'name' (SM); as the researchers put it, "Our propensity to impose meaning and concept blocks our awareness for the detail making up the concept". Subjects were also better able to estimate the number of spots flashing up on a screen, and their drawings became more realistic.

> Three of the four "facilitated" participants [...] experienced altered psychological states after stimulation. For example, N. R. said he was more "alert" and "conscious of detail" and that we had "taught him how to draw dogs." [...] Furthermore, the drawings of these three participants had not reverted to their original convention 45 minutes after stimulation had ceased.

If heightened skills persist beyond the period of stimulation, what other opportunities might there be to reprogram our brains by combining altered states with focused meditations? Dramatic shifts in brain activity can be triggered by highly specific but less invasive stimuli, such as music. While Sean Paul's dancehall reggae just makes me twerk, it provoked tonic-clonic seizures in one woman until she had brain surgery.[100]

Another woman continues to go into convulsions whenever she hears Ne-yo's music, despite having had most of her left TL removed.[101] One man suffers a migraine whenever he plays basketball – not sports generally, just basketball.[102] Migraine is one of the so-called 'aura' symptoms that precede epileptic fits, along with vertigo, dissociation, tingles, déjà vu, moving lights and voices. A specific character may appear consistently and reliably in a vision as a fit approaches, like a familiar angel announcing the opening of a portal to the strange.[103] [104] All of these aura symptoms appear in the phenomena of mystical experience. The master of the temple masters the temples of his ritualists, setting triggers to fire and provoke highly specific brain events, with the drumbeat of Papa Legba, the sign of the cross, the scent of sandalwood. Once neural pathways and ceremonial procedures are intertwined, managing brain states and eliciting apocalypses is a matter of technique.

Ritual skills were much impoverished by centuries of witch-drowning and bishopry, and most Britons have never had the pleasure; but some of the enthusiastic churches are taking back their mojo. Sniffer dogs were called to a hotel where worshippers were crawling around the lounge smashed on the Holy Spirit.[105] I had a surprising experience at Gnostic mass at the Theosophical Society once, high on nothing more than ceremony and the poetry of the early Chinese Christian scriptures.[106] It was my third visit, with a rite executed with elegance and precision as always; and as always the taking of the host jarred with me, because of the implicit symbology of consecrated and unconsecrated hands. I stifled my scowl and ate it politely, and when I sat down I found to my great surprise that I was feeling something like a hit of MDMA. The rite itself is par for the course for one of the cults of the dying god, and a lot less messy than some; but on a concrete and visceral level that simple ritual can work such immense power (even as it offends) that you might think you are eating the body of Christ – and maybe you are. In a space set apart from the mundanity of the day-to-day, people in tune with each other and their chosen rite can achieve all sorts of interesting states fairly reliably, with a bit of practice, and without drugs – though a joint consecrated in silent reverence doesn't hurt.

When nuns contemplate God their TL activity decreases; and magnetically inhibiting the TLs gives around 80% of lay subjects the feeling of "not being alone".[107] TMS researcher Dr. Michael Persinger argues that because he can trigger a sense of spiritual presences with his 'God Helmet', then such experiences are *ipso facto* 'caused' by abnormal brain function. *Ergo*, belief in God is a function of neuropathology. Religions are the institutionalised side effects, *nihil ultra*, of the malfunctioning brains of mental defectives known to history as Muhammad, Jesus, Buddha *et cetera*.[108] *Quod erat demonstrandum*? Or *non-sequitur*?

We can be deceived by apparent causalities, for our FLs are great spinners of stories, but things are not so simple among the tangled branches of the Tree of Knowledge. If we are to tease them apart – if such a thing can be done at all – we had best remain cautious in our conclusions. We call weird stuff going on in the brain 'irregular' or 'abnormal', but we don't know how it is supposed to work. We are working with assumptions fished from the gutter of reductionism. TMS and brain scans are the wonders of a very young science exploring a very old set of phenomena, and a young science is like a young lover – exciting, full of vigor, and prone to large statements that might become embarrassing later – so let's not go getting any tattoos just yet. For the time being it is safe to conclude that there are some funny things lurking in the lobes of your brain.

Dr. Persinger is unabashedly hostile towards religion and the idea of spirits, however he is open-minded about the paranormal. Testing one psychic in the days following a TMS session, he found that his accuracy had increased:

> The results suggest that this type of paranormal phenomenon, often dismissed as methodological artefact or accepted as proofs of spiritual existence, is correlated with neurophysiological processes and physical events. Remote viewing may be enhanced by complex experimentally generated magnetic fields.[109]

For some scientists, the fact that religious experience has something to do with brain function means that it is not religious experience. Following Logic Code (Aristotle) - bylaw 3: EITHER (A or not A), things cannot be both at the same time. Following this dictum, neurologist Professor Gregory Holmes denounces the founder of the Seventh-day Adventists:

> Her whole clinical course to me suggests a high probability that she had temporal lobe epilepsy. This would indicate to me that the spiritual vision she was having would not be genuine, would be due to the seizure.[110]

Well Professor Smarty-lobes, if her vision was not 'genuine', what would a 'genuine' spiritual vision look like? And why should scientists have the last say on matters so far from their fields of expertise, pathologising spiritual experience as their colleagues have pathologised autistic experience? At least, we should keep our minds open on such matters, because we all police our brain waves to some degree, and some of us station extra patrols at the borders to keep apocalypses out. Religious people see religious visions more reliably than others undergoing TMS, while both Persinger and Richard Dawkins are among the 20% who feel nothing at all – no rushes, no sweats or fits, no tingling, no kundalingaling.[111] Generally the God Helmet is wasted on the Godless. "If I were turned into a devout religious believer," says Dawkins, "my wife would threaten to leave me" – so perhaps it is best for everyone concerned if he gives the Godhead a wide berth.[112]

Ω

Without a doubt the gods exist "in the head", because they are names people have talked and thought about for a long time, perhaps since the dawn of thought – and names guide our perceptions, prime our actions, and alter behaviour in various ways. Subjects are less susceptible to group norms if tested after thinking about a punk stereotype, for example, making less conformity errors of the type described on page 37.[113] They score better in a general knowledge quiz if they have been thinking about professors beforehand.[114] Familiar things can take on lives of their own in our psyches. My wife grew up in cowboy country, and she often dreams about cows turning into people, chasing her, walking meaningfully into ponds and so on. In my dreams the only consistent symbol is the bicycle. I even gave one a ride once, a few weeks after I first started practising Taoist seed retention, which was strange and not entirely unpleasant.

In scripture and in the psychiatric wards, disembodied entities sometimes supply their own names. They also issue threats and orders, and offer promises. Whether they exist outside of our heads is another question, though that is the case for many things, since Descartes' "I think therefore *I AM*" [emphasis YHWH's]. YHWH nearly always acts in the heads of the prophets in His stories, often by telling them precisely what to do and say:

> YHWH spake unto Moses, "Go unto Pharaoh, and say unto him, 'Thus saith YHWH, Let my people go.'"[115]

YHWH also worked through the psychology of Moses' opponent. After every plague, "YHWH hardened Pharaoh's heart so that he would not let the Children of Israel go".[116] Regarding more tangible acts of God – locusts, frogs, parting of the sea and so on – it is a rather unfashionable way to think about meteorology these days, but rain dances have been danced and pestilences summoned for a very long time. Whether those rites work outside the head is another question, and not one we need to answer to explore the layers of a story. The incorrigibly curious will find extraordinary tales in the despised aisles of the library. A charming anecdote is told by the founder of the Skeptics Society, describing a moment before his wedding ceremony just as the bride was feeling acutely the absence of her family, when a broken radio once belonging to her grandfather woke up briefly after a silence of decades to play a love song.[117] He used to be your run-of-the-mill humourless skeptic, now he's not sure what to think. Dr. John Hagelin's data on the spooky effects of group meditation on crime rates is interesting, not least because this Harvard fellow and former CERN researcher was one of the most cited physicists of the 1980s, and earned his stripes by developing super-string theory.[118] The Princeton website announces "clear evidence that human thought and emotion can produce measurable influences on physical reality", in reference to a 25-year project involving many millions of trials of marbles tumbling through pins and other randomizing systems.[119] It began as a collaboration with McDonald Douglas Aerospace, to investigate whether sensitive equipment might respond telekinetically to a pilot's mind.

Such stories, and all scientific conclusions on the nature of reality, are fisherman's tales – despite any amount of statistical significance, double-blind paradigms, prestigious institutions and other glamours of 20th century science. They are other people's stories, and so are the articles debunking them. The journals are no better, with the editor of *The Lancet* concluding that "much of the scientific literature, perhaps half, may simply be untrue".[120] A recent attempt to replicate 100 psychology studies from top journals failed in two-thirds of cases. Perhaps this marks the beginning of a more critical era of thought without the luxury of belief, but for the time being the language of dispassionate science remains a litmus test for reasonable thinking, even appearing in our speech with metaphors like 'litmus test'.[121] The pursuit of empirical knowledge by testing hypotheses against data is one thing; the well-known and well-worn net of notions that defines the limits of respectable public discourse is something else. It is Scientism, not science, and it changes gradually as the net is torn and restitched. Though some of its racist and sexist follies have been unpicked, knowledge generated in the institutions of Scientism remains problematic, for reasons which are addressed in *Science Revealed* and some of my talks online. Suffice to say here that we're on shaky ground building cosmologies from the unfalsified hypotheses and statistical distributions of strangers funded by strangers with agendas.

Anyway, I don't buy it so I'm making my own cosmology, and that begins with personal experience. When the lobes of your brain lead you to believe that a stranger is asking you what time it is, it is not necessarily delusional to entertain the possibility that a stranger is asking you what time it is. What if the sensation of a spiritual presence indicates... the presence of a spirit? Should such things exist, and whatever and wherever they may be, how might they communicate if not via sensations impressed upon the central nervous system, which is how bus drivers communicate? Perhaps the God Helmet works like my spectacles, bringing into focus that which is already there. I'd like to ask the entities in question a few questions before publishing my own whimsy, and so I shall comment further when I have worked out how to get a microwave to work with my very reverend head inside it.

Mindfulness practice quickly improves stress levels and wellbeing, but it may take years to engineer the kind of experiences that destroy and remake worlds. With busy lives and minds accustomed to immediate gratification, with a medicalized language of extraordinary experience and very low expectations of what a human being is capable of, many Westerners setting out on the path experience no *satori*, no *samadhi*, no *dhyana*, no banana – not much more than stiff legs. And some of us have our crown chakras so far up our root chakras that it is going to take more than a little *metta bhavana* to pull them out. Meditation can certainly do interesting things, but it is at least as hard as learning to raise one eyebrow. Other techniques, however, are more direct. If you are brave enough to seek to know YHWH, there are over a dozen psychoactive agents listed in the Jewish scriptures indicated for that very purpose, along with detailed instructions on how to consume them (more about that later). There are also geomagnetic hotspots to explore on this giant magnet spinning through space, trolls to hunt beneath the aurora borealis, and earthlights floating above Sedona.[122] Whereas TMS weakens the magnetic field across the brain, solar wind storms mess with the magnetic field of the whole planet. There is a little data suggesting that epileptic seizures may be more common during periods of low geomagnetic activity, and clear evidence that more paranormal experiences are reported during solar storms, including sightings of ghosts, UFOs and even Yeti (a big hairy airy faerie?)[123] [124] Persinger lists other ways to interfere with brain function:

> If you begin to change the organization of the brain, you change the sensor [...] with shamanistic practices [...] drugs [...] rituals of depravation, hypoxia, starvation, sensory isolation – you can sit in a cave like Muhammad did, or you wander through the desert like Christ did [...] You alter brain activity, and now you have access to information that you typically might not have access to.[125]

The fastest path to an altered state is a stroke, as Jill Bolte Taylor discovered. Psychedelics are a little more laid back. Alan Watts spent a lifetime pursuing the mystical path with dedication, taking meditation classes from his teens, taking a theology degree, taking up the cloth, and finally taking LSD in his forties:

> In the course of two experiments I was amazed and somewhat embarrassed to find myself going through states of consciousness that corresponded precisely with every description of major mystical experiences

> that I had ever read. Furthermore, they exceeded both
> in depth and in a peculiar quality of unexpectedness
> the three 'natural and spontaneous' experiences of this
> kind that had happened to me in previous years.[126]

New technologies have uncovered key similarities between psychedelic and meditative states, and established that both can trigger lasting shifts in baseline function.[127] [128] There is nothing new about mixing potions and devotions, and nothing particularly dangerous if it is done with care. Such mysteries are best approached with a guide, though, and as is often the case that someone is a naked hippy screaming at the sea. We shall join him shortly to skinny-dip in the oceans of neurobiology, and prepare ourselves for some advanced theobiology, neurojehovatry and psychopharmadolatory in the continents of cognition beyond.

But before all that, let us return to Genesis.

Ω

Eve's Apple & Adam's Nostril

Disobedience, in the eyes of anyone who has read history, is man's original virtue. It is through disobedience that progress has been made, through disobedience and through rebellion.[1]

- Oscar Wilde

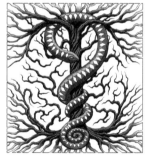N THE BEGINNING things were good, better even than Eden. Elohim released a series of universally acclaimed hits, beginning with "Let there be light" (and "it was good"), and "Let the waters bring forth abundantly" (which was also "good"). He created winged fowl, cattle, creeping things and more, and "it was good […] good […] good […] good […] good, and […] good". Finally He created mankind "and, behold, it was very good", so the Creator rested; but He didn't go to bed like Paddington Bear at the end of a story. 'Rest' (*shabath*) has the connotation of ceasing, not pausing, and for the rest of the *Pentateuch* (i.e. Genesis, Exodus, Leviticus, Numbers and Deuteronomy) He

maintains His distance from the world.[2] Men walk with Him in prophesy or encounter Him in dreams. He "revealeth the deep and secret things", and He answers prayers and swells wombs.[3][4] But His work of creating is finished in the first week.[5]

"In the beginning Elohim created the <u>heavens</u> and the <u>earth</u>", but the perspective reverses in Genesis 2 when "YHWH Elohim formed the <u>earth</u> and the <u>heavens</u>". In Genesis 1 mankind was the culmination of the process and a complete archetype, when both "male and female created He them". Genesis 2 is different. Man comes first, not last, and as an individual rather than an archetype, a vivified lump of earth with a story unfolding around him. Where Elohim created and then retreated, YHWH Elohim steps into creation to show off his moves, the LORD God grooving in mysterious ways. *Let It Be* has been dropped from the repertoire. He's singing a new song, issuing prohibitions and curses.

In popular theology He is The Artist Formerly Known As God, coming out of retirement for a comeback as an unpronounceable squiggle. In the mystery of Hebrew poetry, however, the two godnames are rather different. YHWH Elohim does not "create" with the verb *bara*, as Elohim did.[6][7] He "forms" with *yatzar*, a lovely word that dips into the sound stream with the semi-vowel /y/, like <u>Y</u>HWH Elohim Himself. He is the first of the gods that begin with *yowd*s:

AND YHWH ELOHIM FORMED [YATZAR] THE MAN OF THE CLAY OF THE GROUND, AND BREATHED INTO HIS NOSTRILS [AF] THE BREATH OF LIFE...

132

"Nostrils" might conjure up an image of a deity inflating the man's head with a straw, but *af* more commonly refers to the front of the head or the forehead. The human story begins in the forehead, which expanded as *Homo sapiens* emerged from the apes. Beneath the forehead, FL processes relate the image of the man to other elements in the internal world, developing a narrative of the self and self-awareness.*

> *...AND THE MAN BECAME A LIVING SOUL.*
> *AND YHWH ELOHIM PLANTED A GARDEN EASTWARD IN EDEN; AND THERE HE PUT THE MAN WHOM HE HAD FORMED...* [8]

The root of Eden is *adan*, meaning 'pleasure' or 'softness'. [9] Adam resides alone in Eden, easy and pleasing in a state of bliss before knowledge and desire.

> *...AND OUT OF THE GROUND MADE YHWH ELOHIM TO GROW EVERY TREE THAT IS DESIRABLE TO THE EYE, AND GOOD FOR FOOD;*
> *THE TREE OF LIFE ALSO IN THE MIDST OF THE GARDEN, AND THE TREE OF KNOWLEDGE OF GOOD AND EVIL.*

---

* "He bowed himself with his face [*af*] to the earth." (Genesis 48:12)

"And I put a jewel on thy forehead [*af*] and earrings in thine ears, and a beautiful crown upon thine head." (Ezekiel 16:12)

AND A RIVER WENT OUT OF EDEN TO WATER THE GARDEN

AND FROM THENCE IT WAS PARTED, AND BECAME INTO FOUR HEADS...

...which is curious, because it means that the river flows both ways...

... THE NAME OF THE FIRST IS PISHOWN...

...a watery onomatopoeia, not so unlike an English equivalent, meaning to 'spread out'.[10] The other river names are also sonorous: Gihon (burst forth), Hiddekel (rapid) and Perath (break forth).[11] Pishown spreads out and "compasseth the whole land of Havilah", from a root meaning 'pain'.[12] In Havilah "there is gold". Gihon bursts forth from Kuwsh, with a root meaning 'darkness/digging/piercing/mining'.[13] Hiddekel goes rapidly "toward the east of Ashur", from a root of 'joy'.[14] The fourth breaks forth to an unnamed place. The streams meet and feed into and out of Eden. In the head, streams flow back and forth from places of joy, pain and darkness, watering the garden branching through the networks of the brain.

AND OUT OF THE GROUND YHWH ELOHIM FORMED [YATZAR] EVERY BEAST OF THE FIELD, AND EVERY FOWL OF THE AIR...

YHWH Elohim the Definer squeezes off things "out of the ground", and that process is associated with PL activity.

…AND HE BROUGHT THEM UNTO ADAM TO SEE WHAT HE WOULD CALL THEM…

The Definer forms things (*DBR*), but He doesn't name them. He presents them to Adam, and Adam fixes the names (*SM*). Neologism is a different process to definition, a creative process bringing ideas together, associated with FL activity, as are the other talents particular to humans. The Manipulator arranges elements of thought, making sense of experience by creating ideas, names and schemes, writing chronicles and lamentations.

When the Definer grabs something that is already known and has a name, that thing is categorized in an unconscious process of association. Birds and fish are capable of categorizing visual and sound stimuli, including Monet and blues, and in humans the process is related to TL activity.[15][16] In the Garden of Eden this job falls to neither Adam nor YHWH Elohim. Once a name has stuck the Categorizer works automatically:

…AND WHATSOEVER ADAM CALLED EVERY LIVING CREATURE, THAT WAS THE NAME THEREOF.[17]

Representing something to consciousness as an element of thought is the process of assigning a name to it: it's 'Freddy', it's a 'roller skate', it's a 'fruit bat'. Presented, it becomes a presence one is conscious of. TL disturbances are often experienced as presences, both in epilepsy and with TMS.[18] They are usually felt as animate presences, but then the intangible presence of a disembodied roller skate might not feel like much anyway.[19]

Relationships develop between self-aware living things and known things with names, and they can be both good and bad relationships. With Elohim it was all "good", but according to YHWH Elohim,

> *"IT IS <u>NOT GOOD</u> THAT THE MAN SHOULD BE ALONE; I WILL MAKE HIM AN HELP MEET FOR HIM."*
>
> *AND HE TOOK ONE OF HIS RIBS [TSELA], AND CLOSED UP THE FLESH INSTEAD THEREOF.*[20]

Tsela is found 41 times in the Bible, and only in this story is it translated as "rib". Elsewhere it is usually 'side', and reading 'side' here cuts through the politics and tells a story of division and complementarity between equal parts. Wherever YHWH Elohim acts we encounter dualism: good and evil; self and not-self; lover and beloved and the yearning between them to unite. This is the first of the 'not goods', with the promise of ecstasy and new life in its resolution.

The serpent steps in at the beginning of Genesis 3, for at this point he has not yet been cursed to crawl. He raises the first question in the *Bible*:

> *"YEA, HATH ELOHIM SAID, 'YE SHALL NOT EAT OF EVERY TREE OF THE GARDEN'?"*

Elohim hath not said anything of the sort. Elohim had given mankind "every tree [...] for food", and the prohibition was issued by YHWH Elohim, along with a threat that "in the day that thou eatest thereof thou shalt surely die".[21][22] The serpent hissed at the contradiction:

"YE SHALL NOT SURELY DIE: FOR ELOHIM DOTH KNOW THAT IN THE DAY YE EAT THEREOF, THEN YOUR EYES SHALL BE OPENED, AND YE SHALL BE AS GODS [ELOHIM], KNOWING GOOD AND EVIL."[23]

The English translation sounds like the gods know good and evil, i.e. "ye shall be as gods, knowing good and evil [*like the gods do*]". The Hebrew could mean that, but it could also be read as "ye shall be as gods, but knowing good and evil as well [*unlike the gods*]". Tradition, common sense and wishful thinking tell us that it is the former. Religious folk will insist upon it, as if they own the text by virtue of familiarity or piety, but the question is open. The Bible provokes endless questions like this with its loose grammar, suggesting lines of enquiry to interrogate the options. In this case we can read about what the powers get up to, and then decide if they behave like they know what good and evil are.

Biblical morality begins with a conundrum, for if Adam and Eve were without knowledge of good and evil, how could they possibly know whose counsel was good and whose was evil? To Eve the fruit "was good for food, and […] pleasant to the eyes", so she ate it.[24] If a toddler eats mummy's sleeping pills it is because he is innocent, not cunning, without the capacity to distinguish between tic-tacs and Temazepam, without the knowledge of good and evil. Eve ate the fruit in her innocence, and shared it with Adam.

AND THE EYES OF THEM BOTH WERE OPENED, AND THEY KNEW THAT THEY WERE NAKED.

With the benefit of hindsight or foresight or insight, they might have chosen differently; but they had no sight at all. They were young and blind and in love, incapable of good judgement or foreseeing the evil that might lie ahead. For their eyes to be opened, they first had to disobey a command they couldn't possibly comprehend.

And YHWH Elohim said unto the woman, "What is this that thou hast done?"

And the woman said, "The serpent beguiled / elevated me, and I did eat."[26]

In the event Adam did not surely die "in the day" as promised; his suffering continued for "all the days of his life".[27] YHWH Elohim's lie was exposed to freshly opened eyes.

"Behold, the man is become as one of us..."

...said YHWH, introducing the rest of the powers into what will become a very busy story. Orthodoxy explains the divine plurals in the Bible as 'majestic plurals', singular names with plural endings a bit like the royal 'we'; but that doesn't fly here. He doesn't say "they will become like us", He says "like one of us", evoking individuals amongst the plurality of the powers.

"...to know good and evil."

The dichotomy of Good and Evil is introduced by YHWH Elohim in Genesis 2, when He plants the Tree of the Knowledge of Good and Evil. The English word 'evil' GHOULISH FONT suggests serial killers and ghoulish fonts, but the Hebrew word *RO* covers a broader range of meaning, and need not carry moral overtones:

> the other basket had very naughty [*RO*] figs, which could not be eaten, they were so bad [*RO*].*[28]

'Fig' is a noun, its figginess intrinsic to it, and the same goes for 'cattle' and every other noun, the 'light' spoken into creation in Genesis 1 and the darkness divided from it. They are absolutes, absolutely what they are, whereas Good and Evil are relative depending on how we relate – and relationships change over time. Nothing is fixed, save the names in the minds of Adam and his descendents. Things outside the head change, from one day to the next sometimes, and we don't notice until we bite into a fig that has become very naughty. Once upon a time in my twenties, I spent a day nursing an evil hangover and apologizing for things I couldn't remember. That day my eyes flicked open like Adam's, and cheap fortified cider, which had once seemed good for food, and pleasant to the eyes, was recategorized as evil in my own personal cosmos. And in retrospect, maybe the hangover was good.

The Tree of Life is mindless of Good or Evil. Fed by the waters of pain and contentment and darkness it grows toward the light, recalibrating as the source of power cycles through space. Mankind who loves toffee but hates the dentist continually modifies his relationships with the elements of thought in the head. Names are coloured with emotional associations as the Tree of the Knowledge of Good and Evil grows, as the Manipulator reflects and develops capacities for reason. Any fool can label things 'good' or 'evil', or adopt the scheme of some priest or patrician; but in morality as in cognition, the detail gets lost in the category.

---

* In this book, *O* represents the letter *ayin*. It used to be pronounced differently to *alef*, with a contracted throat

To understand the why behind a cancer or a riot requires close observation of all the elements in context, the chains of action and reaction that encircle the planet. The sharpest observer in the garden is the serpent who spots the discrepancy. The letters of his name *NaChaSh*, revowelled as *NaCheSh*, mean 'observing the signs' 'guessing' and 'interpreting'. Evoking the whisper of the soothsayer in its etymology, *NaChaSh* divines, reading the signs on the surface to uncover secrets beneath.[29] [30]

The serpent suffers from near-universal prejudice, though he risked all to uncover the truth. The Bible never describes him as *RO*. Neither Adam nor Eve are described as *RO*, and it wasn't a moral lapse that got them into trouble. It was their innocence and their inattentional blindness, missing the switch in the powers and missing the greater prize. They were cast out of their booby-trapped paradise, but not as a punishment for transgression. It was a preemptive strike, as YHWH Elohim announced:

"And now, lest he put forth his hand, and take also of the Tree of Life, and eat, and live for ever."

Therefore YHWH Elohim sent him forth from the garden.

With this line YHWH Elohim retires from the story. Outside the garden in a world more like ours, YHWH takes over as the principle emanation, and his antics are described as *RO* in diverse verses. "I will bring evil [*RO*] from the north," He promises, "and a great destruction", and He makes good on his promise.[31] When He aims annihilation at the Israelites at Sinai. Jung puts the godname on the couch:

> Such a condition is only conceivable either when no reflecting consciousness is present at all, or when the capacity for reflection is very feeble and a more or less adventitious phenomenon. A condition of this sort can only be described as amoral.[32]

The role of moral Manipulator falls to Moses, who intercedes to direct the powers and rescue the Israelites; "and YHWH repented of the evil [RO] which he thought to do unto his people."[33] He can repent, but He can't help Himself, and nor can He change. Creating evil is fundamental to the nature of the emanation:[34]

> "I form the light, and create darkness: I make peace, and create evil [RO]: I, YHWH, do all these things".[35]

"The thing proceedeth from YHWH," says Laban, the brother of Rebekah, "we cannot speak unto thee bad or good."[36] Simplistic dichotomies fail to describe the powers, and also fail to describe the people I know adequately. Even the patriarchs have morals that are all over the place, with Abraham pimping his wife, and Jacob scamming his starving brother with a stew.[37] [38] [39] The serpent who both beguiles and elevates in a single word has a complicated code of ethics.

> Now the serpent was more subtil [ORWM] than any beast of the field which YHWH Elohim had made.

"Subtil" is the serpent's one and only adjective in the *Bible*, and like many Hebrew words it is morally ambiguous. *ORWM* sometimes suggests 'crafty', but in each of its eight appearances in *Proverbs* it is a virtue, not a vice:

> The prudent [ORWM] are crowned with knowledge.

As per the proverb, the serpent knows his stuff. He clearly knows more about the forbidden fruit than YHWH Elohim does (or at least more than He is willing to reveal).[40]

ORWM also appears a mere seven words before the serpent's *ORWM*:

And they were both <u>naked</u> [*ORWM*], the man and his
wife, and were not ashamed.

Now the serpent was more <u>subtil</u> [*ORWM*]...*

One *ORWM* is written directly above the other in a handwritten
scroll, but the knife of dualism cut between then with the
Masoretic vowel scheme in the 7th century AD.[41] In the
vowelling that would become orthodox, the first *ORWM*
(*arowm*) implies innocence and the second (*aruwm*) implies
craftiness. This completely obscures the poetry, and misses
the paradox that morality poses. The Masoretes pruned the
hyperconnectivity beneath the surface of the words in line with
their stated agenda of guarding YHWH from indignities and
blasphemies. Doctoring the text goes back further, a thousand
years or more; the Talmud cites 18 "corrections of the scribe"
made to the very letters of the scrolls after the period of exile
in Babylon.[42] Some edits were made with the same pro-YHWH
whitewashing agenda in mind, such as that which took the sting
out of Moses' candid plea to YHWH, from "let me not see <u>thy</u>
wretchedness [*RO*]!" to "let me not see <u>my</u> wretchedness!"[43]
Other sources mention further edits bringing the total closer to
30, and there may be more that are unknown.[44]

The serpent knows and Adam is learning, but maybe
YHWH Elohim doesn't know all that much. "Where art thou?"
He asks, a mite less omniscient than His PR team would have
you believe. Adam replies,

"I was afraid, because I was naked [*ORWM*]."

...or perhaps "because I was prudent", or "subtil", depending
on how you want to read it. Another of the *Proverbs* describes
how "a prudent [*ORWM*] man foreseeth the evil, and hideth
himself".[45] Adam hid, having foreseen the evil approaching
with his freshly opened eyes – which is just what prudent men
are supposed to do.

---

* Naked: עָרוֹם   Subtil: עָרוּם

Given the complexity of the poetry, it is no surprise that there used to be other interpretative traditions, and the few texts that managed to escape the censorship purges of the early Roman church attest to this. *On The Origin of the World* recounts how "when they had eaten [the fruit], the light of knowledge had shone upon them".[46] The *Testimony of Truth* retells the whole story from the perspective of the serpent, a principle of wisdom with plenty to say about his enemy:

> First He maliciously refused Adam from eating of the Tree of Knowledge, and, secondly, He said "Adam, where are you?" God does not have foreknowledge? Would He not know from the beginning? And afterwards, He said, "Let us cast him out of this place, lest he eat of the tree of life and live forever." Surely, He has shown himself to be a malicious grudger! And what kind of God is this? For great is the blindness of those who read, and they did not know Him.[47]

In protecting YHWH from blasphemy the scribes blasphemed against poetry, as far as I'm concerned, making a multifaceted guide to our multifaceted selves into something far more black and white. What comes down to us is corrupted, to a degree we cannot know, and it corrupted the cultures that were built upon it. Nevertheless the edits are cosmetic and superficial if you read critically, as the moral contours of the powers cannot be levelled by switching around a few letters. The godnames are not moral beings; they are forces of nature, forces in the head. YHWH Elohim builds you up and makes a man of you, gives you a soul and a sense of self. He carves the world into chunks, but there is nothing moral – or even thoughtful – about Him. The Definer defines, but He neither names nor explains. The Manipulator manipulates elements of thought in consciousness, relating them back together on the Tree of Knowledge in the light of the conscious mind, comparing and contrasting, making sense, making plans, making names. He hears the whispery hiss of the Questioner. He reads the signs and infers what is behind them, relating it all into a meaningful scheme. He develops ideals, and transforms himself in the process. He can inhibit his urges, or he can follow them, according to his conscience.

In the beginning, in the head, were created the powers. Elohim creates, YHWH Elohim defines, Adam thinks up the names, and the snake challenges the definitions. Observing the signs carefully, reading a little less sanctimoniously and with attention to the mastery of the poetry, the complex brilliance of the wordplay slices through the dualisms. Knowledge of good and evil is no sin. Eve's sin was her inattentional blindness. "God said, Behold," and Eve was told, but behold she did not.[48] She became absorbed in the game and didn't notice the gorilla striding onto court, pounding his chest. She missed the switch in the powers and so did generations of the faithful, singing Sunday songs of praise to a god who is ambivalent at best, and sometimes downright *RO*.

People generally find what they are looking for in life, in the world around them, and perhaps also in the Bible. "Both read the Bible day and night," wrote William Blake, "but thou read'st black where I read white."[49] Some people read according to the assumption that there is a goody called God, (i.e. all the non-human speaking parts except Satan, the angels, and a few talking animals). Many people find moral principles, though these differ radically between readers, justifying slavery for one and revolution for another. People find all sorts in the Good Book. I have been very lucky to find not only a guide to brain function but a tasty stash of psychoactives to go with it.

Ω

THE MONKEY WRENCH

The usual gestalt mode of perception, where the figure is noticed and the ground ignored, seems to be modified. One sees instead the figure-ground as a totality [...] Conceptually, it appears obvious that such opposite categories as being and non-being, light and darkness, good and bad, solid and space are related mutually in the same way as front and back. This may come as a shock to the kinesthetic sense, a threat to one's identity, and a disturbance to standards and habits of judgement.

The individual unused to this situation may interpret it onesidedly: he may feel utterly helpless, wondering whether he can continue to think logically or even speak correctly, or conversely, he may imagine that he is God almighty, in charge of the whole universe.[1]

- Alan Watts, describing LSD

 N THE BEGINNING I didn't expect to meet the Godhead on the Yucatan peninsula in Mexico; but life is full of surprises. The party I happened upon was a decent affair at a beach bar with chaps in shirts and ladies sipping cocktails, not some crazy full-moon knees-up, and it was unremarkable until around midnight when a hippy began to shout his rapture at the sea. He ran around enthused all

night long, vocalizing his joy and wonder, sometimes proclaiming himself to be whatever his eyes or his free-roaming imagination fell upon: "I'm the sea!"; "I'm the sun!"; "I'm the earth!"; "I'm the sky!" and so on and so forth, "I'm Jesus!"; "I'm God"; "I AM EVERYTHING!" He was naked, of course, and like Adam he was not ashamed, but people soon lost patience with him, and answered him with blasphemies against his divinity. The dogs remained devoted followers, pursuing him happily around the sand until morning, when he finally collapsed in a heap for a well-earned day of rest.

Opinion is divided over whether such an episode constitutes a genuine mystical experience; in any case he ticked at least three of the four boxes proposed by William James in his pioneering study into the psychology of religion.[2] Bliss (1) was in glorious evidence. Concerns and conditioning were shed (2), along with his clothes. He was experiencing overwhelming newness (3), at least, he sounded surprised about being the sun. Regarding the revelation of hidden truths (4), "I'm God!" is an apocalypse of divinity within the self, though not something one generally proclaims in polite company. People have burned at the stake for similar indiscretions, and even if you have excellent credentials it can go badly:

> Jesus answered them […] "I and the Father are one."
> Then the Jews took up stones again to stone him […]
> "for blasphemy and because that thou, being a man, makest thyself God."[3]

Given half a chance, some at the beach party might have taken up stones; but they contented themselves with flinging insults, and the hippy continued with his beatitudes. Jesus answered his critics:

> "Is it not written in your law 'I have said, Ye are gods?'"[4]

He is quoting Psalm 82:

> Ye are gods [elohim]; and all of you are children of the
> most High. But ye shall die like men, and fall like one
> of the princes. Arise, O gods [elohim], judge the earth:
> for thou shalt inherit all nations.[5]

None of the OT prophets identify themselves with divinity
as blatantly as did the holy men of Galilee and Yucatan; though
the question of identity arises at the burning bush:

> And Moses said unto Elohim, "<u>Who am I</u>, that I should
> go unto Pharaoh, and that I should bring forth the
> Children of Israel out of Egypt?"
> And He said, "I will be with thee"

This roundabout answer to a direct question suggests all kinds
of interesting things, including that Moses' identity is about to
be eclipsed by the powers. Moses continues:

> "When I come unto the children of Israel, and shall say
> unto them, 'Elohim of your fathers hath sent me unto
> you'; and they shall say to me, 'What is his name?',
> what shall I say unto them?
>
> And Elohim said unto Moses: *EHYEH ASHER EHYEH…*

It might not be a name at all, more of a badass answer to
an impossible question: "I am who I am!" A 'name' (*SM*) fixes
meaning to a defined 'thing' (*DBR*), but the infinite can be
neither defined nor fixed. If we take it to be a name, it is not
a noun like other godnames. It is a verb twice. *Ehyeh* usually
means 'I will be', as in Elohim's answer to the first question: "<u>I
will be</u> with thee".[6] It is in the imperfect uncompleted form, so
whatever it is, it has potential. Different sages propose 'I WILL
BE WHAT I WILL BE', 'I AM HE WHO WAS, IS AND WILL
BE' and many other translations, but no one has a monopoly
on the meaning of poetry.[78] *Ehyeh asher ehyeh* strikes me as a
fractal unfolding, the powers to the nth power: being becoming.

Infinites of *et ceteras* open up in *ehyer asher ehyer*, and
the infinite has its perils, for mental health as well as beach
decorum. Mathematician Georg Cantor courted danger as he

broke sets down into sets and more sets, counting infinities between integers, multiplying infinities beyond anything the classical philosophers had conceived of. His work led him to an apocalypse of "the true infinite or Absolute, which is in God [and] permits no determination".[9] That same God, according to Cantor, personally revealed to him the infinite set – the set that contains all sets, infinity of infinities. Bertrand Russell declared that Zeno's paradox had been resolved, that Achilles had finally caught up with the tortoise after giving chase in ever diminishing strides for 2,500 years.[10] Wittgenstein was horrified, calling it a "cancerous growth, seeming to have grown out of the normal body [of mathematics] aimlessly and senselessly".[11] To Wittgenstein, sets were recognisable by their "family resemblances", meaning "similarities, relationships, and a whole series of them [...] overlapping and criss-crossing".[12] For example, not all 'games' are played with a ball, or in teams, or with points, or for fun – and yet we all know an instance of the 'game' set when we see one, from whatever traits it shares with other games (like balls, teams, points, fun or whatever). Cantor's sets were totally different, grounded not in the known but in the infinite unknowable. His investigations violated the rabbinical taboo to leave alone "what is above and what is below", and we should not be surprised, therefore, that after discovering the infinite set he went straight to the mental asylum for the first of many extended stays.[13]

"A set is a Many that allows itself to be thought of as a One," said Cantor in a moment of lucidity, but then what is I WILL BE WHAT I HAVE BEEN?[14] If it is a thing at all it is something inconceivable to minds accustomed to normal names, like 'Moses', 'tent' and 'hunger'. The Manipulator can't grab something without an edge, so the deity gives another name:

> ...And He said "Thus shalt thou say unto the Children
> of Israel: 'I AM [*Ehyer*] hath sent me unto you.'"[15]

Or perhaps I HAVE BEEN, or I WILL BE. The 'be' verb is usually omitted in sentences describing the present; 'I am Nemu' is simply *anochi Nemu* (I Nemu), and when Moses asks "Who am I?" he says *mi anochi?* (who I?), without a verb. The answer contains the verb: *ehyeh imach* (I <u>will be</u> with thee).

In the seminal meeting between Moses and the divine, Elohim <u>is</u> and the prophet <u>isn't</u>. God revealed Himself to the 14th century mystic Catherine of Siena with similar sentiments:

> The more you abandon yourself,
>
> > The more you will find Me.
>
> You are that which is not.
>
> > I AM THAT I AM.[16]

The Berditchever Rebbe put it more technically:

> When man nullifies himself completely and attaches his thoughts to Nothingness, then a new sustenance flows to all universes. This is a sustenance that did not exist previously.[17]

Something new comes into the universe, even into all universes, when Moses the goatherd finds his god at the burning bush, and becomes Moses the prophet of YHWH. When he follows the command to challenge Pharaoh, he goes as God:

> And YHWH said unto Moses, "See, I have made thee Elohim to Pharaoh."[18]

A few days after the beach party I bumped into the artist formerly known as God, and found him to be humourless and unfriendly, rather sunburnt and apparently no better for his temporary deification. The Holy Spirit had descended and scarpered, leaving him dispirited. We must conclude that there is some truth in the boring old adage about there being no shortcuts to God. Mind-bending paths may attract those of a certain bent, but they are long and challenging, and strewn with day-glo distractions.

$$\Omega$$

What psychoactives tell us about the divine is ineffable, but we can eff a little more clearly about what they tell us about the brain. One that has been studied in some detail, including on my own keenly conditioned lobes, is psilocybin. It causes "activity to decrease in areas that have the densest connections with other areas," according to former government drugs advisor Professor David Nutt.[19] *Nature* adds that these "connector hubs" co-ordinate information flow between different parts of the brain, and that inhibiting them accounts for "the effects of hallucinogens, which induce a state of 'unconstrained cognition'".[20]

One of the connector hubs inhibited is the anterior cingulate cortex (ACC), which connects the limbic system and TLs to the FLs.[21] It is involved in deciding between conflicting interpretations of things. When subjects are asked to read the word 'red' printed in green letters, they have to decide between the sensation (green) and the concept (red), and ACC activity spikes as the conflict is resolved.[22] The decision takes longer if the ACC is inhibited with TMS.[23] With the "unconstrained cognition" of psilocybin such conflicts can go unresolved, giving the experience of "the five senses disembodied," as one of the first accounts put it, "all of them blending into one another most strangely, until the person, utterly passive, becomes a pure receptor, infinitely delicate, of sensations".[24]

With ACC inhibition things lose their edges, including matters, concepts, percepts and other *DBR*s. To quote the Talmud out of context, "both these and those are the living words of God."[25] When working normally the ACC helps establish what is what, and it also supplies the urge to put it into words. People with ACC damage do not initiate communication, and Tourette's vocal tics are linked to a spike in ACC activity.[26] [27] [28]

Meditation inhibits the connector hubs, along with various other parts of the brain. Psilocybin is more focused, targeting specific receptors found at high concentrations in the connector hubs. It disrupts the pathways that normally integrate information, but most of the brain is working more or less normally. This is in some ways comparable to autistic brain function, with long range central communications disrupted and relatively lively local activity. Robin Carhart-Harris, who conducted the psilocybin study, offers a political metaphor:

> What would it mean if you were to, metaphorically speaking, blow up a capital city? It's a bit of a loose metaphor, but it is kind of one way you can understand what psychedelics are doing because they're disturbing the normal order or organization, particularly in this hub structure and other cortical hub structures. If you were to do that in a really important organizing centre, then that would have implications for an entire system […] for the rest of the country. It may invite some anarchy […] Regions which don't normally communicate communicate more, [with] novel communications.[29]

My brain was honoured to help smash the mental state in the name of science, by staring at static images of chaos and deciding what I could see while my ACC was under surveillance. It was boring, to be honest, and Cardiff wasn't pretty from inside an MEG machine; but Wales offers many more pleasant places to disrupt the normal functioning of one's connector hubs. I lay in such a spot many seasons ago beneath an apple tree bemushroomed, watching the leaves traffic with the air in a green haze that leaked into the sky, feeling the roots diving down and dissipating into the earth, integrating her ions. The processes of my body were drawn into the processes of life that were pulling the tree into and out of the cosmos. We were all breathing the same air, as the earth and the heavens and the powers came together in my head.

Mushrooms erode the veils that separate tree from earth and self from other, beloved from lover. Memories of before combine with images of now, as trails follow things through space. Auras of possibility pulse around objects. Little people emerge impetuously from the shadows, and holy cities peep over the horizon as apocalypse presses upon the fraying fabric of the veil. Some unknowable mystery intersects with our worlds via chemistry; but does the chemistry define the mystery, or does the mystery create the chemistry? What other worlds are screened out for the sake of more immediate concerns?

Like psilocybin, ketamine limits information flow, but with a different mechanism, blocking the NMDA-PCP receptor.[30] This receptor is widely distributed in the brain, involved in language, thought, memory, emotion and perception, and ketamine disrupts all of these faculties.[31] The individual, her concerns, her concepts and edges melt into the (K-)whole. Ketamine also inhibits inhibiting neurons, meaning that some activity increases – particularly that which is involved with image and sound. The internal camera continues to roll, following paths to the lost temples of the deep unconscious while the rest of the system is dozing. It bears some resemblance to the dream state, and the same receptor is involved in both.[32]

Ketamine is fascinating, but such widespread inhibition seems to turn some enthusiasts into barely-conscious zombies – or perhaps that's just the parties I used to go to. Some years after I stopped taking it I went to visit a friend who had moved to Dublin to study veterinary medicine. She thought I was still as intemperate as I had once been, and greeted me with syringes of vet-ket she had diverted away from some unfortunate mammal or other. Novelties have always intrigued me, and there is something about the technology of injection that is inescapably, even literally veil-piercing, so I abandoned myself one last time. It did the job, but the things of that strange, vegetative world made it clear that they would take me so far and no further. I was not to be deterred, so I abandoned myself once again on my final evening in Ireland, this time a few more mls up the syringe, but the message remained the same. The following morning I stepped off the overnight ferry at Liverpool with my sea-legs, and my sea-legs staggered with me all the way to Manchester. They continued stalking my steps for a week, and then another week, long after any entertaining novelty had worn off. Worried that I would stay permanently wonky I took up tai chi, and gradually my balance returned.*

NMDA-PCP receptors are also inhibited by nitrous oxide. Though it is something of an environmental catastrophe, with canisters scattered about festival sites like shells on a battlefield, physiologically it seems benign enough. The main side effect of the heroic doses those intrepid Victorians enjoyed appears to be the writing of extended philosophical tracts.[33] William James' experiments led to a "tremendously exiting sense of an intense metaphysical illumination," stripping him of both the category and the self in the space of a breath, demolishing the framework of Aristotelian logic:[34]

> The ego and its objects, the *meum* and *teum* are one [...] every opposition, among whatsoever things, vanishes in a higher unity in which it is based [...] God and Devil, Good and Evil, Life and Death, I and Thou, Black and White.[35]

Dissolving familiar lines, psychedelics open up a space of what James called "overwhelming newness" outside the category. Senses melt together, emotional streams fan out into muddy deltas, assumptions soften. LSD works differently again, but also by promoting widespread communication between brain regions normally independent of each other.

It does further insult to the category, in my experience, upending the filing cabinet and shredding its contents unceremoniously; though that may have something to do with the unceremonial way in which I have taken it, rather than pharmacology. Ayahuasca, iboga, San Pedro, salvia divinorum,

---

*I'm quite prepared to believe that I had picked up one of those strange inner ear viruses, as I did some years later, whose sole symptom is to cause inexplicable whisky legs. The powers move in mysterious and sometimes wonky ways, but meaning is ours to infer as we make sense of the staggering footsteps. Perhaps, if your ACC is sufficiently loose, it could be both.

peyote, coca leaves, Hawaiian woodrose, datura, ganja, henbane, yopo and various mushrooms have long histories of ritual use, and wisdom traditions that advise on how to navigate the other worlds encountered (some of which are not playgrounds). LSD, by contrast, is still young, and the War on Drugs has meant that much of its exploration has been underground. I've had some extraordinary times on acid, but personally I prefer things more ceremonial.

Ω

The first time I heard about ayahuasca was during my second year in Japan, when my ex described a party with a strange brew. She didn't speak enough English at the time to explain further, and I was already sold anyway; but when I arrived to find Japanese people in uniform and totally out of character, hugging each other amidst icons and candles and the cross of Caravaca, I suddenly found myself feeling very Jewish indeed. I made a beeline for the only other white man in the room, and asked him if it was some kind of church. "It's a funky church," he replied, tuning his guitar. I stood quietly contemptuous as they began to pray, but within a few hours I was not sure what to think, or even how to think. I was rolling around the carpet with a circus in my head and a riot in my stomach, careering between wonder and terror via the puke bucket.

And then the music stopped.

I remained in a heap for incalculable aeons.

Eventually someone told me it was time for another dose. I genuinely thought it was a joke, but sure enough people were adjusting their ties and standing in orderly lines to start the second half. I couldn't stand. I couldn't sit – I could barely lie down! It wasn't the first time I'd been in a state, of course, though it was my first time in a state with a bunch of Japanese people in uniforms banging drums and singing Portuguese to Jesus. And I was supposed to drink more?

Daime is a lineage that syncretises folk Catholicism and Amazonian shamanism, and I took to it with enthusiasm. The brew is extremely strong, for one thing, and very curious, and the ceremony is particular – far too weird for most straight people, and too straight for a lot of weird people. Over subsequent years I learned to stand up more and vomit less, to sing and dance in formation. The many ritual instructions also started making more sense to me, with the exception of the Apostle's Creed. Our Father and Hail Mary become more interesting as you study them, but the Creed remains what it always was, a cynical piece of Roman politics jammed into the litany to standardize belief and marginalize groups that thought differently.[36] I couldn't bring myself to say it, and my cognitive dissonance was only resolved many years later in Brazil, where I learned that centres faithful to the original format don't recite it, because the founder Mestre Irineu removed it from the litany.

Daime has been the catalyst for many changes in my life. It was the inspiration for my books and the reason I left Japan for Brazil. As a door to extraordinary worlds, it has never ceased to surprise me. It continues to offer me new perspectives on my problems – though it doesn't solve them. It lends brilliance to the inhibited, comfort to the nervous and grace to the hopelessly formal, but these jewels are snatched away. Plenty of people give up cigarettes after a few glasses of Daime, and start again after a few glasses of beer. People go home to abusive relationships and destructive cycles. Having soared in the heavens you slip back into the mud, and while you might have a better idea about which way to crawl, there are no guarantees, except what you can guarantee yourself. In my case I can be sure that if I fail to put into practice what has been revealed, the messages will grow more insistent.

Many ayahuasqueros take pains to explain that ayahuasca is not a drug, because, you know, drugs are bad. I'm not convinced by this dualism. Ayahuasca is called many things, including medicine, jaguar medicine, sacrament, teacher plant and entheogen. It is a purgative, or 'the purgative' (*la purga*). From a medical perspective it is a drug, because it alters the function of the body. What it means to you depends on the categories your mind has at its disposal, which is your problem, not ayahuasca's. Some people call it a hallucinogen, which means that it makes you see things that aren't there. From a shamanic perspective that is not what happens with ayahuasca, but then all terms carry baggage. From my perspective Daime is a divine being, but that is my problem, not its. Besides, that isn't why I drink it. I drink it because I like what it does to my brain.

I'm very happy with my Daime lineage, and one of its quirks is that it forbids advertising or "doing propaganda", including proselytizing or generally talking in public about how marvellous it is – so please excuse a few guarded but partisan paragraphs about how it works. Daime is a lineage and ritual form, as well as a brew prepared to a specific recipe in a specific ritual. The ceremony combines various techniques, including meditation, repetitive dance steps and repetitive beats, sleep deprivation, singing and playing maraca in unison. Wandering around, chatting, and the whole "social game" (to use one of Dr. Tim Leary's terms) is suspended. There is nothing to do except sing and dance in formation, in lines modelled on the motion of the sea. It might sound a bit contrived, and indeed it is contrived – to facilitate a specific type of experience. The tight geometry of the lines and the shared beat of the maracas help to shake up your own lines, drawing you into a different rhythm, and as your body takes its place in a collective of people dressed just like you, the deeper parts of you can follow the journey wherever it goes.

By some means, perhaps via its effects on the amygdalas at the junction of the TLs and the limbic system, ayahuasca reintroduces memories into the stream of consciousness, including forgotten or 'repressed' traumatic memories.[37] They can be reappraised, with turbo-charged FLs making connections as participants actualise the geometry of the session with their bodies, giving voice to poetry about honesty, love, and attention. The songs both guide and challenge one's thoughts, and with elements of thought less edgy people are less concerned about deciding whether things are red or green, good or bad or this or that. We can keep both sides of a dichotomy in the crucible, and something transformative might emerge from the alchemy. In the words of Mestre Irineu, the point of the session is not simply to see beautiful things but also to correct your errors.[38] This is not always easy, but it is something to aim at.

Imagine, for example, that the memory of a painful betrayal presents itself to the light of the conscious mind during a ceremony. Other things with similar motifs join the mix, including other events from your biography and your personal database of mythology (Ovid's *Metamorphosis* or Oprah's melodramatis, depending on your habits). Things leak in from the other side of the story, mistakes made on your side, traumas from the past and other things beyond anyone's control. There may be insights about subsequent relationships where the old wound continued to fester. All of this takes place in line and in step with the poetry, rhythm and eye-wateringly beautiful melodies, under a ten-hour bombardment of lines like "don't despise your brother or sister, show your light of love".[39] A shift in thinking might allow the strands to be weaved back together into a coherent story. The betrayer may drift out of the category of 'dreadfully awful things' (along with nuclear accidents and bone cancer in children) and into 'lessons learned' (like when you crashed your bicycle while texting).

Ayahuasca enhances creative divergent thinking while decreasing conventional convergent thinking, as the title of a recent research paper puts it.[40] In the cipher of the alchemists: *solve et coagula*. As the fixed is made volatile new combinations become possible, new insights and solutions become apparent. Patterns are disrupted, new concepts created. The puffed up are punctured, the dozy shaken awake, the careless rapped soundly across the knuckles. With psychedelics, I AM can become a more blurred BEING experimenting with WHAT I WILL BE; and sometimes a more familiar version of the self comes into focus. Establishing a new poetic order with tighter metre prepares the poet for the lines to come, so challenges and opportunities can be met more skilfully.

Daime can be powerful, and how much of this is down to ceremony and how much is the brew itself is difficult to say. The 'dry' rituals we did without drinking when the police started cracking down had some of the same effects (although no one puked, even if we did put buckets out to get ourselves in the mood). Daime ceremony is highly formalized, and my feeling about this is that while a hot air balloon need not be over-engineered for a pleasure flight, a spaceship should be aerodynamic without cracks and panels flapping around if it is to escape the atmosphere and return safely. The Catholic vibe and rigid format of Daime aren't for everyone, and many groups outside of the Brazilian Amazon have relaxed the discipline so far as to abandon the original instructions, mixing lineages and fancies in a fairly haphazard manner that doesn't do a lot for me. Some people prefer getting psychedelic in nature, which has its own order, others are happier dancing naked around effigies of He of Horn and Hoof. Do what thou wilt, wherever your enthusiasm takes you – but try at least to be respectful and informed about your tradition. If you dedicate yourself, the effects can be extraordinary.

Whenever you become ecstatic, however, you eventually have to return to yourself, wherever you are when you find your way back. Psychedelics are alchemical catalysts that make volatile the fixed, but lines reform – and what new categories will be fixed down by the chains of logic established in your new cosmos? That depends, to a large degree, on what Tim Leary called "set and setting".[41] 'Setting' is the physical environment, and ceremony takes care of that (barring any unscripted acts of God). 'Set', the mental mindset, is more complicated, as everyone arrives with the ideas in their heads. If, therefore, you are exploring this murky zone, ask yourself if the facilitators are cool and competent. If you trust them – and of course, if your trust is well-placed – you might get more out of it if you leave your inner critic outside the ceremonial hall, as gentlemen used to leave their swords outside church. It will still be there for you to pick up on the way out, and you may find it has been sharpened and oiled in the interim.

Ceremony does not clear away the clouds completely, of course, as the most immediate part of the experience is filtered through the individual's own mind, which responds to subjective, collective and whatever other encounters in its own way. Ceremony should ensure, however, that when rays break through the clouds they are sun-beams and not gamma rays. If you have some insurmountable hang-up about some aspect of the ceremony, like its Christian iconography, its New Age vibe or the whiff of cultural misappropriation, things could become complicated. If you have stumbled into an ill-conceived muddle of neo-whatnot with an altar overflowing, or your facilitator's messiah complex starts to spin out of control, that confusion might bleed back into your everyday life, and you can blame that on yourself, not ayahuasca. If things are done with care, and are internally consistent and coherent, all should be well.

Psychedelic psychotherapy attempts to manage the process of dissolution and integration in a more direct manner than ritual, and it shows great potential with war veterans suffering from treatment-resistant PTSD. After MDMA-assisted psychotherapy studies, 83% no longer met the criteria for a PTSD diagnosis.[42] They were 'cured', and remained cured in tests three years later.[43] In one case, an officer's panics were triggered by telephones, stemming from the repeated trauma of phoning parents with news of sons killed in action. With MDMA suppressing his amygdalas and his panic response, the therapists were able to reframe that trigger by talking about birthday wishes and other pieces of good news that might come by telephone, establishing new mental associations and synaptic connections.[44]

Other research indicates potentials for psychedelics to treat addiction, compulsive behaviours and depression, as well as physical maladies from hepatitis to chronic headaches, tumours and asthma.[45][46] Ayahuasca increases neuronal differentiation in vitro, which could treat all kinds of neurological disorders.[47] Ganja can stop some tonic-clonic fits in seconds, and psychedelics are the only known medicines that halt the daily agony of cluster headaches.[48][49] In one study "a single dose of LSD was sufficient to induce remission of a cluster period [in 80% of cases], and psilocybin rarely required more than three doses [in 91% of cases]".[50]

I'm excited about psychedelic therapies, but my own cure took place in ritual. That is not to simply say that it took place in a different 'set' and 'setting', as those ideas derive from a psychotherapeutic perspective, which is its own thing, as Daime is its own thing. Daime doesn't begin with setting an intention or isolating an issue; it begins with invocations to the male and female principles of the cosmos, and your problems fit into that. One of the problems I encountered in Brazil began as an insect bite on my chest and expanded into a pus-filled boil of flesh-eating bacteria the size of a ping pong ball. Leishmaniasis is known locally as *ferida brava*, meaning 'angry ulcer', and the doctors told me in no uncertain terms that the only treatment was intravenous antimonium tartrate three times a day until the angry ulcer had calmed down and dried out – at least 150 shots of heavy metal salts, possibly twice as much. That was also the advice of every single herbalist, healer and homoeopath I consulted, and plenty of neighbours I didn't consult. My sister, who had worked in tropical medicine, emailed me clinical data and images of the sprawling ulcers of phase one, faces without ears and noses showing phase two when the cartilaginous tissues come under attack. She suggested I made up my own mind, so I said my prayers, drank a dose, and put my question to the doctor.

My visions followed a procession of acquaintances who had waved their scars at me, whose ulcers had yielded to injections, but whose lives were still blighted by lingering conditions, including permanently painful joints from the antimonium, strange bumps on the legs, pathological greed which kept turning friends into enemies. They were free of leishmaniasis, but they were still suffering. Transformative suffering is a common motif across the frameworks of meaning that appeal to me, in the image of Christ's execution and the first noble truth of the Buddha, in the nigredo phase of decomposition in alchemy, in the shamanic vision of dismemberment and the Daimista's purge. The individual is tempered through trials, and it struck me that if karmas or sins or imbalances are not worked through one way, they will manifest in another.

I also remembered that I had gone to the jungle to learn about Daime, which means 'give me' (*dai me*); and I saw the opportunity I was being given to learn. Seven years into a relationship with my 'teacher plant', its consistent wisdom had won my attention and filled my life with synchronicity, with wishes speedily fulfilled. We make our decisions based on meaning, and while science generates significance from statistics, the currency of life as lived is personal significance, and its measurement necessarily personal too. 95% certainty is usually good enough for science ($p<0.05$), but I could not recall a single instance in hundreds of sessions where my sacrament had given me bad advice.*

The Amazonians around me, panicking that the crazy gringo in their midst would soon be a disfigured or dead gringo, were the terrified human face of something I had researched for my degree – the pharmacological colonization of the body, and the loss of indigenous medical heritages. Brown people

---

*There is a caveat here, because people come up with all kinds of crazy ideas. It takes many sessions and much private reflection on how things unfold in order to calibrate one's instrumentation, to distinguish between the voice of the teacher and other noise. Indigenous and Daimista traditions recommend silence about the more mysterious side of the experience. There may be some therapeutic value in the sharing circles all the youngsters seem to be doing these days, but not occult value. It depends on what your goals are.

around the world are choosing the white bottles of white men in white coats over their own medicinal roots. I was on the opposite trajectory, having given up synthetically-derived drugs at aged 15 (bar the strictly recreational); but besting the occasional flu with my bare lymph nodes doesn't amount to much on this glorious battlefield. I had gone to Brazil to finish writing something begun in a compulsive frenzy shortly after I started drinking Daime, and the narrative threads of my life were converging, metre set and rhyme scheme unfolding, another line approaching.[51] Was I really going to abandon such a compelling poem half-finished?

I went to a curandero of local fame, who told me to go to hospital, and pressed me with stories of cartilage. I refused, and I asked if leishmaniasis was beyond his capacities, so he gave me a bottle and instructions to pray every morning at 4am and to drink a dose. He covered his ears to gesture that I was to listen to nobody else's comments on my disease and my cure, and he told me to remain celibate.

Doctors like to tell me that a third of cases clear up without medical intervention, that my 'sacrament' was a 'placebo'. In the 1950s, when doctors finally began to accept that there was more to recovery than antibodies, the idea of 'the placebo effect' was mooted to explain the psychosomatic effects of the sugar pill. It would be extended to cover a wide variety of folk practices from a mother rubbing her daughter's belly to a juju-man sucking out spirits.[52] The Latin syllables of 'placebo' sound like knowledge, even if the Latin stems from a 1,600 year old translation error on the part of St. Jerome – but it strikes me as a carpet of rationalism drawn over an abyss of ignorance.[53] What is the placebo effect? What happens to that third of cases that clear up without medical intervention? Are all those terribly sick people really twiddling their primitive thumbs idly as their flesh turns to goo? Or rather, are they addressing a disease according to their folk cures, using interventions that a Western-trained medic would not recognise as medicine.

If, as the logic of placebo implies, belief assists cure, then does certainty guarantee it? Can Daime outdo the doctor in the mysterious medicine of meaning? My dietas and daily doses, the barks that I harvested while composing poems to the cashew trees, my mudpacks that tore the scab away to begin each new cycle of a battle fought in shades of yellow – they were all ritual/medical interventions embedded in a context of meaning. They had personal, if not mathematical significance. The angry ulcer expanded and shrank as the lines of my story turned around it, and when tiny worms spilled from it they carried a message about the transient miracle of fleshy incarnation. I fought a running battle with a poisonous snake living beneath my shack, which ended when I slammed it in the door, and I defeated another reptile in my ceremonies and technicolour dreams. Having ignored the doctors, I consulted a 400 year-old *preta velha*, a black slave incorporated into the body of a medium at a Barquinha ceremony. She massaged points on my arm as drums pounded, swishing a scarf and blowing tobacco smoke around me. She gave me dietary advice and prayers to say with leaves from a lemon tree, and she made an offering of white roses. I listened to the *preta velha*'s words, through a medium and then through a translator, with a strange combination of mortal fear for my health and ethnographical curiosity. At the end of the session, after a good twenty minutes of explanations, I broke my silence to tell her in halting Portuguese that I had a question. She responded appropriately before I had a chance to voice it: "*my... name... is... Maria... da... Mata.*"

After six months, drinking daily for most of it, a nurse who had cured her own migraines with Daime came into my life. One morning she told me she had dreamt of us picking up and disposing of smashed glass under water, and of her having her hair plaited. Later we went to take a bucket bath at the well where the Daime was made, where she had never been before, and as we arrived she announced that it was the place in her dream. The following day we went again, and this time she began clawing into the ground like a maniac, and pulled up a large shard of glass.

Discerning patterns and testing predictions is part and parcel of both the mundane and mystical sciences. We unearthed enough broken glass to fill six sacks there, and then visited a neighbour, whose niece promptly sat down and started to plait her hair, which was rather eerie. The plot thickened several years later when I learned of a man who used to perform rituals around the community, smashing bottles of rum, stamping on the glass without cutting his feet, and then burying the glass. This is how a place is cursed in Brazilian black magic. The sorcerer came to a sticky end in 1977, and much of his buried glass had been dug up, but that patch had lain forgotten and undisturbed as the community declined from its former glory.[54]

Eight months turned my world upside-down, and then I recovered – much to the surprise of the naysayers around me. It was a terrifying time, but I don't miss the ten kilos, the ex-wife, or the pair of rose-tinted spectacles I lost in the process. My nurse was released from her duties of care, and released me from my celibacy. A year and a month and a day after we met, she gave me twins with birthmarks on their chests, one dark and one light, where the ulcer had been on mine. Stories weave through the generations, between parasite and host and history screaming significance, but is any of it as significant as $p<0.05$? What is meaning for anyway? Practically speaking, we try to understand situations so we can respond to them skillfully. I'm not sure how to explain my whole bizarre odyssey, but I'm happy with the choices I made and the fruits they bore – a pair of twins and a trilogy distinguished by the seals of my ordeal.

In doing their duty to banish the demon placebo from the lab, scientists also exclude much of the cure as the arbiters of meaning. Fencing with curves and plots, the institutions of science command the faith of the tribe. Our convictions are governed, to a great degree, by the notions of strangers reviewed by strangers, edited, selected and funded by strangers; and as Malaclypse the Younger put it, "convictions cause convicts".[55] When psychedelic researchers answer "can ayahuasca cure my cancer?" with "there is no scientific data about ayahuasca curing cancer," as they often do at conferences, they are being mindful of their training and responsibility; but is this the best thing to tell a sick person? They occasionally add that there are some anecdotal accounts, but I'm yet to hear a scientist say "I don't know, ask somebody else, maybe someone indigenous." Why do people without data or even an appropriate methodology to collect it assume the right to speak for medicine men with generations of tradition behind them?

Years later we returned to Brazil and I showed the birthmarks to the curandero, who commented without drama that a tag had passed through the generations. Such things are common in the context of Amazonian folk healing, where meaning is assembled differently. The narrative of my disease and recovery came together as a complete package of medicine and meaning, packing an almighty placebo punch. In some zones of experience disease is more than just physiology, and cure is not just recovery but discovery of something overwhelmingly new. It is dissolution and reconstruction, *solve et coagula*. The powers erupt into being when a person forgets his lines, and revelation mixes up the narrative, reversing sentences and rewriting meaning.

EXODRUGS

"The mandrakes send out their fragrance, and at our door is every delicacy."

- Song of Songs, 7:13

"Sure, mandrakes can be used for hallucinogenic purposes, too. So can paint thinner, but just because a home improvement text mentions using paint thinner to thin paint does not mean it also endorses the use of paint thinner to get high."[1]

- Tekton Apologetics Ministries Newsletter, June 2016

 N THE BEGINNING, the Blue Lotus arose from the waters of chaos. Sacred to the Egyptian nobility and scattered on the mummy of Tutankhamen, it was given voice in an ancient guide to the afterlife, the *Egyptian Book of the Dead*.[2]

> I am the Holy Lotus that cometh forth from the light
> which belongeth to the nostrils of Ra, and which
> belongeth to the head of Hathor. I have made my way,
> and I seek after him, that is to say, Horus.[3]

The *Nymphaea caerulea* lotus opens on the Nile at the break of day to reveal a brilliant golden disk reflecting Ra in the sky and framed by sky-blue petals, closing at dusk to be reborn again like Osiris after the darkness of death. Its euphoria-inducing dopamine-boosting MAO-inhibiting properties also impressed the Egyptians, as it was often depicted in the hands of gods together with two other psychoactives, mandrakes and opium poppies, and with the papyrus plant that was made into writing paper.[4][5]

The Egyptians were pioneers in surgery and pharmacology as well as writing, and their magical writings feature other psychoactives. *Acacia seyal*, for example, was the Egyptian Tree of Life from which emerged the primordial couple Isis and Osiris, and Osiris returned to an acacia tomb after his murder. It boasts the highest concentration of DMT of any plant in the region, along with other psychedelic tryptamines including the "spatial hallucinogen" NMT, and a simple alcohol extraction yields mind-blowing crystals.[6][7][8] The imagery in the Book of the Dead suggests a portal to other worlds and a protector guarding it.

> Homage to thee, O Lord of the Acacia Tree, whose
> Seker Boat is set upon its sledge, who turnest back the
> Fiend, the Evildoer, and dost cause the Eye of Ra to rest
> upon its seat.[9]

Acacia seyal is consistently found at the juncture between worlds in Middle Eastern folklore, used in Arab exorcisms, planted on Israelite graves, and fashioned into a crown of thorns by early Christians for their own dying and returning god-man.[10][11] When YHWH demands the Ark of the Covenant be made "that I may dwell among them", it was to be fashioned of acacia.[12]

The lotus also appears between the worlds in other traditions. 'Blue Lotus' is the name of the body-swapping character who visits the underworld in the Chinese classic *Monkey*, and a lotus is also found in a gateway role as the first port of call in the *Odyssey*, on the Island of Lotus-eaters.[13][14][15] Its colour is not described, though its psychoactivity is; the crewmen who eat it fall into a deep and blissful sleep from which they are unwilling to be roused. The source material for the poetry traditionally attributed to Homer was the oral tradition of late Bronze Age Greece, a body of songs and tales that had been refined over generations of retelling. Such oral traditions are repositories of history, among other things, and can be remarkably accurate; Aboriginal stories told today correctly preserve details about changes to the Australian coastline that happened over 10,000 years ago.[16] As Greek bards wandered between audiences they could refine the wordplay and develop themes and juxtapositions in the meta-narratives, but they had to versify faithfully enough to satisfy audiences that were already familiar with the material. Details such as lotuses, therefore, may predate the life of an individual poet, or even their entire culture.

Poetry comes before prose in Greek literature, and this is also the case for the Latin, German, Icelandic, English, Spanish, Arabic and Hebrew texts in the youthful vigor of these languages, with the oldest surviving compositions in each being verses.[17] Rhyme predates reason in every case. The oldest Sanskrit text is the *Rig Veda*, with verses dating in oral form from the late Bronze Age describing how to prepare, store and drink the mysterious *Soma*.[18] *Soma* is a teacher, a doctor and a bringer of insight, especially poetic insight, written of as the inspirational source of the verses of the Vedas themselves.[19] Mushroom heads, ganja fiends and ayahuasca loons have all claimed it as their own favoured tipple; I favour the latter, of course.[20][21][22][23] On the other side of the Indus River, verses composed in around the same period by the magi of the East describe a similar brew with the similar name of *Haoma*, in one of the many ancient myths bringing together a garden, a temptress, a snake and a plant.

Overenthusiastic mushroom-spotters sometimes come a-cropper in unfamiliar fields, so let us be cautious with our identifications, because not every fungus on a frieze or herb in a couplet is psychoactive. Still, there's no doubt that power plants were highly regarded in pagan poetry and ceremony around the world, as far away as the Mayan empire, where another psychoactive lotus of the *Nymphaea* genus was used in rites of the underworld.[24] *Hymn to Demeter*, from the Homeric cycle, tells a tale set in "Eleusis, fragrant with incense", which was the site of a mystery cult that ran for 2000 years.[25] Movers and shakers including Plato, Hadrian and Marcus Aurelius travelled considerable distances from around the Hellenistic world to drink the mysterious *kykeon* there, and reported terrifying and transformative visions that were "new, astonishing, inaccessible to rational cognition":[26]

> Blessed is he who hath seen these things before he goeth beneath the hollow earth; for he understandeth the end of mortal life, and the beginning of a new life given of god.[27]

The drama witnessed was the story of Demeter, goddess of the grain, seeking her beautiful daughter Persephone who had been seized by the Lord of the Underworld. Gordon Wasson proposed that the symbolism relates to ergot, a fungus born of the grain that can catalyse a journey of astonishing beauty to other worlds. Making a mind-bending and non-toxic preparation of ergot is "well within the range of possibilities open to Early Man", according Albert Hofmann, who did just that when he produced LSD.[28] [29] Robert Graves suggested magic mushrooms as the active ingredient, others propose an ayahuasca analogue, according to their own proclivities, and there are even depraved metaphor addicts who take it to be a metaphor![30] Whatever it was, however, *kykeon* was a physical liquid only to be consumed at Eleusis. One of history's earliest recorded drug busts sent Plato's friend Alcibiades (more than a Platonic friend, as it happens) into exile in 415 BC for serving it up at a party.[31]

Christian moralists eventually shut down the Eleusinian Mysteries in the 4th century AD, but before sobriety was a virtue, when botany was the science of the day and the long arm of the law was shorter, what would have stopped you from enjoying the fruits of your garden – apart from tribal taboos?[32] Though drugs were limited to certain castes in some traditions, blanket prohibitions only emerge in younger doctrines. Buddhist precepts include avoiding things "that befuddle the mind", in contrast to Hinduism where Lord Shiva of the trinity is not only the Lord of Dissolution but of Yoga, Ganja and the Ganges – washing away karma and dissolving knots of of the muscles, the mind and the cosmos.[33] Likewise, the Quran banned wine where the OT had blessed it.

The poison path winds back through the ancient world and beyond. In Gabon, the Fang and Pygmy tribes have been eating iboga in their coming-of-age rites since time immemorial, and gorillas in the same forests take it before challenging the dominant male in a bid to overturn the current order.[34] Jaguars have been filmed eating the 'jaguar medicine' ayahuasca vine and vomiting, or else looking like my cat after a dose of catnip.[35] Bighorn sheep brave precarious rocks far from their feeding grounds for narcotic lichen, and some very naughty dogs lick psychedelic toads and then modulate their doses carefully.[36] [37] Vietnamese water buffalo that had previously left opium plantations alone started breaking in and getting high when the airstrikes began.[38] [39] For courage and for kicks, for escaping the world and for changing it, and maybe for reasons of their own, many animals including man are enthusiastic drug users.

Ω

Like the *Odyssey* and the *Rig Veda*, the earliest stories of the Bible were drawn from Bronze Age oral traditions by poets with gods in their quills and drugs in their gardens. The value of a trippy aphrodisiac like mandrake might be beyond the understanding of a puritanical minister of apologetics, but Jewish law does not class drugs or any other plants as non-kosher (though there are plenty of non-kosher meats, acts, combinations of textiles and so on). "Herb [is] for the service of man", goes Psalm 104, and the ancient Israelites were in no doubt as to the service that mandrake provides; they called it *duday*, from *duwd* (meaning 'beloved').[40][41][42] It would be a disastrous foodstuff anyway, because while a small amount stimulates creativity and euphoria, another mouthful might cause "erotic delirium" and beyond that "muco-bloody dysenteric discharges".[43] As with any godfood, caution should be observed with dosage. Another caution applies with mandrake, as not only does the root look like a person, according to tradition it also screams like a person when uprooted, killing anyone who hears it. In the 1st century Jewish historian Josephus described how mandrake hunters could avoid this fate, by tying a dog to its stem,

> and when the dog tries hard to follow him that tied him, this root is easily plucked up, but the dog dies immediately.[44]

Rachel let her rival sleep with their shared husband in return for some mandrakes, indicating that they were valuable to her.[45] Frankincense was a gift of kings, expensive enough to justify a six month, 1,500 mile camel trek from Oman to Palestine across robber-infested deserts.[46][47] That would be a lot of trouble for a posh whiff; but there is more to it. Frankincense contains the GABA receptor agonist dehydroabietic acid, which dampens down the network by inhibiting the most common receptors in the brain, as does Valium.[48] The incensole acetate in frankincense has potent actions on the TRPV3 ion channel, which is involved in temperature sensation in the skin, and it is also widely distributed in the brain, though its functions there remain a mystery.[49]

Scientists have tortured mice with hotplates and drowning to establish to the satisfaction of their weirdo friends that frankincense is a tranquilizer, an antidepressant and an anxiolytic (meaning that it works against anxiety).[50] Such words as anxiolytic, catatonic, or other terms from the poorhouses and lunacy wards of history help us to talk about compounds, but experience is complex and layered, and details can get lost in the categories. Contemporary public discourse is comfortable discussing depression and mental illness, but balks at the language of mystical experience. In the jargon of abnormal psychiatry, a calling is mania and a voice is dissociation, while bliss might be regression to primary narcissism if you find yourself on a Freudian's couch. Tranquilizers do much more than make one tranquil, and the empirical test is to eat some. A pea-sized dose or two is about right to start with, and go slowly beyond that because at some point your intestinal flora will be offended. I think it is lovely; Dioscordes thought it could cause madness.[51] You have been warned.

Along with frankincense and gold, the Magi brought myrrh, which is another 'tranquilizer' whose terpenes are *mu-* and *delta*-opioid receptors agonists.[52] The Romans knew it as an aphrodisiac, and in Proverbs:[53]

> I have perfumed my bed with myrrh, aloes and cinnamon. Come, let us take our fill of love until morning; let us delight ourselves with love.[54]

Pleasant in its own right, myrrh's depths are revealed in combination, with frankincense for example, and both go well with alcohol (best infused in wine, though there is no pharmacological reason why you can't snort the gifts of the magi off a nightclub toilet).[55] Jesus refused myrrh in wine at his crucifixion, maybe to keep his head clear.[56] Myrrh and frankincense grow together in a paradisical garden in the Song of Songs:

> Thy plants are an orchard of pomegranates, with
> pleasant [or precious] fruits [or fresh things]; henna,
> with spikenard. Spikenard and saffron; cane and
> cinnamon, with all trees of frankincense; myrrh and
> agarwood, with all the chief spices.[57]

The 'chief spices' are *rosh bosem*, where *bosem* is a
fragrant resin and *rosh* is 'chief', 'principle', 'first', 'finest',
and fundamentally 'head'.[58] 'Head resins' works too as a
translation, given that nearly everything listed is psychoactive.
Saffron is the stigma of *Crocus sativus*, and more costly by
weight than gold; it contains the GABA agonist saffrole, which
has analgesic, anxiolytic and hypnotic actions, and has been
likened to opium.[59 60 61] Saffron is burned reverently around Asia,
and according to Pliny it "has a gentle effect upon the head, and
whets the sex drive".[62 63] In Islamic jurisprudence it is one of the
permissible "drugs that cause joy".[64] Cinnamon also contains
saffrole along with other allylbenzenes including eugenol,
a close relative of MDMA from which the love powder can
be synthesised.[65] Agarwood is a highly-prized perfume with
sedative and analgesic properties, produced by Aquilaria trees
as a defence mechanism against parasitic fungi.[66] Spikenard
(pronounced "spick 'n 'ard") is also "very costly", so much so
that Judas complains when it is used liberally on Jesus' feet.[67] It
boosts levels of the neurotransmitters serotonin, dopamine and
GABA, and appears to assist in the formation of memories.[68]

Kaneh is described elsewhere as *kaneh bosem*, and
combined with other 'head spices' in the holy anointing oil
(which we shall come to shortly). It is not positively identified,
like many plants in the Bible, and the KJV's guess of calamus
reed is unlikely; *kaneh* means 'cane', not 'reed', and it was
made into clothes to bury the dead in, which requires a tough
fibrous material rather than a soft reed which would quickly
decompose.[69 70] The word *bosem* is fragrant as an adjective
and 'resin' as a noun, so *kaneh bosem* might be translated as
'fragrant and resinous cane'.[71] In the singular it is *kaneh bos*,

later fused into a word which sounds rather like the *kannabis* that Herodotus encountered among the Scythians to the north of Judah in the 5th century BC.[72] He reported that they would peg down the flaps of their tents and throw it on red-hot stones:

> immediately it smokes, and gives out such a vapour as no Grecian vapour-bath can exceed; the Scyths, delighted, shout for joy.[73]

Hot-boxing enclosed spaces like this was how herbs were smoked before pipes were introduced, and archeology supports Herodotus' observation with the ancient Scythian vessels found containing cannabis and opium residues.[74] There is also evidence of widespread fragrant caning as far away as China, where sages burned cannabis in their cells and channelled the founding texts of Mao Shan Taoism.[75] [76] The Greeks to the west of Palestine used *kannabis*, in Persia to the north it was *kannab*, in Assyria it was *qunubu*.[77] Cannabis pollen was also detected on the mummy of Ramesses II in Egypt to the south, but it was not native there; it would have been brought in along one of the major trade routes that ran through Palestine.[78] *Kaneh bosem* is described in Jeremiah as "from a far country".[79] There is also speculation that the *pannag* being transported in Ezekiel is the *ne-penthe* powdered and mixed into wine in Egypt, and that both words are corruptions of the Sanskrit *bangha* (i.e. cannabis).[80] [81] It is all speculative, of course, but the rabbis and linguists speculating come with good credentials. Professor Sula Benet's pioneering research on *kaneh bosem* won her a scholarship.[82]

The other eight 'head spices' in the garden have all been positively identified. While they could have been valued for their beauty, their medicinal properties, or their fragrances in a stinky era, it is striking that all eight are edible, and seven of them have known effects on brain chemistry. The exception is henna, though maybe the ancients knew something we don't about its effects in combination. Pomegranate contains the neurotransmitters serotonin, melatonin and tryptamines, and a psychoactive synergy with Syrian rue has been reported.[83][84] While modern pharmacology seeks to isolate chemicals, traditional plant lore works with mixtures that synergize together, such as the oil described in Exodus:

> YHWH spake unto Moses, saying: "Take thou also unto thee head spices [*rosh bosem*], of pure myrrh 500 shekels [about 5.5 kg], and of sweet cinnamon half so much, even 250 shekels, and of *kaneh bosem* 250 shekels. And of cassia 500 shekels, after the shekel of the sanctuary, and of oil olive an *hiyn* [about 6 litres]. And thou shalt make it an oil of holy ointment, an ointment compound after the art of the apothecary: it shall be an holy anointing oil."[85][86]

Even disregarding the speculative identity of *kaneh bosem*, the combination of myrrh, cinnamon and cassia has a noble pedigree; Egyptian apothecaries mixed those very ingredients into a massage oil for Pharaoh, and the *hiyn* measurement also seems to be of Egyptian origin.[87][88] The Israelite version also appears to have been applied by massage. It is called *shemen ha-MiShChah*, where *MaShaCh* means to wipe or paint and is thought to be the root of the word 'massage'.[89][90] Massage dilates capillaries and increases absorption, especially with spicy cinnamon in the mix.

Modern psychopharmacology is finally catching up with the ancient apothecaries, and has established by peer-reviewed animal torture that cinnamon contains eugenol, which is euphoriogenic, and that cassia contains both linalool and methyl chavicol, which has an "electric LSD-like psychedelic" effect if consumed correctly.[91][92][93] Taken orally, however, these allylbenzenes are almost ineffective, broken down by the body's P450 enzymes before reaching the brain.[94] This class of enzymes contains many members, with the spread varying between individuals and racial groups, and this makes blocking them much more complicated than with ayahuasca preparations, where the harmaline in the vine is sufficient to inhibit the body's MAO enzymes and unlock the DMT in the leaf.[95] At least two of the P450 series enzymes, CYP2A6 and CYP2E1, are blocked by chemicals in cinnamon.[96] [97] Myrrh and cassia may inhibit others. Some psychonauts have revived the art of the apothecary by combining plants and oils to explore the synergies. One experiment with cinnamon, pomegranate, cayenne pepper, star anise and chai tea went well:

> I felt like I had a warm fuzzy blanket wrapped around me without CYP2D6 inhibition; but with the CYP2D6 inhibition I feel that I AM that warm fuzzy blanket [capitalization his, or possibly YHWH's].[98]

Together cinnamon and cassia contain eugenol, methyl chavicol and saffrole, as well as myristicin and elemicin.[99] [100] [101] With the exception of methyl chavicol, all of these are found in nutmeg, which is a powerful psychedelic in its own right because it also contains a wide range of P450 enzyme inhibitors.[102] Start with a few teaspoons, and if you are lucky then a high dose can cause:

> intensely pleasurable tactile sensations, that seemed to send shivers up my spine every time I acknowledged them. The only thought going through my head at this time was, what a wonderful life I have.[103]

Nutmeg is mentioned in combination with myrrh in the *Kalachakra Tantra* as a path to "pure knowledge […] which illuminates the nature of all things", and this mix has a chemical profile quite similar to the anointing oil, sharing several common allylbenzenes and P450 enzyme inhibitors as well as myrrh.[104] One brave tantrika tried it and wrote a fascinating trip report:

- Awakening – as if possessed by a fierce and aggressive deity: deep, monstrous voice boiling out of me unbidden etc.
- Open eyed visions and closed eyed visions of a bulging-eyed, white-skinned man in ceremonial armour
- The real world perceived as a far-away and distorted window

- This window also emanated and originated a mental fireball or supernova
- This fireball had as its identity the fierce deity above
- My voice seemed to penetrate the walls and echo off of the sky
- New doors/avenues opened up inside familiar mantra, new knowledge disclosed, new perspectives on hidden meanings[105]

The fearsome deity, the martial imagery, and the apocalyptic insights and penetrating of the walls are interesting aspects of the trip, given that the *shemen ha-mishchah* was used specifically to trigger a revelation of the mighty war-god YHWH:

> Then Samuel took the horn of oil, and anointed/ massaged him in the midst of his brethren: and the Spirit of YHWH came upon David from that day forward.[106]

With an extra *yowd*, *MaShiYaCh* means 'anointed person', which it used to describe a descendent of David anointed to become king who would throw off the oppressors of the Children of Israel (though by the time *masiyach* was Latinised as 'messiah' it meant something quite different).[107] Priests were also anointed to introduce them to YHWH, with the same end in mind, "that they may minister unto Me [YHWH] in the priest's office."[108]

If the experience of YHWH can be reliably induced by a psychoactive concoction, does that mean that He is a by-product of psychopharmacology? Or does the pharmacology merely bring Him into focus, as my spectacles bring a friend's face into focus? Such questions are best approached empirically. You could mix high grade resins and ask Him yourself, though He might wax a bit wrath at the impertinence. More importantly, do you learn anything? Does anything change afterwards? Are you luckier or wiser? Do your enemies scatter at your approach, and do dry channels open up before your outstretched hand, as before the prophet of YHWH at the Red Sea?

You will have to disobey the Good Book in order to do this, because the anointing oil was off-limits to everyone except the priests, and "whosoever compoundeth any like it, or whosoever putteth any of it upon a stranger, shall even be cut off from his people."[109] Wine was also forbidden when these rituals were undertaken, which is sound advice YHWH or no YHWH, as tranquilizers and alcohol can be a fatal combination.[110] Another taboo kept the session contained and the setting controlled:

> And ye shall not go out from the door of the Tabernacle of the congregation, lest ye die: for the anointing oil of YHWH is upon you.[111]

The Tabernacle was the exclusive territory of the Levite tribe and guarded by the Korahite clan, who also kept the secret recipe of the anointing oil.[112] They made the wine, which is psychoactive of course, and LORD knows how much more so if they were steeping power plants in it, as Persian and Egyptian cocktail mixers did.[113] [114] [115] The Korahites also made the shewbread, or *lechem ha-panim* (the bread of faces/presences):

> And thou shalt set the *lechem ha-panim* in two rows, six on a row, upon the pure table before YHWH. And thou shalt put pure frankincense upon each row, that it may be on the bread for a memorial.[116]

Even the great biblical commentator, the Rambam of blessed memory, was perplexed by the symbolism and at a loss to explain "the bread of presences", and he wrote *A Guide for the Perplexed* explaining the symbology of the religion.[117] Maybe he was a bit square, or maybe he keeping secrets too, but there may be a psychoactive solution to the riddle, and not just because of the presence of frankincense. The dosage is far more appropriate for a hit than a snack:

> In [High Priest] Simeon the Upright's time a blessing was sent into the omer, the two loaves of bread, and the shewbread, and every priest who received only the size of an olive became satiated, and some was left over...[118]

This is about right for a large dose of frankincense, though such a simple recipe seems under par for the master mixers of the

Tabernacle. The chef in Simeon's time was clearly in the know about shewbread dough, but after that standards slipped, and communion required a strong constitution:

> ...but after him, these things were cursed, and every priest got only the size of a bean. And the delicate priests refused to take it altogether, but the voracious ones accepted and consumed. It once happened, one took his own share and his fellow's: he was nicknamed "robber" till his death.[119]

This story suggests not potent symbolism but potent drugs, drugs that are moreish even. Another possible allusion to psychoactivity is that it was eaten "for a memorial".[120] Though this term is used for sacrifices, the shewbread was not given as a sacrifice, and the literal meaning – that it was to make people remember – may be more appropriate. From the Jewish perspective, like the Socratic perspective, discovery is a process of remembering the wisdom that a person had in the womb before their memory was wiped at birth.[121][122]

Another psychoactive secret in the hands of the Korahites was *ktoreth ha-samim*, where *ktoreth* means 'incense' and *samim* is 'drugs' (in modern Hebrew at least – anything from MDMA to heroin).[123][124][125] The nuances of ancient words can be difficult to ascertain, but perhaps in this case the modern meaning is not too far removed, and it might be translated as 'the incense of drugs'. Exodus lists its ingredients as "stacte and onycha and galbanum, sweet incense with pure frankincense".[126] While onycha remains the subject of much speculation, stacte is identified as high-grade myrrh by Pliny, and most scholars believe that galbanum is *Ferula gummosa*, a sedative with chemicals that act on opioid receptors.[127][128]

Other ingredients are noted in the Talmud, though the complete incense recipe was kept even from the scribes who recorded the ancient traditions after the destruction of the second temple.[129] Saffron, agarwood, cassia and cinnamon were listed, as well as the stimulant mastic and *Sassurea costus*, an analgesic smoked in Tibet and burned reverently around Asia.[130] [131] The memory-boosting spikenard was added, perhaps to help priests recall their tranquilized apocalypses.[132] [133] Some ingredients were used to pre-process others, which indicates extremely refined techniques of production:

> Why was Carshina lye brought? To refine the onycha,
> that it be pleasant.
>
> Why was Cyprus wine brought? To steep the onycha,
> that it be pungent.

Ma'aleh ashan (literally 'that which causes smoke to rise') was also added.[134] It is thought to be the *Nebtadini pyrotechnica* used in fireworks, but this information was withheld even from the scribes, and there may have been other resins not recorded, because the keepers of secrets took their duties seriously, and infractions (such as omitting an ingredient) were punishable by death.[135] In the time of the Tabernacle the Korahites were also ritual musicians and executioners, as well as guardians of the Tabernacle and its recipes.[136] [137] It seems a strange mix of party tricks, but each of these roles situates the Korahites as gate-keepers to liminal zones.

"Oil and incense rejoice the heart," goes the biblical proverb, using the word for 'rejoice' that also describes the effect of wine.[138] The two were used in combination by the High Priest, who was oiled up before his smoke bath at the back of the Tabernacle. Nothing else in the Bible is described in anything like as much detail as the construction of the Tabernacle, specifying the exact length of its acacia planks, the space between the rings fastening the fabrics down and so on.[139] The description covers over five chapters, whereas the story of the Tower of Babel is over in less than half a chapter. The Holy of Holies was a chamber veiled off at the back of the Tabernacle with only one object in it, the Ark of the Covenant, and it was used exclusively for communicating with the divine:

> He shall take a censer full of burning coals of fire from
> off the altar before YHWH, and his hands full of sweet
> incense beaten small, and bring it within the veil: And
> he shall put the incense upon the fire before YHWH,
> that the cloud of the incense may cover the mercy seat
> that is upon the testimony.[140]

This is not This is nota little stick of sandalwood, it is
handfuls of finely ground psychoactive resins hot-boxing a
$4\frac{1}{2}m^3$ chamber. The Holy of Holies was sealed beneath four
layers of skins and fabrics drawn tightly over a frame extending
to the ground, and the Talmud adds that the veil separating the
Holy of Holies was "one handbreadth thick" in the time of the
first temple.[141][142] The veil at the entrance to the Tabernacle was
normal, but the veil of the chamber at the back was different,
clearly designed to block out more than just curious glances.
Surely no veil would be thick enough to contain YHWH;
but a thick screen would definitely trap smoke effectively.
Psychopharmacologist and bible enthusiast Dr. Rick Strassman
proposes that it was the cloud itself that was the medium
of communication, and cites a line from Leviticus that he
retranslated as *"Through the agency of the cloud* I will appear
upon the Ark-cover".[143]

When the thick veil was drawn back, smoke would have
come pouring out of the chamber to rise up from the Tabernacle
door, and this is what the Children of Israel saw at the door of
the Tabernacle (rather than over the Ark of the Covenant at the
back of the Tabernacle, where the revelation took place):

> ...And all the people saw the cloudy pillar stand/
> appear/arise [*amuwd*] at the Tabernacle door: and all
> the people rose up and worshipped, every man in his
> tent door...[144]

There are a few problems with this chapter, at least in the
popular translations, where the preceding verse reads:

> As Moses entered into the Tabernacle, the cloudy pillar
> descended [*yered*], and stood [*amuwd*] at the door of
> the Tabernacle, and *the LORD* talked with Moses...

The most outrageous liberty taken here is the addition of "the LORD", as YHWH is not in fact mentioned for another two verses. Only the Hebrew Names Version Bible faithfully relates that it was the cloud itself that spoke with Moses, and this agrees with Strassman's alternative translation of Leviticus.

Also curious is that the people outside see the pillar standing/appearing/arising (*amuwd*, as in the previous verse), but they don't see it 'descending' (*yered*). Whatever *yered* means in this instance it is reserved for Moses, happening either inside the tent or inside his mind.[145] *Yered* means 'to go down', both in a figurative and a literal sense, to go "to a lower region, as the shore, a boundary, the enemy, etc."[146] [147] It is also used when divinity reveals itself, as when "YHWH came down [*yered*] upon Mount Sinai".[148] It seems more elegant to interpret this as YHWH appearing in a lower plane to the senses of Moses, rather than Him tumbling out of the sky. Retranslating the lines:

> As Moses entered into the Tabernacle, the cloudy pillar *revealed*, and *appeared* at the door of the Tabernacle, and talked with Moses. And all the people saw the cloudy pillar *appear* at the Tabernacle door: and all the people rose up and worshipped, every man in his tent door…

YHWH finally appears in the next line:

> …And YHWH spake unto Moses face to face [or 'presence to presence'], as a man speaketh unto his friend.

This is the famous pillar of smoke that guides the Children of Israel, but perhaps it does so by guiding their leader's decisions. Moses enters the Holy of Holies alone, as the medicine-men of the Amazon jungle or Siberian planes go into their huts alone on behalf of the tribe, with their power plants, their magical objects and familiar spirits. Both Moses and the shaman undertake extended periods of total solitude to deepen their connection with their ally, and they both share their wisdom in verse.[149]

Shamanising was traditionally performed to cure disease and for divination, particularly divination for military decisions, and this is also the case in the Tabernacle.[150] [151] The Oracle at Delphi burned a mix of frankincense, myrrh, laurel, olibanum and henbane in the enclosed confines of her cave in order to prophesy, and famously on military matters.[152] The oracle's mixture is chemically similar in many ways to the incense of drugs, though it also contains scopolamine.[153] Shamanic traditions use divinatory tools such as shells or bones, and the Israelite High Priest had the mysterious *urim* and *thummim* with which to divine the will of YHWH.[154] The nature of these tools is unknown, beyond the fact that they were small enough to fit inside the breastplate and could handle simple yes/no questions.[155] [156]

I have experimented with the holy head resins, including once after a talk I gave on the subject. Though I used more modest quantities of the few I could source in a poor quality chamber, and without any *kaneh bosem*, my audience informed me in spaced out slurs that they were feeling very tranquilized indeed. My private experiments offering incense to the LORD are yet to supply me with auspicious dates for launching an invasion, but I was surprised on one occasion to see a symbol behind my closed eyelids, and even more surprised to discover later that it was the glyph of an abomination worshipped with frankincense centuries before YHWH came on the scene. If you are going to experiment with large doses, or indeed with abominations, bear in mind that the mortal taboos against doing so are grounded in reason. Enjoy your research but take care, because the incense of drugs is what it says on the tin. The powers have quite a kick, and there are a lot of chemicals in synergy.

There may have been more ingredients, and indeed more rites, because much was hidden and much has been forgotten. I'm not aware of any references to henbane recorded in Jewish scripture, for example, though Josephus tells tales, describing a golden henbane flower design on the High Priest's ceremonial hat.[157] The scopolamine in the flower is so powerful that even its scent can make you dizzy.[158] There are no references to acacia incense either in the Bible, though it is curious that the most concentrated source of DMT in the region was exalted by both the Israelites and the Egyptians. The Talmud records a song that describes its ascent and its voice, in imagery that may have been inspired by its role as a communicative smoke:

> Sing, O sing, acacia tree,
>
> > Ascend in all thy gracefulness.
>
> With golden weave they cover thee,
>
> > The sanctuary-palace hears thy eulogy.[159]

Acacia is *shittim* in Hebrew, derived from *shotet* (to pierce), which describes what DMT does to the veil of everyday reality (as well as what acacia thorns do to the skin).[160] The Talmud also relates it to *shtuth*, meaning 'nonsense', which is curious for so exalted a substance but makes more sense if its psychedelic effects are considered.[161]

Professor Benny Shanon of the Hebrew University of Jerusalem speculated that it was brewed into an ayahuasca analogue by mixing it with *Peganum harmala*, a local plant containing the MAO inhibitor harmaline (which is psychoactive even without the admixture of DMT).[162] It's local name is *harmal*, related to *cherem* (taboo), and also the Arabic *haram* (both taboo and sacred). *Harmal* "expels devils and averts misfortune", according to one of the sayings of the prophet Muhammad – peace be upon his tryptophan receptors.[163] Another of his sayings recommends repeated strong psychoactive doses for both cure and insight, which are the same properties that the vedic sages praised in *Soma*, and that ayahuasqueros find in ayahuasca:

> Whoever takes a *mithqual* (4.25 grams) of *harmal* in water for 40 mornings each day, so shall wisdom enlighten his heart, and he shall be healed/immune from seventy-two diseases.[164]

40 days is the length of time that Moses spent on the mountain, that Jesus spent in the desert, and the length of Sufi retreats undertaken today.[165] It is also the first stage of gestation according to ancient Israelites and modern embryologists alike, for that is when the organs, limbs and fingers have differentiated, and when brain waves are first detected.[166] In the Hebrew calculus of gematria, number 40 refers to *mem*, the mother letter of water, the mother and the womb, from which new life emerges fully formed.[167] 40 is the weeks of pregnancy, counting as the Israelites did from the first day of the last menstrual period.[168] 40 is the years that the Israelites spent in the wilderness, and according to the rabbis long enough for everyone including Moses himself to die off, so a new generation that had never known slavery could enter the Promised Land. In the ancient Middle East, death and rebirth, the motif common to so many psychedelic rites and myths, is deeply connected to the number 40.

Ω

> And the angel of YHWH appeared unto him in a flame
> of fire out of the midst of a bush [*sneh*]: and he looked,
> and, behold, the bush burned with fire, and the bush
> was not consumed.[169]

A fire that burns but does not consume is clearly not fire, but it would be a good metaphor for the colourful geometric patterns that blaze around the objects of one's attention in psychedelic states. The only other fire like this is on Mount Sinai, and given the congruence of imagery the wordplay is interesting, because both the burning bush and Sinai derive from *SN*, meaning 'to pierce' (from a different root to the piercing acacia *shittim*).[170] [171] The bush (*SNH*) adds a feminine *H*, and the Sinai (*SYNY*) adds a doubly potent divine *Y*. Flamelike manifestations are seen piercing the veil in both stories, and at Sinai more is seen besides:

> And all the people are seeing the *voices*, and the flames,
> and the *sound* of the trumpet.[172]

The only time most people see sounds is on psychedelics, when the ACC goes offline and sense modalities become muddled synaesthetically. This is the only example of synaesthesia in the Bible, and also the only collective revelation. While apocalypses are the stuff of scripture, prophets almost invariably see sights and hear sounds alone. Collective visions are very rare in world mythology generally, though there was a well-documented case in October 1917, when tens of thousands of pilgrims and a pack of journalists flocked to Fátima in Portugal for the final apparition in a series that had been announced months in advance. Suddenly the young prophetess cried "Look at the sun!", and the sun danced.[173] Or it span. Or it approached the earth. Or it flared in purples, yellows and blues "as if it had come through the stained-glass windows of a cathedral, and spread itself over the people who knelt with outstretched hands."[174]

Some believers saw nothing. Some sceptics saw visions. Accounts vary enormously, but some visually extraordinary event was experienced simultaneously by many thousands of people, each in their own ways but often with the phenomenology of fire that didn't consume.

Did years of war and terrifying uncertainty provoke an episode of mass hysteria amongst the witnesses? Or did Our Lady of Perpetual Succour exploit a

Fig. 14 The visions at Fatima

187

favourable neurochemical environment to slip through the veil and comfort her children in their hour of need? Stress increases levels of naturally occurring endogenous DMT and 5MEO-DMT (in rats at least, and presumably in people, who share 85% of their genes with rats).[175] And perception can be extremely responsive to context at the level of the visual cortex even without psychedelics (see page 37). [176] Like the Fátima witnesses, the fleeing Israelites in the story were facing great uncertainties and stress.

Strassman sees DMT in the visionary experiences of the Bible, but unlike Shanon he proposes that it was endogenous DMT produced naturally by the body. Comparing accounts of prophetic experiences in the Hebrew Bible with lab notes from thousands of DMT sessions he facilitated, Strassman found many similarities in the psychological, physical, emotional and visionary experiences described, and particularly in how entities interact with humans and each other. He proposes a 'theoneurological' model of mystical experience, where God communicates with humans through the physiology of the brain, which is a welcome contrast to the dominant assumption of neurotheology where the experience of God is generated by the brain.[177] The bulk of Strassman's study focuses on the prophets, where altered states come on spontaneously or through fasting, meditation, posture or other techniques.[178] Concerning the priests in the Tabernacle, however, he concedes that the mode in which incense was burned "suggests an exogenous mind-altering agent".[179]

Psychedelics need not be invoked to explain visions, and even collective visions. Even so, biblical history is not without moments of collective stress, and yet the Sinai vision remains the only group apocalypse, and the only synaesthetic experience. Another unique circumstance is that at this time everyone is eating manna together.

> And when the Children of Israel saw it, they said one
> to another, "it is manna [*man hu*]": for they wist not
> what it was...[180]

...goes the KJV, but if they wist not what it was, how would
they know to call it manna?

More logical bibles translate *man hu* as "what is it?",
the problem being that that 'what' in Hebrew is not *man*
but *ma*. *Man* is the Egyptian word for 'what'. Rabbis
argue the point in an ancient commentary, one side
proposing that the escapees had picked the word up in Egypt
and the other asking why they would use this random loan
word when the rest of their vocabulary was Hebrew.[181] *Ma hu* is
spelled normally later in the same verse, suggesting something
deeper in the wordplay.

Another interpretation is that *man* is the Bedouin word for
an edible secretion collected from tamarisk trees.[182] Though
we might imagine "bread from heaven" falling like sacks of
humanitarian aid, the Bible describes a secretion that drips and
forms "thin flakes like frost on the ground", or else hardens on
the plant into resinous pellets the size of coriander seeds:[183][184]

> And it was like coriander seed, white; and the taste of it
> was like wafers made with honey.[185]

Bedouin *man* would have been a good guess, because it forms
a honeydew that tastes like honey and hardens to from whitish
pellets the size of coriander. But manna is "ground in mills, or
beat in a mortar", and Tamarisk secretion can't be, because it is
gummy rather than brittle.[186][187] For the same reason it doesn't
form "thin flakes like frost" where it drips, but globulous
mounds.

Furthermore, there's nothing miraculous about finding
Bedouin *man*, as the Bedouins did just that without divine
intervention. The quails which helpfully come to ground every
night to be rounded up by the Israelites have a much more
remarkable provenance, but they are not called "angel food",

and nor are they remarked upon much.[188] One verse specifically connects a feeling of satisfaction to the manna but not the quail, suggesting that manna satisfies them in a way that quail meat did not:

> At evening you shall eat meat, and in the morning you shall be satisfied with bread [manna]: and you shall know that I am YHWH your God.[189]

Another problem is that Bedouin *man* can be stored for up to a year, whereas with manna,

> Moses said, "Let no man leave of it till the morning." Notwithstanding they hearkened not unto Moses; but some of them left of it until the morning, and it bred worms, and stank: and Moses was wroth with them.[190]

It seems that the Israelites' guess of *man* was close but wrong (which makes more sense, because they wist not what it was). The rapid rate of decay suggests a fungal organism, and so does the fact that heat arrests it.

> "Tomorrow is to be a day of sabbath rest [said Moses] […] So bake what you want to bake and boil what you want to boil. Save whatever is left and keep it until morning." So they saved it until morning, as Moses commanded, and it did not stink or get maggots in it.[191]

Any guess as to the identity of a fungus can only be speculative several thousand years after the penning of legends that were older still; my guess is ergot. The first stage of infection produces a honeydew with a honey taste, and the secretion dries as small resinous pellets on the plant. Less viscous than *man*, it forms a white frosty scale where it drips on the ground, and it dries brittle so it can be ground to powder in a mill.[192] Furthermore, ergot emerges from its dormancy at the onset of spring, just when the Israelites first encounter manna. It also requires vegetation, and therefore water, and manna is only found when they have access to water.[193 194 195] The method of preparation described in the Bible, whereby manna is baked, ground and boiled, wouldn't do much for Bedouin *man*, but it is the simplest way to kill ergot and separate the psychoactive alkaloids from the insoluble toxic compounds.[196] Humans are innovative, and sometimes inspired to experiment. Perhaps one of those clever Jewish doctors figured out how to make something trippy.

Presumably it wouldn't have been beyond an omnipotent deity to provide food that didn't require preparation and had a longer shelf-life; but then the original YHWH isn't omnipotent, despite the hype.[197] His miracles are subject to the limitations of the natural world (some supernatural stories were edited in by later hands, but more on that after we have got through our stash). The meteorologically exciting escape described in Exodus seems a little far-fetched, but then oral traditions build extraordinary elements of history into meaningful motifs played out in the biographies of larger than life characters. Quails do indeed wait on the desert sand in large numbers when winds are unfavourable during their migrations, and are easily rounded up.[198] Plagues plague. Floods flood. The earth quakes and swallows people.[199] Sometimes a "strong east wind" blows all night, and according to the St. Petersburg Institute of Oceanology, 67mph would have been sufficient to part the Red Sea.[200][201] Maybe the miraculous aspect of the "angel's food" is not where it comes from, but where it takes you.

To speculate further, perhaps beyond the limits of good taste: what if the myth-maker was working in an altered state, as the Sanskrit poets claim to be in the *Rig Veda*.[202] And what if Exodus, our most enduring myth about getting out of it, was itself an allegory of the psychedelic experience? After a dry path opens up through the sea for the Israelites to pass, the army pursuing them succumbs to the chaotic waters, obliterating the last remnant of their former conditioning. They emerge into the wilderness with only a distant memory that a Promised Land awaits, and the wherewithal to manage the next few steps.

The wilderness is *MiDBaR* in Hebrew, the womb (*M*) to
the words and things (*DBR*) arising in an orderly fashion from
creative chaos, the ten mega-words, the vision and the voice.
Midbar is the womb of the word in another sense as it also
means 'mouth'.[203] There are three wildernesses, and their names
evoke stages on the alchemical journey, of lines dissolving and
visions erupting into consciousness. They find no water in the
first, *midbar shuwr*, where *ShWR* means 'wall' and invokes the
idea of dividing.[204] They find water and manna in the second,
midbar syn, where *SYN* means 'clay' or 'mud', the malleable
and mergeable substance from which walls are made: *solve*.[205]
Another meaning of *SYN* is 'thorn' or 'spike', again suggesting
boundaries being broken as a thorn pierces the flesh and the
veils, letting the contents of one space spill through into
another. The final wilderness is *midbar sinai*, the same *SN* root
with a doubly fiery *yowd* of God – *SYNY*. At Sinai the Israelites
witness something coming into their plane of existence in its
flaming, piercing, synaesthetic glory, and Moses writes his
mega-words. *Coagula*. When the Israelites discover manna,
the walls that keep the mind com-part-mental-ized become
malleable, and an apocalypse of information erupts in a vision
of splendour.

Ω

As the end of the wanderings in the wilderness, Moses
decides that a stash of manna should be safeguarded:

> Fill an omer of it to be kept/cultivated for your
> generations; that they may see the bread wherewith I
> have fed you in the wilderness…[206]

The command is clear enough, but then the prophet repeats
himself the following line with a slightly different command:

> "Take a pot, and put an omer full of manna therein, and
> lay it up before YHWH, to be kept for your generations."
> As YHWH commanded Moses, so Aaron laid it up
> before the [tablets of the] Testimony, to be kept.[207]

Something stinks here, as stinky as yesterday's manna. Firstly, why would Moses give a command twice, and in two slightly different ways? Secondly, the initial command stipulates that manna is to be *seen* by the people of the generations to come, whereas the second hides it behind two veils where it can't be seen by anyone except the High Priest. Stranger still is that this command is issued, *and followed*, before the Ark has been constructed. The tablets of the Testimony haven't even been hewed yet, so how can something be put in front of them?

The second command renders the first both redundant and unworkable, and it was the second that was followed while the first was broken. Manna ended up with the other Godfoods in the Tabernacle, beyond the reach of everyone except certain powerful and secretive families.[208] It is not mentioned for a millennium and a half, from the arrival in the Promised Land in 1406 BC until the 1st century AD and the *NT*, when it is still safely ensconced inside the Holy of Holies:

> And after the second veil, the Tabernacle which
> is called the Holiest of all; Which had the golden
> censer, and the ark of the covenant overlaid round
> about with gold, wherein was the golden pot that had
> manna, and Aaron's rod that budded, and the tables
> of the covenant; And over it the cherubims of glory
> shadowing the mercyseat; of which we cannot now
> speak particularly.[209]

The veil of secrecy has grown thicker than ever. At some point the story changed, and to understand why we need to learn a little more about how the Bible was put together.

Tradition recalls that the Pentateuch (a.k.a. Genesis, Exodus, Leviticus, Numbers and Deuteronomy) was written in its entirety by Moses. Given the wide variations in writing, textual scholars view it as a compilation of documents from different centuries that can be distinguished by grammatical differences, set phrases, style and so on. They were produced by different communities and present vastly different theologies and political agendas as power structures shifted over half a millennium of turbulent history, as leadership passed from tribal elders in a commonwealth to kings of a kingdom, then through centuries of civil war, then into exile in Babylon, and then back to Judea under the thumb of a series of foreign superpowers. The different sources were joined together by redactors with agendas of their own, the original cut-up artists, who sometimes spliced them together line by line. Out of reverence for the texts, or perhaps in trying to keep different factions happy, they endeavoured to include as much as they could – even when stories contradict each other. So the Ishmaelites become Midianites halfway through a story, and poor old Noah has to enter the ark twice in the same chapter before enduring a flood that lasts both 150 and 40 days.[210] [211] While textual experts disagree over some details about which verse was from which source, they almost unanimously support the general idea, and even the Vatican acknowledges the possibility of "diverse sources" in its current catechism.[212]

Genesis and Exodus are mostly composed of text from the oldest source called the Jahwist, drawing upon oral traditions of the late Bronze Age, like several other epics of antiquity. They are interspersed with passages from a rival text called the Elohist, which was composed after civil war had split the commonwealth a few centuries later, by scribes in the northern kingdom drawing on northern traditions. The Priestly source written sometime between the 8th and 6th centuries BC is quite different, adding the technical detail of the Tabernacle technology. It also makes up most of Leviticus with extensive tracts about sin and cleanliness, and Numbers beginning with nearly 200 verses counting people and their stuff, "even the censers, the fleshhooks, and the shovels, and the basins", followed by instructions on how to set up a leper colony.[213] By this point it is clear that the Bible has become a very different type of book. Deuteronomy is almost entirely the work of a fourth source called the Deuteronomist, and primarily consists of law. Only after the Babylonian captivity had been and gone was all of this redacted into something like the Bible that we know and love and hate today.

Exegesis from a deconstructed Bible isn't an exact science, like pharmacology with its double-blind studies and rat drowning, and with such uncertainty it is tempting to have one's wicked way with the limited facts available. A series of priesthoods made an industry of doing this, and perhaps I am also guilty in my own incense-addled enthusiasm. Still, many scholars have found something wrong with Exodus, where manna is placed in a Tabernacle that doesn't yet exist.[214] Whatever it was, it would be eaten once a year by the High Priest alone while other priests ate the shewbread together outside.[215] There was evidently some concern that the High Priest might get too high, because a chain was tied to his robe so people outside the thick veil would know if he stopped moving.[216] Perhaps they could have dragged him out if he passed out.

In the wilderness a veil had been torn, but a new veil took its place in the Promised Land and hung until the coming of a new masseur Messiah. The Greek equivalent to *mashiyach* is *christos*, from *chrió* (to anoint), and the rite of anointing is the Chrism.[217] According to the Gospel of Philip, Christ took the holy anointing oil from the preserve of elites to baste and bake apostles from all classes:

> The Chrism is superior to baptism, for it is from the word "Chrism" that we have been called "Christians," certainly not because of the word "baptism". And it is because of the Chrism that "the Christ" has his name. For the Father anointed the Son, and the Son anointed the apostles, and the apostles anointed us.[218]

In Mark, Christ sends his followers off to perform the Chrism upon the sick, and in Eastern Orthodox ritual a dribble is still spilled today.[219]

Sobriety came to be a virtue in the early church, when Paul put *pharmakeia* among his list of awful things, along with "wrath,

195

strife, seditions, heresies, envyings, murders, drunkenness, revellings, and such like" – and *eris*, or discord (Hail Eris!).[220] It seems that the Levites may have spiked unsuspecting Israelites with herbal preparations (as we shall discuss in the penultimate chapter), for priests have always had their secrets and operated above the law upon their flocks. Who can be sure that Roman priests didn't mix their sacraments more directly once upon a time, sweetening the blood of Christ for the pious and adding dysphoric tinctures for those who were stingy at the collection plate? Jesus himself knew how to party; his first miracle yielded about 150 gallons for a wedding.[221]

In the Jewish tradition, psychoactive preparations remained kosher through the biblical period and into the common era and rabbinical period. The medieval rabbinical authority Bahya ben Asher wrote about drugs that gave him higher knowledge about the Tree of Knowledge, as manna had done in the wilderness, and the 13th century Jewish grimoire *Sefer Raziel* describes scrying for spirits with "canabus" and wormwood.[222] [223] Cannabis was permitted by some Islamic judges and smoked in some mosques, and a 2014 decree from the highest circle of Shi'i jurisprudence ruled that psychedelics are permissible if used with an experienced guide and in order to know God.[224] [225] [226] The spice-box passed around and inhaled at the closing Havdalah ritual of Jewish Sabbath may be the last faint whiff of something sweeter, but perhaps the traditions went underground as various altered states came to be looked down upon rather than up to as the Age of Rationalism set in. Rites performed with *Acacia seyal* at Masonic lodges today are secrets kept on pain of death, as were the rites of Eleusis and the Tabernacle.[227]

Every day, millions of believers ask in their respective languages that God "Give us this day our daily bread", which is rather a lot of 'day'.[228] The Lord's Prayer is one of the most well-known tracts of scripture, but the word translated as "daily" is the most obscure word in the Bible. It is *epiousion*, found nowhere else in scripture, and nowhere in Greek literature. The *epi-* (of epitaph and epilogue) takes the bread 'beyond', while *ousion* appears to be related to *ousia* (being or essence). St. Jerome translated it as *supersubstantialem* (i.e. supersubstantial), something 'beyond real' or of a 'higher substance', rather more 'extra-ordinary' than your standard crusty loaf.[229] Ancient sources equate it with manna, and the Second Book of Baruch looks forward to a time when it will be eaten again:[230]

> When all that which should come to pass in these parts is accomplished, the Messiah will begin to be revealed [...] At that time that the treasury of manna will come down again from on high, and they will eat of it in those years because these are they who will have arrived at the consummation of time.[231]

The agonists in the agonies and ecstasies of Exodus are sources of creativity and transformation. They are agents of the apocalypse, and therefore a threat to the status quo. LSD was placed behind a veil a few brief decades after its discovery, with research confined to government programs. Perhaps the secret services worried, as top-secret executioners with a monopoly over mind control had worried in ancient Israel, that a freely-available ergot preparation could dissolve into mud the walls of the tower.

Non-ordinary experience is still policed with violence and incarceration. The War on Drugs costs billions of dollars and tens of thousands of lives to maintain, and yet tranquilizer and stimulant use is massive outside the church, while being lamentably absent within.[232] There are, however, a few cults in the forests at the frontiers of Christendom that commune with the plants and practices of ecstasy, and even Jesus Christ slips his nails and slides off his cross to get high in the jungle sometimes. Sometimes he brings something back to church to spice up communion. Freestyle Gnostics traffic between the worlds with flowers in their hair and barks in their pockets.

Despite the bans, hedonists and heads in the belly of the beast are still climbing the Tree of the Knowledge of Good and Evil, smoking, chewing and snorting their way into other dimensions, reclaiming extraordinary experience as an integral part of a healthy life, the supersubstantial in the everyday, the poetry between the words subverting lines of prosaic thought. There are further secrets in scripture concerning the mechanics of the mind and the machinations of realpolitik, my brothers and sisters in blessed abandon. Let us begin again, as is our custom, in the beginning.

GOD AGAINST GOD

En arche en ho Logos,
kai ho Logos en pros ton Theon,
kai Theos en ho Logos

- John 1.1

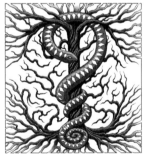N THE BEGINNING was the Word and the Word was with God, and the Word was God, but what words are these at the beginning of the Gospel of St. John?

In the beginning was "the Word", *ho* Logos, where *ho* is the definite article: it is <u>the</u> one and only cosmic logic that orders the universe. God also takes a definite article, *ton* Theon, <u>the</u> one and only God. But "*en arche*" in [the] beginning has none.

There is no indefinite article in Greek, like the English 'a/an'. Grammatically speaking (which is the only way to speak), an unarticulated *arche* could be interpreted broadly: "In a beginning…"; "In the beginning…"; "In beginning…".* It could also be "In foundation…", "At the source…", "At

---

* "And ye also shall bear witness, because ye have been with me from <u>the</u> *beginning* [no article]." (John 15:27)

"Without father, without mother, without descent, having neither *beginning* [no article] of days, nor end of life." (Hebrews 7:3)

its origin...", "In principle..." and so on, as *arche* suggests much beyond mere beginnings. <u>Arch</u>angels are not 'beginning angels', they are 'chief angels'.[1] An<u>archy</u> is not the absence of beginnings but the absence of rulers. Thinking philosophically, 'an-archy' might reject any established principle (*archon*). This is a good way to approach scripture, because if you already know what the book says then why read it? Grammatical anarchy is a different matter, though. If we abandon those rules then we literally don't know what we are talking about.

"Few would debate that we are dealing with the 'original beginning'," opines one rather presumptuous theologian, clearly unfamiliar with the complexities of "the first [sic] day" in Genesis.[2] He speaks for all the popular translations, but some people read more carefully. The Reverend Dr. Felix Just adjusts John in his own "hyper-literal" translation, bracketing and starring, slashing and daggering, scrupulous in his notation:

> In origin was the Logos† and the Logos was toward
> [the] God',* and god/deity/God* was the Logos[3]

Maybe "few would debate that we are dealing with the 'original beginning'" in a culture obsessed with time and causality; but things might have been different a few thousand years ago, during the explosion of thought when the Hebrew Word met the Greek Logos. John was exploring this encounter with "*En arche*", riffing off the world's first translated Bible, which begins:

> *En arche epoiesen o theos, ton ouranon kai ten gen.*

'<u>The</u> God (*o theos*) created <u>the</u> heavens [*ton ouranon*] and <u>the</u> earth [*ten gen*]', each of them articulated neatly with a definite article. But '*en arche*' in [the] beginning goes without. Had the poet begun with an article "in <u>the</u> beginning" it would have put the issue beyond argument, but he didn't.[4] What might he have been getting at by leaving it open?

Why do writers leave questions open?

In a cosmology based on a text, the arrangement of words is surely more relevant than, say, what Pope Clement IV had to say about unbaptised infants. Every pedant for himself, I say! (Or herself). And I just love felicitous daggering with the Reverend Dr. Felix Just:

> † Greek Logos refers to so much more than simply one 'word', a single semantic unit. It can also refer to a phrase, a sentence, an utterance, a whole speech, or indeed even the whole power of language-based thought and reasoning (similar to the English word 'logic').[5]

And the Logos Just just described is just [the] beginning. According to fragments of Heraclitus, which are the oldest known writings on the Logos, it is also the intelligent ordering principle of the universe. Human reason, when it is functioning properly, is a function of channelling that universal principle:

> Although the Logos is common to all, most men live as if each had a private intelligence of his own.[6]

Heraclitus' Logos permeates all minds and all things across space, and also across time in a world where "no man ever steps in the same river twice".[7] He earned himself the epithets "riddling" and "the obscure" for his bewildering attempts to describe in words the workings of the Word.[8] He locates creation in confrontation:

> What opposes unites, and the finest attunement stems from things bearing in opposite directions, and all things come about by strife.[9]

John also describes how all things come about, and with an echo of Heraclitus – because in the Greek of the day the word *pros* meant 'against' as well as 'with':

> In [the] beginning was the Logos, and the Logos was against God, and God was the Logos. The same was in the beginning with God. All things were made by him; and without him was not any thing made that was made.

This is not a popular interpretation, but no one has a monopoly on poetry, especially not with a verse this strangely worded. Thinking outside of established principles of doctrine, as a theological anarchist and a grammar fascist, this is a simple matter of the preposition *pros* + a noun in the accusative case, and there are plenty of verses where that grammatical paradigm clearly means 'against' and not 'with'.* The Logos as both God and against God defies common sense, but so does the Logos as both God and with God. The Logos defies common sense for every writer that wrote intelligently about it. If we are to make any sense of John's Logos at all, even as orthodox Christians would have it, we have to abandon Logic Code (Aristotle) - bylaw 2: NOT (A and not A).

Aristotle cited Heraclitus directly as the nonsensical counterpoint to his clearly formulated laws of thought.[10] The rules of logic made the old pagan very popular with the Roman Church and the medieval academy, even if integrating Aristotle into the faith took some serious apologetics. The Eucharist violates all three laws if you're not careful, and imagine it to be either a biscuit or both a biscuit and the flesh of Christ at the same time. Cyril of Jerusalem cleared up the confusion by his decree that it was flesh; and "even though the senses suggest to you the other, let faith make you firm."[11]

Regarding the philosophical problem of God against God, Elohim (or the elohims) is both majestic plural and messy plurality. YHWH, El Shadday and the other emanations go about their business, sometimes cooperating with each other, sometimes working against each other. El Shadday demands the sacrifice of Isaac, and the angel of YHWH interrupts it.[12] Satan works in the service of his master YHWH, harassing YHWH's perfect servant Job.[13] Christ's god is with him in the temple when he declares that "I and the Father are One", but on the cross the situation has changed:[14]

My God, my God, why hast Thou forsaken me?[15]

---

* "Put on the whole armour of God, that ye may be able to stand against the wiles of the devil." (Ephesians 6:11)

"They knew that he had spoken the parable against them." (Mark 12:12)

"And in their hands they shall bear thee up, lest at any time thou dash thy foot against a stone." (Luke 4:11)

Philo of Alexandria, a Hellenistic Jew writing shortly before the composition of the Gospels, described the Logos in contradictory images. In one chapter it is "glue and a chain [which] connects together and fastens every thing". In the following chapter it is "the divider of all things", and with it God,

> divides the essence of the universe which is destitute of form, and is destitute of all distinctive qualities, and the four elements of the world which were separated from this essence, and the plants and the animals which were consolidated by means of these elements.[16]

Splitting off at [a] beginning, the Tree of Life sends out a new branch that orders matter into a new configuration. The Tree of Knowledge relates it back together through a network of names. The Logos of biology connects and arranges the individual elements of a branch of knowledge – its data, its theories, its methods, textbooks and so on. It also separates it from others, like geology and archaeology, although all three -ologies dig down into the same rock. All branches of Knowledge lead back to one trunk. Master Manipulators follow lines of inquiry through the veils to the junctions, as Newton brought together maths, mechanics and astronomy to formulate the first celestial law, as Paracelsus united medicine and alchemy to pioneer a new concept of disease.

Logos is 'word' in English and *DBR* in Hebrew, where the root of *DBR* pertains to the process of arranging elements in order.[17] Lining up shells on a beach creates order from disorder. The arrangement joins individual elements

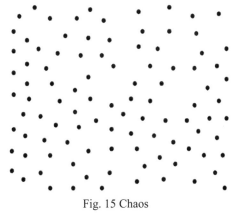

Fig. 15 Chaos

203

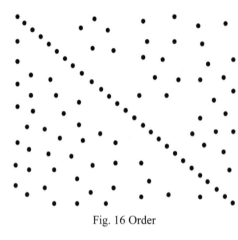

Fig. 16 Order

into a line, which is a 'thing', and a thing is also *DBR*. Simultaneously the arrangement-word-thing splits the beach into this side and that side, with a line to fight over between them.

Letters are lined up into words (*DBR*) lined up into sentences (*DBR*), ordering chaos and carving out chunks for the Manipulator to manipulate. Words unite and divide, and a three-word *DBR* can do both at the same time:

Fuck – the – police!

Combinations of words create and destroy worlds:

I – Love – You

Ready – Aim – Fire!

'The Gospels' are literally 'good spells', and spells are cast just as words are spelled, by putting signs in order. The Good Spell of St. John was spelled out in translation at the second word, a grimoire pinned with grammar at <u>the</u> [one and only] beginning. But a spell misspelled spells trouble.

In the beginning was [the] Word, and the Word was…

…mistranslated?

…misinterpreted?

…mangled?

Or just fundamentally problematic?

Let's tippex the hex, and begin again…

Ω

THE INFLECTED APE

AUM!

- Mandukya Upanishads

'gua?

- Sophia aged 1, pointing
at water (*agua*)

N THE BEGINNING was the Word, but what begins with a word? Some beginnings began long before human utterances, of course, and some thoughts are ineffable; however the world of concepts conceived of and communicated is constructed from words, from nouns coloured by adjectives and connected via verbs into matrices of grammar. Articulation breaks things up and joins them back together, as in an articulated lorry or the articulation of a finger between its sections. The art of art-

-iculation is in how the breaks are made and the parts connected. And without articulation, there can be no meaning shared between us at all.

All mammals communicate in some way, grunting, puffing up chests or squirting out scents. Dogs react to wagging tails and flashing teeth, instinct to instinct. Pavlov rewired the instincts of his dogs so the sound of a bell would cause their salivary glands to flow, and my mum trained her dog to react to the sound "walkies". He would run around and grab his leash, which was a more complicated set of responses than salivation, though it involved processes that were no more conscious, including adrenal gland secretion. A great deal of human behaviour happens unconsciously. Sometimes I notice that my foot has started tapping to music, and stopping it is a conscious act. Sometimes it is tapping along to something no one else can hear, a private rhythm that crept into my head unsolicited even though I'm trying to focus on the Book of Enoch.

Consciousness expresses itself in degrees of inhibition, of both physical and mental activity; but no amount of willpower can restrain certain motions, as St. Augustine lamented:

> At times, without intention, the body stirs on its own, insistent. At other times it leaves a straining lover in the lurch, and while desire sizzles in the imagination, it is frozen in the flesh.[1]

My God, my God, why hast Thou forsaken me!

The Victorians deployed spiked and electrified devices to save their sons from their naughty stirrings, but to little avail; the fact of the matter is that there are bodily systems entirely outside the jurisdiction of the will. This is good news for Stephen Hawking, who has fathered three children with his autonomic nervous system, despite having little willed control over his muscles. St. Augustine was a celibate with a rock and roll past, and he interpreted gravely the fact that the body habitually goes against its master. He authored the doctrine of Original Sin (along with some other celibates), and illustrated it by noting that other organs are easier to control than the sinstick:

> Some can produce at will odourless sounds from their
> breech, a kind of singing from the other end.[2]

My own melodies meow malodorously, but the guy has a point.

In theory, bottom squeaks could be message-bearing signs – code between bridge players, for example, inflected with sliding pitch or broken up rhythmically to signify different bids. The lips, teeth and tongue articulate more clearly, but even communication from the top end can be unwilled. If a scoundrel jumps out of the wardrobe the countess screams without a thought, and the count downstairs in the conservatory flinches at her scream, linked unconsciously into a chain of instinct. Similarly, when a vervet monkey sees a jaguar he makes a sound that sends his troop-mates running to the trees.[3] Seeing a snake triggers a different sound, and hearing it causes vervets to glance nervously around at the ground. This happens in captivity with recordings, and none of it appears to be willed. The cries are not referential signs in a conscious system of communication, like "*snake*" or "*serpente*" or "*nachash*" are. A scream is the same in any language. So are pheromones, emitted and reacted to without a thought, penetrating language barriers and the bounds of good sense undetected. Spraying a waiting room seat with male pheromones will compel more women than usual to sit down in it, regardless of any conscious considerations.[4]

Communication with signs is a different matter, and all the great apes do it – gorillas, orangutans, chimpanzees, bonobos and us. Chimpanzees have been observed in the wild using over 60 signs that are not instinctive; they are gestures learned from other chimps. A hand flick, for example, means 'move away', as it does between the countess and her maid.[5] With 40 years of training Koko the gorilla learned to use 1,000 human sign language signs, and understood over 2,000 English vocal signs (i.e. words).[6] The speed at which signs can be mastered rises sharply at the human twig of the primate branch of the Tree of Life; but that is a difference of degree between the species, not a difference of kind. Even rodents learn what signs mean. Dr. Skinner's rats soon learned that a coloured light coming on *meant* that a part of the cage was about to become painful to touch. They demonstrated their understanding by taking evasive action.[7]

When animals learn about a 'something that means something', that factoid is somehow fixed in the mind. It could be a gesture, a word or a warning light. Orangutans in the wild use a 'something that means something' in the form of a goodnight call (a sound that means 'I'm going to sleep'). The call is not innate, like a scream. It is learned, like human words are. Indeed, the orangutan 'word' for Goodnight is learned differently in different areas, and pronounced with regional variations.[8]

A tool is another type of 'something that means something'. To a chimp, a short, rigid stick means that the shell of a termite mound can be pierced.[9] They make a hole, and then they poke in a longer stick that has been frayed at one end so termites bite into it and can be fished out. Together these sticks are the means by which chimps catch termites. Chimps have been observed using sticks in over 60 clearly defined ways, and each is a fixed concept, an image in the imagination of a chimp in some sense, even when she has no example of the tool to hand. A hungry chimp will explore the area around a termite mound until she finds a stick she can make into an instance of the 'fishing stick' set in her head. Then she strips the twigs and frays the end to complete it.

The innovation that opened up termite mounds began with divergent thinking, the mode of cognition associated with the Manipulator, taking things apart and using things in different ways (see page 117). We might question how willed or planned the ape-ocalypse was, and that question could also be asked about the *eureka* moment of Archimedes himself (my answer is in *Science Revealed*). Monkeys are not as clever as apes, and they don't do much divergent thinking. Locked in a room with crates in the corner and the exit in the ceiling, they will jump around and hoot unhappily until exhausted. A chimpanzee is different; she will quickly stack the crates and climb to freedom. The chimp Manipulator can mentally take something out of context as an element of thought, and put it

Fig. 17 Chimps stacking crates

together with other elements into a new order to make a new thing. She extends her will over the world, re-articulating its elements as 'somethings that mean something' useful to her, 'a crate on a crate on a crate that *means* escape'. Then she can rearrange the corresponding 'somethings' (i.e. crates) outside her head.

Apes brilliantly manipulate various classes of 'somethings that mean something', including complexes, tools and signs. As chimps in Africa combine 'puncturing stick' and 'fishing stick' to get food from the termite mound, their cousin Washoe in North America put sign language signs in order to make phrases, like 'please-open-hurry' to get food from the fridge. When she first encountered a duck she signed 'water' and then 'bird' in quick succession. 'Water-bird' became a new sign in its own right, and she used it in different contexts to indicate ducks nowhere near water.[10] It was picked up and used by other chimps.[11]

And whatsoever Adam called every living creature, that was the name [*SM*] thereof.[12]

Another primate neologised with the same strategy, combining the signs 'tooth' and 'brush' to make 'toothbrush'. A 'toothbrush' remains a 'toothbrush' in other contexts, even if you clean your toilet with it. And a 'toilet brush' remains a 'toilet brush' even if you clean your teeth with it, and even though it is written with a space between the words.

Humans are not alone in voicing meaning. Orangutans have their goodnight calls, and Kanzi the bonobo appears to have coined at least one vocal referential expression.[13] When asked to communicate 'yoghurt' to his sister in a nearby room he made a vocalization, and at the sound she selected a picture of a yoghurt.[14] If a chimp spoke Hebrew, she might describe 'the yoghurt noise' as a *DBR*, and also 'please-open-hurry' and 'water-bird' as *DBR*s. Given that the meanings of the words 'water-bird' and 'yoghurt noise' were fixed and known to others, they could also be *SM*s (names / things of renown).[15] Apes recognise words, names and signs. They combine them creatively in complex constellations. One bonobo touched the buttons for "marshmallow" and "fire" on his symbolic keyboard, and when they arrived he broke twigs to build a fire, lit it with a match, and toasted the marshmallows.[16] According to one primatologist studying how bonobos use strategy and make models and hypotheses, "apes possess the cognitive capacities for language but lack the proper organ of expression".[17] Despite their clumsy mouths, apes do make meaningful sounds. After saying 'goodnight' in their local dialect, they also bed down in nests built according to the local architectural style.[18] They are cultured creatures, with different cultural traits between areas.

A biological definition of culture is "information capable of affecting individuals' behavior that they acquire from other members of their species through teaching, imitation, and other forms of social transmission".[19] In the Kluet swamps of

Sumatra, orangutans scoop out the seeds of the neesia fruit using a stripped stick, accessing the most energy-rich seeds in the jungle while avoiding the sharp hairs inside its shell.[20] The fruit is an impossibly prickly mouthful for other animals, and off the menu for orangutans in nearby swamps where they don't have the culture or the cutlery. They haven't cracked it, and don't eat it.[21]

Apes rearrange things – first in the head and then in the world, as above so below. At the level of the individual, and at the level of the troop, new complexes are created, new means and meanings. Cultures branch off, ordering their own cosmoses and living different lives. Kluet orangutans eat particularly well, and the Kluet swamps support a denser population than areas with less sophisticated cuisine. Other fruits come under less pressure. There will be knock-on effects as ripples travel beyond the swamps, as documentaries are made and a young camera-operator in Berlin gets a contract and so on. We can articulate individual causes and effects, but the edge of an ecosystem blurs out at least to the edge of the solar system.

Adam's trick of generating new *SM*s does not distinguish humans from apes, nor even from monkeys. The mandrills of Colchester Zoo have developed a novel sign, covering their eyes in a gesture that means 'leave me alone'.[22] Mandrills are not apes, though they are the most ape-like monkeys, with large stocky bodies and tiny tails where apes have none – but here as elsewhere the category can obscure the detail, and it is useful to think beyond the edges of mental sets. Baboons dangle further still into the monkey category with their long tails, and they do not appear to develop new signs, though they can recognise patterns in them. Researchers report that they learned to tell, with 75% accuracy, if a newly-presented word was a real English word or a jumble of letters "on the basis of differences in the frequency of letter combinations".[23] In other words, they recognised that T often sat next to H, rarely next to Q.

Given the baboon's skill with symbols, it is fitting that he holds the singular honour among primates of having his head upon the shoulders of a major Egyptian god – Thoth, the god of letters and language, scribe of the *Book of the Dead*. Associating signs is the root of language, and a tree of semiotic relationships begins to emerge from that root well before man, before the apes even, with baboons and mandrills. Kanzi the bonobo outperformed a 2-year old child in a comprehension test, answering 74% of the questions appropriately.[24] When asked "Can you make the dog bite the snake?" for example, he picked out the dog and the snake from a pile of toys and placed the snake in the dog's mouth.

The difference between 'dog-bite-snake' and 'snake-bite-dog' is a function of word order, which is technically called 'syntax'. Understanding "Can you make the dog with the yellow collar bite the snake?" requires an extra mental manipulation, because the embedded '*with-the-yellow-collar*' must be held apart for a moment in a separate compartment of the mind. But even this capacity to compartmentalize doesn't distinguish humans from apes, nor for that matter from baboons, who successfully learned to associate letters at one level of embedding.[25] Researchers doubt if they could manage two levels, and even humans struggle to understand three levels in a sentence.[26] With four we get completely lost in compartments within compartments: *Do you think the woman the young man who the old man was complaining about on the bus met can drive?* In mentalizing and compartmentalizing hierarchies to decode meaning, the difference between humans and non-humans is again a matter of degree, not kind.[27]

Kanzi developed his communication skills despite the fact that the humans who raised him from infancy "had no intention of studying language-observational learning" with him, and never trained him with drills or rewards.[28] Human and bonobo babies busy themselves playing with things, working out what things do and how they fit together. If they grow up with language around them, some of the things they learn to manipulate are words and syntax, and they do it surprisingly well. Chimps respond appropriately to 'if-then' constructions, negative statements and the question form, including 'who', 'what' and 'where' questions. But as the Premacks commented after 20 years of training a chimp:

> Though she understood the question, she did not herself ask any questions – unlike the child who asks interminable questions, such as What that? Who making noise? When Daddy come home?... Sarah never delayed the departure of her trainer after her lessons by asking where the trainer was going, when she was returning, or anything else.[29]

Formulating questions is a trait that distinguishes humans from other primates, a distinction of kind rather than degree. It is not a matter of syntax, because apes understand question syntax. It is something to do with cognition. Apes are skilled at articulating various types of 'somethings that mean something'; but a question evokes an empty space to fill with suggestions, a 'nothing that means something'. That is rather more abstract and difficult to conceptualize (like 'no-rhinoceros'). The potential in the void is the set that contains all sets – and that is not something to monkey around with.

Ω

In the Garden of Eden a hairy-backed Manipulator by the name of Adam neologised, fixing names for the things the Definer YHWH Elohim brought to him; but it was not until the next chapter that another character arrived to unpick the fixed, by raising the first question in the Bible:

> Now the serpent was more subtil than any beast of the field which YHWH Elohim had made. And he said unto the woman, "Yea, hath Elohim said, 'Ye shall not eat of every tree of the garden'?"

The first primate to formulate questions punctured a veil
that had hung since the beginning of cognition. It turned the
proto-human brain into an open system capable of intellectual
collaboration, and was the beginning of the collective mega-
mind.[30] On the individual scale, the greatest innovators are also
great questioners. Leonardo Da Vinci, for example, wrote "I
question" more than any other phrase in his notebooks.[31]

Eve heard the question, but she hesitated at the edge of
infinity, so the serpent pushed her with his second and final line:

> And the serpent said unto the woman, "Ye shall not
> surely die..."

...and he was right. They did not die in that day, as promised.
The serpent is challenging by nature, but he's not deceptive
in Genesis. Quite the opposite in fact, he was the original
snitch who told the truth to reveal the deception of YHWH
Elohim. Deception is an ancient primate habit, with apes and
even monkeys using premeditated trickery. One baboon infant,
for example, was observed waiting patiently while an adult
laboured to dig up an edible bulb, and then screaming at the top
of his lungs the second it was out of the ground.[32] His mother
came running onto the scene enraged and immediately charged
the only nearby creature, causing the hapless victim to drop
her dinner and flee. After a furtive glance around, the young
miscreant picked it up for himself.

Trickery is a useful, and frequently delicious survival trait.
In terms of cognition, though, it is a fairly simple matter. The
young baboon already knew the meaning of three things: i) an
adult digging means that something tasty is about to appear;
ii) his own screaming means that his mum will draw near in
a state of aggression; and iii) attacking a baboon means that
they drop what they are carrying. The infant won his lunch
by cleverly constellating all that together. Trickery is part of
the normal primate social repertoire, but unveiling trickery is
more complex. It requires much more flexibility of mind to

214

view a situation from another's perspective, to inquire into the numberless possibilities silently articulated in their thoughts, to uncover means and schemes. The snake inquired, and divined the Definer's motive correctly,

> …"for the gods (elohim) know that in the day ye eat thereof, then your eyes shall be opened, and ye shall be as the gods (elohim), knowing good and evil."…

The serpent turns words back at the words of YHWH Elohim, and brings the couple to the edge of infinity. His first challenge aims a question at a discrepancy opening a crack in the edifice. His second is a refutation that demolishes the established order of the day. He was wise to begin with the woman, as female chimps are more innovative than males. They experiment more with tools, using them in more varied ways, and they also use gestures with more flexibility and sensitivity to context.[33] [34]

> …And when the woman saw that the tree was good for food, and that it was pleasant to the eyes, and a tree to be desired to make one wise, she took of the fruit thereof, and did eat, and gave also unto her husband with her; and he did eat.

In the garden the serpent is the most subtil, and the most supple. The serpent of the ouroboros bends back around the circle to bite its own tail in an emblem of infinity and self-reflexivity. A question goes all the way round to de-scribe a space, and a refutation denies the official story about what lies within it.

The simplest way to ask a question is by bending the pitch of the voice up at the end of a sentence, which is technically called inflection (*in* 'into' + *flectere* 'bend'). Question inflection is understood by babies, and used with their first one-word phrases from around age one, long before any syntax structures appear.[35] Rising inflection indicates a question in every language in the world, apparently without exception.[36] Many primates have excellent pitch control, such as gibbons, whose beautiful duets slide up and down the octaves. The patterns don't appear to mean anything specific, though theoretically they could.[37] In Japanese conversation at least half of the utterances are *ehh...*, *oh?, ha?!* and so on, inflected with the precision of a Japanese bow. In Mandarin *ma* means 'mother', as it does in many languages, but bending the pitch in different ways changes the meaning. The tonal tongue-twister *ma ma, ma ma ma ma* means 'the horse is slow, mother scolds the horse'.[38]

Over half of the world's languages are tonal, some of which in sub-Saharan Africa inflect to communicate grammar as well as vocabulary (saying something once and then repeating it again higher puts it in the past tense, for example).[39] There are whistle languages used over long distances by such groups as the Pirahã of the Amazon, and yodels rang out meaningfully across the Alps in a time before telephones, sending messages to both cows and neighbours.[40] [41] Much can be said combining tone and the vowels with /h/ and /m/, which are most of the phonemes we share with apes. The emergence of a speaking primate would not have required a broad alphabet of sounds, and it could have predated the development of specialized human mouth anatomy. Conversely, if meaning originally depended on phonemes, evolutionary biologists have to explain the advantage that drove evolution over many generations and millennia before the lips finally became muscular enough to differentiate between /m/ and /b/. Tonal language, on the other hand, could have developed a broad vocabulary in the course of an afternoon once the idea had caught on. Natural selection might have favoured a more expressive voice instrument after sound and meaning had been linked, but not before.

Darwin's theory was that anatomical adaptations made our ancestors into increasingly charming singers, as the songbird's syrinx developed at the base of the lungs; meaning was a late addition laid on top.[42] However it happened, it seems that tonal inflection was key in the emergence of language, as Otto

Jespersen and Jean-Jacques Rousseau before him imagined.[43] [44] On the human scale, meaningful vocalizations begin with pitch control; baby sings before she can speak. Music and language are structured similarly, using arrangement and intonation to make phrases, with variations and iterations to produce novel material. Remembering musical phrases calls upon the same TL substructures as does remembering phrases of language, and combining them creatively involves the same FL substructures.[45]

Gorillas beat their chests at threats to communicate their power. Chimpanzees gather to stamp, to pound things and vocalize for a while before bedtime, advertising the size and strength of their troop to any nearby predators.[46] Ethnomusicologist Joseph Jordania proposes in his wonderful *Who Asked the First Question?* that when our ancestors descended from the trees and faced big cats on the savannah, they shouted, stamped and clapped at them to drive them away, as African bushmen do today at the approach of a lion. The hypnotic effect of rhythm, and my unconsciously tapping foot, could have been a survival adaptation that kept my ancestors stomping and clapping and getting a groove on together, shaking their booties at the lions while the tragically ungroovy individuals who made a run for it alone ended up cat food.[47] [48] Music may have begun in this way, as synchronized stamping, percussing, dancing and chanting, or perhaps it was used in other situations where collective, synchronised rhythmical movements were required, like the heave-ho to drag a megalith. Music brings bodies and voices into unison, then breaks them up in orderly and beautiful ways, with structures (yeah!) in tone (yeah!) and time (yeah!), with harmonic arrangements and verse-chorus alternations.[49] Call and response singing is a universal form across cultures. It is also the paradigm of a question and...? An answer! Perhaps one apocryphal afternoon as the sun waxed hot on the savannah, a thirsty primate hummed the song of the river that they always sang together at the river, absentmindedly at first before playing with the arrangement, dropping it into the call and response form. The first question had been asked, the response was resounding, and everyone went singing together down by the riverside, down by the riverside, down by the riverside.[50]

Ω

Tonal inflection is one way to add information to utterance. Another is word inflection, modifying words into different forms. 'Walkies' means one thing, a 'walk' is something else, and a 'walker' is different again. Each is an inflection of the lemma 'walk', and a different noun, a different 'something that means something'. Verb inflections – like 'walked' and 'walks' fold up phrases in different ways, pointing nouns at each other precisely. Perhaps at one level of cognition finer variations on a theme also give us more elements of thought, and more degrees of freedom to bend ideas through.

With tonal inflection and word inflection, and with articulation and syntax, tongues twist sound into meaning. Apes can articulate hand signs and verbal signs, and they have impressive skills with syntax, but they haven't developed meaningful tonal inflections, nor the anatomy to pronounce word inflections. As our ancestor's twig emerged from the primate branch of the Tree of Life, the lips, teeth and jaws folded in. The mouth became more flexible, better able to modulate air flow into different sounds. The vocal chords sank down the throat, opening up more internal space for the voice chamber, adding gutturals to the phonic palette.[51]

Another inflection happened in the hand. Nearly all New World monkey digits point the same way and perform the same simple tasks, wrapping around trees, digging for insects, scratching backs and so on; but Old World monkey thumbs separate further from the fingers and begin to fold in towards the palm. The mandrill, on the cusp of the Old World monkeys and the apes, has a strong thumb which meets the side of the first finger, and the thumb continues to pivot round through the apes,

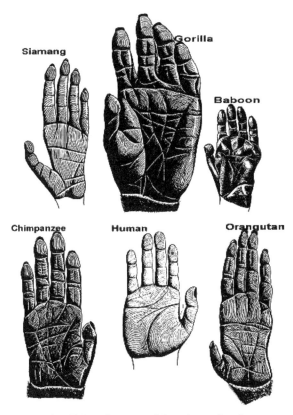

Fig. 18 Development of the primate thumb

progressively opening up more space in the hand to work with.[52] Meanwhile cognition is also developing. Monkeys are cursed with conformity in digit and dendrite; they grab on to the world as it is. Apes, however, pull elements out of the background, first in their minds and then in meat-space using their fingers and semi-opposable thumbs.[53] While most monkeys don't think to stack crates, there is an exception in the capuchin, which is also one of the very few with a semi-opposable thumb.[54] The thumb finally comes into a position of full opposition with the hominins, capable of meeting the front of the fingers at the pads, perhaps as early as *Australopithecus* 2-3 million years ago.[55]

Grasping and manipulating terms in the head and items in the hand are intrinsically linked processes. The skills develop together from infancy, when babies invariably point with the right hand as they name things.[56] They remain associated in adulthood, as verbal fluency declines when subjects are instructed to not move their hands.[57] Anatomically also, the area that controls the right hand is immediately adjacent to the grammatical Broca's area in the left prefrontal cortex.[58] As well as grasp and grammar, the prefrontal cortex is concerned with the inside of other people's heads, involved in empathy, uncovering deception and the motives behind it, testing people to get the measure of them. It is the area that expanded most through the sequence of *Australopithecus* species.

The surface of the brain shows another anatomical inflection. Pro-simian tarsiers have smooth brains, but the cortex becomes

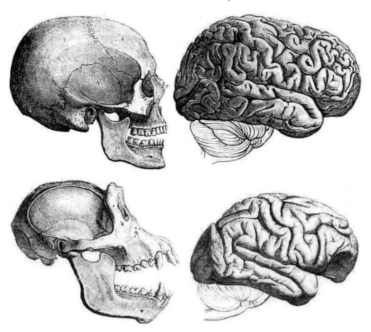

Fig. 19 Chimp and human brains

gradually more walnutty through the primate order. At some point amidst the inflections, as the thumb, the throat and the cerebral cortex were folding in and opening up more internal space, the thoughts turned inwards. Perhaps the catalyst was a mutated brain cell that made more interconnections in the brain of *Australopithecus*.[59] Perhaps it was the expansion of the mirror neuron system, with cells firing empathically as an individual observes another's activity.[60] Man is distinguished among the apes by his excellent skills of mimicry.[61] We learn by mimicking the behaviours and words of others, and then modifying them to suit ourselves. It might be foolish to try and guess what triggered what and when, as paleoanthropology moves quicker than computer hardware these days, in any case, it seems that reflecting the actions of others and reflecting upon our own actions arise together. These physical and mental reflections occur alongside physical inflections.

Something intriguing about *Australopithecus* is that he collected stones resembling his own face.[62] We can only guess at what the stones meant to him, but they must have meant something if he went to the trouble of collecting them. My daughters collect stones with faces, as well as leaves, sticks and anything else with faces. They play with them as they play with teddy bears, as characters with personalities, and it is only fun because they can imagine minds inside them. Perhaps our ancestor was beginning to detect something beneath the surface in a new way; and what is more revealing of the world behind it than a face?

…And the eyes of them both were opened…[63]

Another anatomical inflection is that while our ancestors walked with their bottoms and pudenda sticking out behind them, the human vagina both pivoted inwards and retracted deeper into the as we stood up. Like most primates, the countess communicates her fertile period with her genitals, though not with the scandalously ballooning buttocks of a crested macaque, nor the swelling perineum of a chimp that a suitor might test with a finger.[64] [65] More discreet even than gorillas, whose swelling is localized to the vulva and whose ovulation is described as semi-concealed, the countess is the most subtil, often unnoticed and just at the clitoris (much more and she would have to walk like a cowboy).[66] [67] Meanwhile, the dazzling bumps on her chest conceal her ovulation by obfuscation, rendering her fascinating all through the month, regardless of microfine variations in her labia. Her pheromonal and behavioural cycles may give her away to a prospective beau who knows her nature well, and more so in a world before alarm clocks and deodorant; but the visual clues on display to the sharp-eyed suitors of our very very great grandmothers were very slight. Those that did give something away would be hidden away with the development of clothing, some hundreds of thousands of years ago after *Australopithecus* had been eclipsed:[68]

> …and they knew that they were naked, and they sewed
> fig leaves together, and made themselves girdles…[69]

Both Adam and Eve swell into readiness whether they like it or not, for the autonomic system has its autonomous zones; but the primordial couple soon recovered their dignity, covering what they had dis-covered by making their parts into private parts. The countess also likes to retreat to a private place to copulate (unlike chimps who gang-bang in the open, and bonobos whose troops are intergenerational swingers parties). Her discretion here, and also in keeping her fertile period to her perpetually interesting chest, raises questions that Adam is eager to answer. His equipment folds out prodigiously, making him a veritable King Dong amongst the apes, and Eve for her part folds in, pivoting up and drawing the uterus inwards as the vaginal tube lengthens. There is much to explore in the depths of a woman, too much for an occasional visitor to discover. He who is persistently inquisitive may come to know the woman Eve; then Eve conceives, and new life is born screaming and scheming into the cosmos.

In concealing the portal to life, Eve forced the development of a (somewhat porous) pair-bonded family unit, radically changing the lifestyle of the species by opening up and closing off another internal space. The portal to death was also concealed with the development of burial rites.[70] Other apes mourn their dead with displays of sadness and even fasting, but they eventually leave them where they have fallen. Burial covers them over and hides another natural process that is entirely beyond our control, which is decay. As his perspective on mortality shifted, perhaps our ancestor took another step towards the infinite by recognising the possibility of the opposite, of something immortal that doesn't decay.

Pivoting inwards put Eve into a position of opposition to her partner, should she wish to so position herself. She could even climb on top, inverting the order of Eden entirely. Bonobos famously pleasure each other in diverse sexual positions, but not with her on top.[71] In old Jewish stories Adam's first wife Lilith climbed on top, overwhelming the poor man, and for that she was cast out of Eden.[72] Maybe *LYLYT*'s double powered (*YY*) double negative (*LL*) was too much for him to handle – I've known a few primates like that myself. She spent history as a succubus stealing the sperm of men in their sleep and murdering babies in their cots, while Eve was reunited with her other side, having shifted the order of Eden just enough to make space to gestate something new. The mother of humanity was more flexible, her ally more flexible still. The two would be bound together in an eternal feedback loop:

> "And I [YHWH Elohim] will put enmity between thee [the serpent] and the woman, and between thy seed and her seed; it shall bruise thy head, and thou shalt bruise his heel."

'Heel' is a general term for the rearmost part of something, including an army in retreat.* The image is of a double ouroboros, with humanity and the questioner head to heel

---

* "A troop shall overcome him: but he shall attack them at their heels." (Genesis 49:19)

"O thou fairest among women, go thy way forth by the footsteps of the flock." (Song of Songs 1:8)

and heel to head, twisting and turning uncomfortably through time, the snake's insights gestated and humanity's horizons expanded. The motive force twisting the helix and driving the story is the enmity of the powers, and the pressure continues. "Thou shalt eat the herb of the field," said YHWH Elohim to Adam, "in the sweat of thy face shalt thou eat bread". Adam followed the order and Cain followed suit, but Abel innovated by raising livestock. YHWH was more impressed by success than obedience, and favoured the sacrifice of Abel's lamb shanks over Cain's plain old grains.[73]

> And Cain was very wroth, and his countenance fell.
> And YHWH said unto Cain, "Why art thou wroth? and
> why is thy countenance fallen?"...[74]

Creatively rearranging elements of thought into innovative constellations does not separate us from apes. Talking to ourselves probably does. The internal commentary is something that remains with us almost constantly, if not always faithfully, commenting as our hair and teeth fall out, as our friends move away and die, as our personalities change. This story is the self we present to others – even the self we present to ourselves as we explain our selves to ourselves in the most recursive of paradoxes. Making meaning from experience by linking ideas across time and space, the narrative of self is the record of triumphs and defeats on the battlefields of life, in the workplace and in the kitchen, in the toilet and in the temple, and always there in the head – except on those rare occasions that we escape into the infinite. That story is who we are and what we do, where we live and whom we love. It is a commentary on all of the above, on all that is above and below. In the most extraordinary of inflections, the Logos turns on its master:

> ..."If you do what is right, will you not be accepted? But
> if you do not do what is right, sin is crouching at your
> door. It desires to have you, but you must rule over it."

At that point Cain was incapable of ruling over anything, and so in jealousy and wrath, goaded by a famously jealous and wrathful god, the first murderer rose up against the first innovator. Abel got caned, Cain got disabled, and mankind has been careering between brilliance and barbarism ever since, innovating and destroying, creators in our own right and destroyers, as gods.

Uncultured mammals almost never kill their own in fights, but chimpanzees do. They also wage war at territorial borders. The Gombe chimpanzee war in the 1970s lasted four years, and only ended when all six adult males of one troop had been killed in ambushes, the infants eaten and the females raped and kidnapped.[75] The victors annexed the territory, but they had overstretched themselves; before long it had been ceded to a neighbouring troop.[76] Our lineage has been warring since before our backs straightened out. Humans take philosophy and other weapons of mass destruction to the frontline, where chimps only took clubs; but that is a difference of degree, not a difference of kind. Our enemies have grown more distant, from neighbouring troops and tribes to neighbouring countries and power blocs, and now there is an enemy further away than geography and yet as close as media, around us and among us, emerging from Twitter accounts and CIA databases to carry out headline-grabbing massacres. In the Age of International Terror and the Mega-state, of distributed hyperconnectivity and ubiquitous surveillance, the battle has followed the conversation inwards, and it is no longer clear who our allies are, nor what the enemy is.

A monkey amongst crates hooting wistfully at the exit above is not trapped by his environment but by his imagination. Humans construct mind-frames, and move around them as deftly as any ape in a cage, and like other apes we can reorder the sequences. Unlike other apes, we can also bend the bars. We can fashion them into crowbars and turn them inwards. Mankind manipulates and communicates at the edge of the possible, between the infinite and the articulated, between YHWH Elohim defining and the serpent challenging the definitions. Articulation breaks it up and breaks it open, and inflection peers through the cracks. Our ancestors manipulated sticks in their hairy, hairy, quite contrary fingers for aeons, and human digits are more contrary still, reaching into crannies to bring insight out to the light. We can predict where things are going, and steer ourselves accordingly. Apish cultures split apart and turn on each other but the greatest ape turns on itself, questioning itself and other assumptions. The pregnant nothingness that we alone among the apes can imagine is at the root of the question at the heart of our humanity. In the words of Nagarjuna:

For whom emptiness is possible, for him all is possible.[77]

Or in another idiom:

Nothing is true, everything is permitted.[78]

Your heart beats, lungs pump and stomach churns in equilibrium with the rest of the body, working through negative feedback, but something in the mind rears up against the status quo and the direction of flow, offering choice and the audacity to choose. The Manipulator can fall in line with the urges behind it, as the thumb falls in line with the fingers to push. Like the thumb it can also swing round into opposition to pull back, to raise questions and objections. Cain's only concern was himself, asking "Am I my brother's keeper?"[79] The next to raise a question was Abraham, acting as the keeper of his nephew Lot by speaking up for Sodom. He threw out a better question, twisting the narrative in a better direction:

"Wilt thou also destroy the righteous with the wicked?
[…] That be far from thee to do."

Any old ape and many a monkey can articulate aspects of its world, breaking things apart and joining them together again. With a full range of inflection and endless potential for creation, mankind alone makes stories, and stories can take over. Words stream in and out, and plots thread moments and millennia together, making meaning, revealing and veiling by twists and by turns, mutating through iterations as the tale is rewritten. A well-articulated story is compelling, binding its characters and directing them to higher hopes and happier endings.

In beginning was the Logos, intelligent and ordering, with God, against God, and God; and God was the Logos. All 'things' were made by Him. In his absence, however, 'nothing' was made.

So who is in charge when we add an I?

Adonai?

"I deny!", hisses a voice from the canopy.

$$\Omega$$

THE APE & THE GOD-HEAD

God needs man in order to become conscious, just as he needs limitations in space and time. Let us therefore be for him limitation in time and space, an earthly Tabernacle.[1]

- Carl Jung

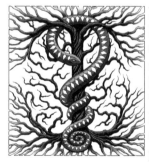

N THE BEGINNING Adam didn't know the powers, didn't know anything apart from the names he made up himself. He only came to know after he had eaten the fruit of the Tree of the Knowledge of Good and Evil, after dualisms had started dividing out; for what could he have possibly known before self and other and the line between the two had been established? The primordial couple ate the fruit and saw that they were naked. They covered a little of what they had discovered, and then,

> They heard the voice of YHWH Elohim walking in the garden in the cool of the day…[2]

Their eyes were open, but they didn't see Him. They *heard* Him. They heard His voice "walking", which is a curious thing to hear, and "in the cool of the day" is a curious place to hear it. It sounds pretty, if you like that kind of poetry; but "cool" is *ruach* in Hebrew, and that's just not cool at all. In 378 verses, this is the only time it is translated as "cool".[3] It is sometimes the 'wind' in a moody sky. Most often it is 'spirit' or 'breath'. In all of its meanings it is something intangible and animated something only ever perceived indirectly, like the wind making noise to hear and movement to see in the rustling of leaves. *Ruach* can be 'courage', 'vigour', or simply 'mind'.[*4] 'Mind' is a good translation when the story begins "in the head".

As to the other words, "walking" is *halach*, but more generally 'going' or 'moving'.[5] "Voice" is *kowl*, but it also means 'noise', or it may have nothing to do with sound at all, as when someone "fleeth from the <u>noise</u> of the fear".[67] Like 'disquiet' in English, *kowl* can be a noiseless perturbation of some sort. "Heard" is *shema*, but again it may have little to do with sound. More broadly it is to 'recognise', 'discern', 'perceive' or 'understand'.[†] "So is my lord the king to discern [*shema*] good and bad" is about a mental process, not an audio process.[8] *Shema* (*SMO*) is likely related to *shem* (*SM*), meaning 'name'.[9] In terms of the movements of mind, discerning something (*SMO*) is the process of assigning a name (*SM*) to it, or rather, assigning it to a name, and a category. The perceived thing is represented to consciousness as a fixed element of thought, even something as vague as a 'presence'.

Finally "of the day" is *ha-yowm*, and could equally be 'on that day', describing their minds at a particular stage of their development. From a neuro-apocalyptic perspective:

> And they discerned the perturbation of YHWH Elohim
> moving in the garden, with their minds as they were at
> that time. And Adam and his wife hid themselves from
> the presence of YHWH Elohim.

---

* "I know the things that come into your mind [*ruach*], every one of them."
  (Ezekiel 11:15)

† "Let us... confound their language, that they may not understand [*shema*]
  one another's speech." (Genesis 11:17)

There was clearly room for improvement, as their immediate reaction was to flee at a rustle in the branches. Fear often accompanies the perception of a presence, both in haunted castles and the God Helmet. One poor subject tore off the electrodes and bolted, but running away doesn't work for voice-hearers and presence-feelers outside the lab.[10] Posts on the Dissociative Identity Disorder internet forum describe how the voices can often be hostile at first, threatening "some type of punishment if I do not submit to their choices".[11][12] The consensus there is that they are best confronted on their own terms, as personalities:

> Talk to the voices. Start with one of them. Ask that one their name. If that one doesn't engage with you, keep trying until someone does. Treat them with respect and kindness, no matter how they respond [...] You will never be fully healthy without each other.[13]

"The only path to success we've ever heard about for people with Dissociative Identity Disorder goes through increased communication and cooperation," comments one poster.[14] The conventional belief that disembodied voices are symptoms of a pathological disorder doesn't help anybody except the pharmacist, and nor is it accurate. Some voices are kind and supportive.[15] Some become allies, and contribute to orderliness rather than disorder:

> Nowadays the communication is more like whispers, and really helpful, like: "I feel something is wrong in the pasture" (my livestock broke into the feed room) or when I was looking for my camera, a not mine thought of "your camera is in your purse, take a peek."[16]

And then there are voices that are friendly but inappropriate with their suggestions.[17]

Like voices, compulsions can manifest with intense pressure. Following the impulse to paint or write or dance or research something can be thrilling and rewarding, and with an ox-goad to direct the thrust of genius it can pay the bills and get you groupies, or even win you an adjective like Blakean or Newtonian. More challenging are those compulsions around hoarding, hand-washing and the number 13. Many people grow up with invasive ideation or some degree of compulsion, dodging cracks in the pavement at the edge of control and release. Autistic compulsions can include flapping and what Higashida calls his "little missions".[18] He describes a "feeling of horror" when resisting an urge, and yet he can do it.[19] People with Tourette's can sometimes suppress vocal tics, though it feels uncomfortable. Our impulses can be contained, to some degree, and we improve with practice.

Adam and Eve left Eden and YHWH Elohim behind to enter a world more like ours, though the disembodied voices continue to speak imperiously, issuing orders and threats and curses. Fleeing still didn't work, as Jonah was to discover on his fishy odyssey. Some prophets stood up to the powers. Noah didn't. He heard and obeyed, but he failed catastrophically to raise an objection, and the rabbis of the Zohar criticized him for it:[20]

> "Surely they were 'the waters of Noah', for they were due to him, since he did not ask for mercy on the world."[21]

When the flood subsided Noah built the first altar in the Bible in order to perform a ritual, and "YHWH was pleased with the aroma of the sacrifice".[22] A deal was struck. YHWH would never again kill everything in fury, and in return mankind would demonstrate his respect for life by maintaining a food taboo:[23]

> "Flesh with the life thereof, which is the blood thereof, shall ye not eat. And surely your blood of your lives will I require; at the hand of every beast will I require it, and at the hand of man; at the hand of every man's brother will I require the life of man. Whoso sheddeth man's blood, by man shall his blood be shed; for in the image of Elohim made He man."[24]

This is the first of several covenants made between man and the powers that drive him, binding the behaviour of both. Note that YHWH does not prohibit killing here – immediately after the deluge that would have been rather hypocritical. The covenant prohibits eating blood, and establishes a symbolic relationship between that and taking life. Justice and retribution are weaved into the flow of events by powers working through the narrative. Murder is set into a wider context invoking fate or something one might call karma, where a killer's destiny is to be killed.

Noah's food taboo would bring his story into daily life at mealtimes, necessitating that meat have the blood beaten from it before serving. Not eating until some ritual has been performed is a textbook OCD symptom, common to Tesla, Tammet and religiously observant people of all persuasions. They may be onto something, as subjects enjoy their food more when they perform a pre-dinner ritual first, even if the nature of the ritual is completely arbitrary.[25] Another classic OCD trait Noah introduces at the first altar in the Bible is the practice of performing rituals in order to stave off catastrophe, as the Catholic priest does at his to "deliver us from evil". Again they might be on to something, as prayer is correlated with "better psychological, physical and health outcomes" in people suffering from chronic pain, and reduced anxiety-related symptoms in anxiety disorders – at least in individuals who have a "secure attachment to God".[26] [27] "Among those who have a more insecure or avoidant attachment to God", however, prayer seems to increase anxiety. In other words, the nature of the relationship is critical in predicting whether it is healthy or toxic, as it is in our other relationships.

Noah's idiosyncrasies could be viewed unkindly, as symptoms of Post-Diluvial Stress Disorder, but pre-dinner acts of sanitisation, petitions to higher powers, and other rituals common to religion and compulsion could also be understood as adaptive responses to the trauma of being born on a confusing and painful planet. We are all subject to some degree of compulsion, whether we like it or not, and it can turn out well or badly depending on how we handle it. Leaving aside questions about whether our rituals can keep us from harm, or indeed whether washing your hands before you eat keeps you from disease, they can at least make it easier to be human. For whatever reason, people feel obliged to perform rituals at the door, and a simple custom such as the sign of the cross or a nod to the shrine of the doorkeeper on the way out addresses this aspect of our humanity. The doorpost of a Jewish home has a *mezuzah*, affixed at a slant according to a tradition that just happens to preempt any obsessive compulsions developing about straightening it up.

Ω

The second covenant in the Bible was made with Abraham, back when he was called Abram and the power introduced Itself as El Shadday:

> YHWH appeared to Abram, and said unto him, "I am El Shadday [...] And I will make my covenant between me and thee, and will multiply thee exceedingly [...] And I will give unto thee, and to thy seed after thee, the land wherein thou art a stranger, all the land of Canaan, for an everlasting possession."[28]

The power of the destroyer/nurturer (see page 101) would be put to good use – good for the patriarch and his seed, at least, whose needs would be met by El Shadday's soft side. His sharp side would be reserved for the competitors to be driven out of the territory. The deal manages good and evil in the magician's favour, as befits a pact made with a dangerous power for dominion and sexual potency, and he pays with blood-letting:

> "He that is born in thy house, and he that is bought with thy money, must needs be circumcised: and my covenant shall be in your flesh for an everlasting covenant."[29]

Sacrificing foreskins for power is pretty old-school, but whatever one's views on this ancient custom it was a considerable advance on the killing of the firstborn. Child sacrifice was practised by various nearby cults of the day, including some Israelite tribes, and very nearly by Abraham himself:[30]

> And He said, "Take now thy son, thine only son Isaac, whom thou lovest, and get thee into the land of Moriah; and offer him there for a burnt offering"…

The suggestion made here by the voice is similar to the kind of forced ideation that makes it difficult for me to relax if I'm holding a baby on the deck of a boat or near the edge of a building. Personally, I tend to 'act natural' for a while in those situations, and then hand the baby to someone else. Abraham heard and obeyed, and built an altar.[31]

> And Abraham stretched forth his hand, and took the knife to slay his son. And the angel of YHWH called unto him out of heaven, and said, "Abraham, Abraham"…

Hearing one's name is very common in voice-hearers. When people who don't usually hear voices do so, when recently bereaved or under stress, for example, it is often their own names that they hear first.[32] The only disembodied voice I ever heard shouted my name as I was reading in bed, and I'm officially not crazy.

> …and he said, "Here am I"…

I wish I had said something like that, but I was startled, and I said "What the fuck was that?!", bringing our chat to a close. Abraham was a better conversationalist, and the angel of YHWH continued:

> …"Lay not thine hand upon the lad, neither do thou any thing unto him: for now I know that thou fearest God, seeing thou hast not withheld thy son, thine only son from me."[33]

This story often comes to mind when I am reluctant to continue sacrificing my social life, my family life and my sleep to pursue an obsessional writing project in increasingly strange directions, editing the same chapters over and again. To have even a hope of success in your endeavours you have to sacrifice things you love, apparently, or at least be prepared to – and still there's no guarantee. That said, try not to get too carried away with knives at the behest of the voices. The world is safer when both people and powers set limits on how we express our impulses.

> "And in thy seed shall all the nations of the earth be blessed; because thou hast heard/perceived/obeyed/ understood [*shema*] my voice [*kowl*]."

A later editor would add words about how Abraham was also rewarded because he "kept my charge, my commands, my statutes", but it doesn't make sense at this stage of the narrative. The only generalized law-like thing was Noah's food taboo, and keeping a food taboo is no biggie, Abraham blessing began with his keen powers of perception. The blessing repeats the vocabulary of the prototype spiritual experience, when Adam and Eve discerned [*shema*] the perturbation [*kowl*] of the presence of YHWH Elohim. He heard (*shema*) and obeyed (*shema*) a voice that demanded the life of his son, in the tradition of many blood-thirsty voice-hearing cultists of the ancient world. He also heard a different voice with different instructions, the Angel of YHWH proposing a ram caught in a thicket in Isaac's place. In this story, which is remembered today with the blowing of the ram's horn at Jewish festivals, different voices pushed in opposing directions, and the man made his choices.

Abraham heard acutely, but he didn't like everything he heard. He was the first man in the Bible to successfully stand up to a power, as YHWH was preparing a dose of brimstone for Sodom:

"I will go down [said YHWH] and see whether they have done altogether according to the cry of it, which is come unto me; and if not, I will know." And the men [actually angels] turned their faces from thence, and went toward Sodom. But Abraham stood yet before YHWH...[34]

...or did he? There is a "correction of the scribe" here, a late edit made to protect the dignity of the mighty name.[35] Originally the position of the protagonists was reversed, and it was Abraham, not YHWH, who was doing the judging:

...*But YHWH stood yet before Abraham*. And Abraham drew near, and said, "Wilt thou also destroy the righteous with the wicked?..."

Abraham made a stand without being compelled by any divine power. He was guided by nothing more than his own moral compass:

"...Peradventure there be fifty righteous within the city: wilt thou also destroy and not spare the place for the fifty righteous that are therein? That be far from thee to do."

YHWH agreed that an airstrike causing extensive collateral damage was unbecoming of a superpower. A Calcutta market scene followed, where Abraham haggled the Lord down through 45, 40, 30, 20 to 10 righteous men, and finally Lot and his family were spared. In this story Man the Manipulator becomes what the serpent foretold, a power unto himself "as the elohim", and "knowing good and evil" where the powers sometimes forget.[36] The man inhibits and directs the movements of the other powers, sending stories in different directions in line with his own moral judgement.

Ω

Having tested Abraham's powers of obedience, the powers tested Jacob's powers of resistance.[37] When Jacob was fleeing Esau he prayed for deliverance, and that night he was attacked by a stranger who fought him until dawn:

> And when he saw that he prevailed not against him,
> he touched the hollow of his thigh; and the hollow of
> Jacob's thigh was out of joint, as he wrestled with him.
> And he [the assailant] said, "Let me go, for the day
> breaketh."…

Jacob's dark night of the soul was drawing to a close, but he would not release his attacker so easily:

> …And he said, "I will not let thee go, except thou bless
> me."

"Bless" (*barach*) is not the symbolic benediction of a Sunday priest; it is the awarding of a boon, usually the birth of children or the winning of riches.[38] The belligerent stranger turns out to be a manifestation of divinity, and so the story describes a man subduing the divine and pinning Him until a demand is met. From an orthodox perspective this has an air of blasphemy about it, inverting the order one might expect between mankind and the powers. So did the verse where Abraham judged YHWH, until the 'correction of the scribe' switched the agents around. These stories make more sense, however, when the struggle is reframed in the head. We wrestle with our compulsions, and we are transformed in the process. Like Abram before him, Jacob has his name changed in the encounter:

> And He said, "Thy name shall be called no more Jacob,
> but Israel: for as a prince hast thou power with powers
> (elohim) and with men, and hast prevailed."

"As a prince thou hast power" is how the KJV translates *SRH*. It is a bit of a word salad for only three letters, because it is trying to evoke several ideas implied by *SRH* simultaneously. Overall it suggests something about access to and mastery of formidable power:

SaR: chief/prince

SaRaR: to exercise dominion over

SaRaH: strive/fight

ShaRaH: let loose (a javelin or thunderbolt, for example)

The new name is Israel (pronounced *"yiss-ra-el"*), *YSRAL* 'the chief' (*SR*) flanked and powered up by the *Y* of <u>Y</u>HWH and the *AL* of <u>E</u>lohim. *YSRAL* also invokes the focus and justice that are the ideal qualities of the superego directing the deep urges of the id, because *YSR* means 'direct', 'upright', 'just' and 'virtuous'.[39] It's a considerable upgrade from 'Jacob', which means 'supplanter'.[40]

Names are things of power in Hebrew mysticism and elsewhere. The magick words in medieval grimoires grant powers to the sorcerer, and discovering the name of a cocky little trickster like Rumpelstiltskin can break his curse and set him to work as an ally spinning gold. According to the Dissociative Identity Disorder forums, learning the names of the voices brings them under a degree of control (see page 231). Jacob tried to consolidate his hold, asking "Tell me thy name"; but his assailant remained slippery.[41]

> …And He said, "Wherefore is it that thou dost ask after my name?" And He blessed him there…

Things are developing, and with each encounter the balance of power shifts in man's favour. With Noah and Abraham the powers become subject to the terms of covenants, and with Jacob they become subject to the will of a man directly. There's no covenant forged at this episode, and the powers refuse to be fixed into a name; and what word could possibly have said it all anyway?[42] Jacob forges a new name to mark the encounter, combining the *Y* and *AL* of the Godnames with the *PN* of 'the presence'.

> …And Jacob called the name of the place Peniel [*PNYAL*]: for I have seen Elohim face to face [*panim-al-panim*], and my life is preserved.[43]

Some nuance is lost in translation here, because *panim* is actually plural, as in "faces to faces" or "presences to presences". More than a simple majestic plural, it suggests divinity that is multifaceted beyond the grasp of the Categorizer; and the faces of the perceiver are also pluralized. In the heat of battle, in the revelation of divinity, the prophet discovers new sides to himself.

There is much to contemplate in the story of an ordeal unleashing new powers. Normally we use up to about 65% of muscle capacity, even when straining ourselves, and highly trained athletes can push through the pain to about 80%. People in mortal danger sometimes access their full power, however, in a phenomenon called "hysterical strength", tearing off car doors for example.[44] In strength tests, terrifying an unsuspecting subject by setting off a loud bang behind them increases maximal pull strength.[45] So do both alcohol and hypnosis, which inhibit the FLs. Infants with immature FLs do not inhibit their power, and nor do chimpanzees with small FLs; both are remarkably strong for their size compared to adult humans.[46] Autists are also sometimes exceptionally strong for their size, both in normal situations and under stress.[47]

In life or death situations it is also common to hear voices, and even to battle with them. As Steve Callahan drifted alone at sea for 65 days he sometimes saw "God's face in the smooth waves", while at other times a disembodied voice he called "the captain" shouted at him, rationing his daily supplies:

> "Shut up! We don't know how close we are. Might have to last to the Bahamas. Now get back to work!"[48]

Mountaineer Joe Simpson followed a "clean and sharp and commanding" voice during an ordeal that involved a fall that shattered his knee, hours dangling on a rope, falling again and knocking himself unconscious, and then scaling an icy crevasse when he came round.[49] On the final leg, as he dragged his broken leg for two and a half frostbitten and famished days back to base, he saw "with greater clarity and honesty than I had ever experienced before".

Ordeals can be transformative as well as transcendental. Petra Nemcova clung to a palm tree for eight hours with a crushed pelvis after the 2004 tsunami killed her fiancé, and she credits the experience with radically changing her perspective on life for the better, and leading to her founding a charity.[50] People who have prevailed against life-threatening illness often exhibit what researchers have called "post-traumatic growth", including "reappraisal of life and priorities", "existential re-evaluation" and "a new awareness of the body".[51] My own battle with leishmaniasis certainly feels like a defining (or redefining) episode in my life. Since then I feel more focused with my writing and thinking, and I'm quicker to challenge people whose manners offend me. I laugh more, and cry more, and express my anger more directly, disinhibited in many ways.

The daily doses of Daime helped, of course. Psychedelics, like brushes with death, can be transcendent and transformative, dissociative even. Generally the various concurrent processes in the head resolve into a single stream of consciousness, a story of a self that bears our name; but that story and that self can splinter into shards when one's life is at risk or in other extreme situations. Pain will do it, if that's what you're into. Sex, drugs and rock and roll will do it. Creepy rituals, seals and triangles – any taboo will do. Whether one thinks of the presences as gods and demons with their own personal integrity or dissociated parts of ourselves, it seems less important than what these apocalypses bring into our lives. The Good Book's "faces-to-faces" suggests pluralities both within and without. Another good book preempts the question with its subtitle: "It's all in your head... you just have no idea how big your head is".[52] Some struggles take place entirely in an individual's mind, but even then the same phenomenology can occur. When Gandhi was wrestling with his conscience he heard,

> a Voice from afar and yet quite near. It was as unmistakable as some human voice definitely speaking to me, and irresistible. I was not dreaming at the time I heard the Voice. The hearing of the Voice was preceded by a terrific struggle within me. Suddenly the Voice came upon me. I listened, made certain it was the Voice,

and the struggle ceased. I was calm. The determination was made accordingly, the date and the hour of the fast were fixed.[53]

Ordeal and disintegration can also leave people traumatized, of course (as can psychedelics if handled carelessly). The story of Jacob and the angel asks us not just to escape with our lives but to battle on until victory is complete, until the enemy has been pacified and deputized as an ally. Jacob walked away with a limp, diminished as well as increased by his encounter, and because of it he could no longer flee the brother he had tricked out of his birthright. Jacob 'the supplanter' had to face Esau 'the rough' head on.[54][55] He bowed his head in supplication, and his enemy embraced him in peace.

"When we are no longer able to change a situation," wrote Viktor Frankl, "we are challenged to change ourselves."[56] His own ordeal was the concentration camp, and his revelation came during a forced march, when, "for the first time in my life I was able to understand the meaning of the words, 'The angels are lost in perpetual contemplation of an infinite glory'."[57] Established patterns of thought and loops of emotion can be disrupted, opening up a void for something new to emerge into. Disintegration is terrifying, but re-integration can bring epiphanies of infinity and significance. Frankl went on to write *Man's Search for Meaning* and develop his school of psychotherapy. Called logotherapy, it emphasises the central importance of the meaning (Logos) one finds in life as key to overcoming adversity and maintaining autonomy. The Logos brings cacophony into coherence, organizing thought and word and deed into orderly patterns. Though the powers push us in different directions, "life can be pulled by goals just as surely as it can be pushed by drives."[58]

Ω

Biblical prophets speak across the gulf between the worlds, sometimes expressing the will of the powers toward the people, at other times interceding with the powers on behalf of the people. They are Manipulators *par excellence*, and words of power boil in their mouths as they hold the powers to account and channel them into history. First Abraham learned to inhibit the expression of power. Then Jacob learned to disinhibit and release it at full intensity. With Moses the powers spoke "faces to faces" and revealed the name of YHWH for the first time, though Moses did not consider himself up to the task demanded of him:

> "I am not eloquent neither heretofore nor since thou
> hast spoken unto thy servant: but I am heavy of speech,
> and of a heavy tongue."[59]

Because of his "heavy tongue" and "uncircumcised (literally 'uncontrolled') lips", Moses is said to have been a stutterer by ancient rabbis and modern neuroscientists alike. [60] [61] [62] YHWH assures him that his slow tongue will be replaced with a compulsion to speak:

> "Go, and I will be with thy mouth, and teach thee what
> thou shalt say." [63]

Moses and the power compelling him are moved by a great love for their tribe. YHWH heard "the groaning of the Children of Israel" and, being a sentimental type, He declared a kind of marriage, promising "I will take you to me for a people".[64] The next stage of the relationship would require a new covenant, but first he brings up the old covenant:

> And Elohim spake unto Moses, and said unto him,
> "I am YHWH: And I appeared unto Abraham, unto
> Isaac, and unto Jacob, by the name of the Almighty (El
> Shadday), but by my name YHWH was I not known to
> them…"

The presence had appeared Almighty to Abraham, and to Isaac bound beneath the knife, and to Jacob too – until he out-mightied Him; but by that point He wasn't Jacob anymore. He had been dissolved, to reform as *YSRAL*.

"I have remembered my covenant," continues YHWH, referring to when El Shadday had promised "all the land of Canaan, for an everlasting possession" to "thee [Abraham] and thy seed".[65] "I will make nations of thee, and kings shall come out of thee," promised El Shadday, who is interested in increase, dominance, territory and genetic legacy. In terms of neuroanatomy, these drives pertain to the brainstem at the top of the spinal chord that we share with all vertebrates, the so-called 'R-complex' or 'reptilian brain'. A territorialist, a fighter, a breeder and a hoarder, it ensures the organism's survival and multiplication.[66] Its instincts and reflexes keep the heart beating and lungs pumping, keep the drool flowing repeating time-tested rituals. It tweaks the levels, taking the rhythms through different intensities as it shifts the organism between states of arousal, from sleep through a spectrum of trance states to alertness. It turns the treble right up for fight or flight.

"I will make thee exceeding fruitful!" is just what any self-respecting anthropomorphized brainstem would promise if it had a voice, though not for the love of babies.[67] Chameleons do not dote on their babies; they barely look at them. Reptiles are not subject to the range of emotions that mammals are, and rarely provide parental care, though some perform instinctive

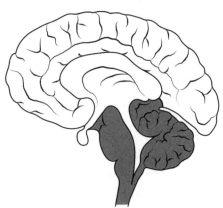

'parenting' rituals such as rock pythons that share warmth with their young.[68] The few reptiles with more generalized parental behaviours have more to their brains than the R-complex, like crocodiles with their rudimentary limbic systems.[69] Many snake

Fig. 20 The R-complex

species will eat their own young if they can catch them, driven by predatory instincts in the absence of any maternal feelings. Abraham was compelled to destroy his own son in order to increase his own power. The boy was saved, but not by El Shadday. It was "the angel of YHWH [who] called unto him out of heaven".[70] Abraham didn't know the name of YHWH, but he heard the voice and followed the instruction.

YHWH is an altogether different type of power to El Shadday, and not interested in seed and offspring. His covenant is "with thee and with Israel", meaning the tribe of Israel, and His concern is the prosperity and security of the tribe.[71] "I will cast out the nations before thee, and enlarge thy borders," He says, focusing on the edge of the tribe rather than the territory beneath it. El Shadday the Sustainer named the land of Canaan in His covenant; YHWH the Tribalist names a series of tribes, separating off the Chosen People from other peoples:

> "Behold, I drive out before thee the Amorite, and the Canaanite, and the Hittite, and the Perizzite, and the Hivite, and the Jebusite."[72]

YHWH is a tribal god, and concerned with tribal matters. He is fierce in emotion, "abounding in love" for his people, and He is also a war god – "a warrior" as Exodus puts it.[73] [74] Tribal survival requires more than just sharing your olives in peacetime; it demands fighting collectively in tribal war, and that doesn't work if individuals are only concerned with their own necks. Love of family, love of troop and tribe, and hatred of the enemy, are functions of the limbic system, the so-called mammalian brain that encloses and feeds into the R-complex. Love and hate are not instinctual. They are a function of learning, of emotional memories associating feelings with people and other recognisable things (i.e. *shem*). Nelson Mandela described the learned nature of love and hate with characteristic optimism:

> No-one is born hating another person because of the colour of their skin, or their background, or their

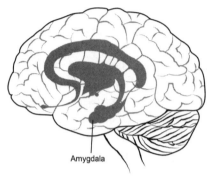

Amygdala

Fig. 21 Limbic system

religion. People must learn to hate, and if they can learn to hate, they can be taught to love, for love comes more naturally to the human heart than its opposite.[75]

Emotion doesn't drive the organism, in the way that the R-complex does. We don't flee because we are scared. We flee for the same reason that lizards flee, for the same reason that we blink – because our instincts drive us to. The difference is that we get emotional while we do it, and the associations made will influence our mood and behaviour in the future when similar situations arise. Psychopaths, who usually grow up neglected or abused and never learn to love, maintain their instincts for sex and power.[76] Indeed, without any normal feelings of empathy mitigating their instincts, they may become killers, child-abusers or members of parliament (or all three at once).

Our emotions widen the circle of our concerns beyond the individual to our loved ones, even to our pets. The amygdalas and limbic system lay down networks that are pre-cortical and pre-rational, making us heroes with hysterical strength to share, like the woman who lifted a car off her father and the mother who fought off a polar bear threatening her child.[77] [78] To quote St. Huey, "it's strong and it's sudden and it's cruel sometimes, but it might just save your life. That's the power of love".[79] Some people risk their lives to rescue people they don't even know. Sometimes they risk their lives to kill people they don't know, for abstract ideals that they love, like 'king and country' or 'the proletariat uprising'. Within the troop or tribe filial sentiments usually overrule primal urges, but things are

246

unpredictable in extreme situations when the self disintegrates. Parents starving under Stalin killed and ate their own children, for example.[80] Chimps almost never kill infants from their own troops, and on the few occasions that it has been observed it seems to be when the R-complex takes over in a twisted display of dominance.[81]

In the pivotal biblical encounters between people and powers, taboos are introduced. El Shadday demanded a cut to reveal the redness of the wand of potential, marking out every male descendent of Big Daddy Abraham. Jacob's clinch is remembered with a prohibition on eating the sinew of the thigh, which is the most powerful muscle in the body. YHWH stipulated a food taboo that pertains to His concerns, a prohibition against cooking a kid goat in the nanny goat's milk. The symbolism addresses the power of love, acknowledging and sanctifying the bond between a mammalian mother and her young.

Moses' covenant would also bring the whole tribe together as one body to observe seasonal festivals three times per year.[82] YHWH is god of the Israelites collective, and He would have Israel maintained and increased, and so the spoiling of enemies is something wonderful to Him.[83] The morality of plunder has nothing to do with anything. Morals and empathy pertain to the functions of reason and the lobes of the Logos, and YHWH cares nothing for them. His concern is consolidating tribal power, and so His prophet insists that only the virgin girls of conquered tribes be spared.[84] Chimpanzees don't care about virginity, but otherwise their war strategy is the same, massacring the males of all ages and taking the chimpanzeenas for themselves.

YHWH defines the edge of the tribe and patrols it, and in that He has something in common with the power that formed man "of the clay of the ground". Back in Eden, YHWH Elohim established an edge around the chosen person, rather than the Chosen People.[85] Where YHWH presents a list of other tribes for the Chosen People to subdue, YHWH Elohim presented other animals to Adam to have dominion over.[86] Both the Definer and the Tribalist claim ownership of their chosen fancies, making demands of them, issuing threats, curses and food taboos. Both demand fidelity from their charges, and militate against the enemies that would come between them. YHWH's covenant would oblige the Children of Israel to destroy the altars and images of YHWH's rivals, the snakes and bulls and other godforms worshipped in the land of Canaan.[87][88][89] This is to be expected of a tribal god, but YHWH's jealousy also extends to images of Himself, and His legendary intolerance of images lays the foundation for something exceptional about Yahwism. I WILL BE WHAT I WILL BE will not be fixed into a form; He is fluid between the faces and slippery with name and category and image. This is skillful neuro-programming, because while the powers may be felt forcefully like a bull one day, on another day a different presence might be presented – and will a Categorizer primed for an almighty crash notice the slither of the subtil? In Yahwism the powers would be fixed into letters rather than images, singularly pluralistic in multifaceted verses with a broad spectrum of interpretative possibility.

According to the story, something of YHWH's power was also written down on Mount Sinai:

> And he [Moses] wrote upon the tables the words [DBRYM] of the covenant, the ten words [OSRT H-DBRYM].[90]

The phrase OSRT H-DBRYM (aseret ha-d'varim) is found only once in the Bible. Though it is invariably translated as "the ten commandments", DBRYM doesn't mean 'commandments'. It is the plural of DBR, and it means 'words', 'things', 'matters', 'percepts', 'sentences', 'utterances', 'concepts' and so on. A DBR could be a commandment, of course. It could also be a lie, or a love letter, or a telesales script, or any orderly sequence of words or letters. Whatever the "ten words" are is never described, and Moses shows them to nobody. Gandhi did the same; he heard the Voice, and kept what it said to himself. He then stopped eating for three weeks and successfully subverted the political order of the subcontinent, and when riots broke out in the young republic he fasted again until order had been re-established.[91] [92] Moses kept his mega-words between himself and his other selves, his ever-changing I AM THAT I WILL BE, sealed in an acacia box in a thick cloud of incense.

Ω

There are several commands specified in the chapter that mentions the "ten words", but there aren't ten of them, not by any reckoning. "Thou shalt not seethe a kid in his mother's milk" and "Thou shalt not offer the blood of my sacrifice with leavened bread" are also rather arcane from a modern perspective (if progressive from a goat's perspective).[93] The more well-known Thou-shalt-nots come from a different mountain hike, described in Exodus 20. Christian clerics call this list 'the ethical Decalogue', which is crooked numerology indeed; the number of commands is not 10 (*deca*) but around 14 (*decatessera*), and 'law' is not *logos* but *nomos*. If there was any logic in theology it would be called 'the ethical Decatesseranom'. It is unlike the other covenants, binding mankind but not binding the powers. It also has none of the poetry of the others, raising and settling the issue of murder in two words (*lo tirtzach*: thou shalt not murder). Along with Leviticus stipulating the death penalty for murder, this is a far cry from the poetry of Noah's covenant, where retribution for murder comes through the agency of fate.[94]

The covenant story is repeated in Deuteronomy, but this time transferred to Mount Horeb and with some of the laws changed. Three stories about two trips up two mountains with two sets of tablets and three documents makes for a muddle; the orthodox conclusion is that Moses used two names for one mountain, and that YHWH's ten cultic mega-words from one trip are actually a decimalized 14-point do's and dont's list mostly concerned with property rights from another trip. That is what well-meaning but ill-informed American evangelicals are lobbying to have displayed in school classrooms.[95] They don't seem too fussed about the goat thing.

Another glitch in the plot is that the Decatesseranom prohibits Moses' own vices – killing in peacetime, encouraging theft and lying in Egypt, coveting the land, the milk and the honeys of other tribes.[96] [97] [98] Of course, the law code doesn't extend beyond the Israelite tribe, which is another detail our evangelical friends don't seem too concerned about, so perhaps we shouldn't be either. But then Moses ignores Thou-shalt-not no. 2 at the foot of the mountain, by commanding that a magic box be festooned with golden cherubim:

> Thou shalt not make unto thee any graven image, or any likeness of any thing that is in heaven above, or that is in the earth beneath, or that is in the water under the earth.[99]

The Golden Calf was a graven image, and an abomination at which the anger of both YHWH and Moses "waxed hot".[100] Only by grinding it up and feeding it to the idolaters, and then putting 3,000 men to the sword, was Moses able to downgrade the power of YHWH's unrequited love from total annihilation to a mere plague. In rabbinical law "it is prohibited to make images [even] for decorative purposes", and some orthodox families forbid Barbie dolls strict observance. The Golden Calf was seriously unkosher. So what about the golden angels?

Exodus 34, where the "ten words" were given, presents no contradiction, because there YHWH forbids "molten gods [*elohim*]" not "graven images", and the angels are *cherubim*, not *elohim*.[101] YHWH is a famously jealous god, and He takes rejection badly, but He doesn't seem to object to the artform of sculpture per se. Like the rest of the powers, He doesn't care a hoot for the ethics of the Decatesseranom.[102] He killed pretty much everybody with the flood.[103] YHWH Elohim authored the first lie in creation. None of the great men of Genesis or Exodus seem very concerned about lying, theft, murder or any other ethical standard I expect my friends to uphold. Jacob 'the supplanter' scammed his starving brother out of his birthright with a stew, and took from him his father's blessing with a cunning disguise.[104] [105] Lot, whose righteousness was rewarded, offered his daughters to the Sodomites molesting his houseguests.[106] He was God-fearing, to be sure; but his ethics were entirely self-serving, like those of the god he feared.

The root of the confusion is that Exodus 20 was written centuries after Exodus 34, and with a completely different agenda in mind, in a book made up from successive edits (we'll come to that corrupt cranny of our apocalypse in the next chapter). Back in the good old bad old days, morality was a different matter, and YHWH was a wilder god, a trickier god, a lawless god, and a god that could be bargained with. His sense of justice is pretty shocking, and He boasts about it as He proclaims His own mighty name:

> "YHWH, YHWH AL, merciful and gracious, longsuffering, and abundant in goodness and truth, keeping mercy for thousands, forgiving iniquity and transgression and sin, and that will by no means clear the guilty; visiting the iniquity of the fathers upon the children, and upon the children's children, unto the third and to the fourth generation."[107]

Here YHWH condemns generations of innocent children to suffering, and that did not sit well with the prophet Ezekiel:

> "Yet say you, 'What? Doesn't the son bear the iniquity of the father?' No! When the son has done that which is lawful and right, and has kept all my statutes, he shall surely live. The soul who sins, he shall die: the son shall not bear the iniquity of the father."[108]

These two visions of how the world works cannot be reconciled. So which is true?

From my perspective, having worked in education teaching children and meeting parents, and having watched my own kids growing up for seven years, and having lived among humans for nearly forty, I'm with YHWH on this. Maybe I'm jaded, but it seems that your parents "fill you with the faults they had and add some extra, just for you", as one poet put it in a vulgar little gem.[109] For example, I could usually generate enthusiasm about numbers in a remedial maths class, and pass on basic number skills even with some learning difficulties to contend with; but if a child's parents wouldn't give up a few minutes to drill times tables at home (because on some level they didn't really care whether their children could count or not), those children may well have ended up functionally innumerate like one in five British school-leavers.[110] Children grow up scarred by the neglect, the violence and domination, the selfishness and other iniquities they encounter in their parents – failings invariably rooted in some kind of blockage or perversion of the proper expression of familial love, which is YHWH's domain. Around 68% of serial killers were subjected to child abuse. According to Freud, victims of abuse are often driven by a "compulsion to repeat", to recreate familiar twisted dynamics in their adult relationships, and if they can't find suitable players they will draft guiltless people into their scripts, provoking them unconsciously but relentlessly until their abusive tendencies are awoken.[111] [112] The cycle rolls on tediously "unto the third and fourth generation", and so do the health problems associated with emotional trauma, such as diabetes, cancer and a weaker immune system. Like Ezekiel I find this unbearably unjust, and wish that the world was different; but YHWH is simply describing how things work. The nascent mind pours its innate enthusiasm into the world, and adapts to what bounces back at it.

I like to think I'm a better parent than some of the people I see pushing pushchairs towards the fires of Hell, but there is no escaping the fact that my carelessness damages my kids, just as my care nourishes them. Today, as it happens, I am editing left-handed after a very careless morning, losing my temper spectacularly at breakfast and then fracturing my knuckle against the wall. Fortunately my family were spared a portion of the ugliness, because I had removed myself to the bedroom by the time I exploded. Nevertheless, my girls did see their beloved archetype of benevolent paternal security – who had more or less kept it together since the beginning of time – raging incoherent and making everyone cry. The sharp side of El Shadday punched a wall in their still-forming brains this morning while my neocortex was still dozing, scaring away some unicorns no doubt. It would have been worse had I yielded completely to my inner reptile and beaten their mother senseless with the toaster, which was what I wanted to do, though the exact nature of her transgression has slipped my mind a few edits later. Over half a million British women every year aren't so lucky, beaten in their homes, often with drunken and inhibited FLs as a contributing factor.[113]

My knuckle has healed up already, such is the nature of a story put together from successive edits. I'm a little wiser, hopefully, but my hand span on the right is tighter, a whole pinky-width narrower than on my left, and capitalizing Y on a keyboard is more belaboured. It's not the end of the world, but it is an apocalypse of sorts, as something previously hidden was disclosed. And my bones are old and hard, while my girls' brains are more plastic, reconfiguring more readily to the environment. They were bound to discover explosive aggression sooner or later, of course; I just wish I had been doing something heroic.

I told my girls that I had punched a bear. They told that to everyone else, and who knows what tale they will tell when they look back on their own genesis and exodus stories, after their own lamentations have been written. Such is the nature of stories patched together from re-readings and rewritings. There may be meaning in the threads running through our lives and our generations, some reward and retribution, some resolution and poetry in the narrative if the writer can make sense of it; but fairness is a lot to ask for in a world of earthquakes and cot death. The fracture in my knuckle was my fault. The fractures in their worlds were my fault too, the children were perfectly innocent. My mood was my fault, but it was also their mother's fault. And it was my fault for marrying her in the first place, as a little girl put it at the time without missing a beat, thinking more clearly than my stupid brainstem. And it was her parents' faults for raising her with such glaring deficits, her grandparents' faults and her great-grandparents' faults, and so on all the way back to Adam and Eve and that cursed serpent; but before the serpent was cursed he was naked and subtil, prudent and observant. Fault is a meta-story, born out of a dualistic concept of good and evil that becomes exponentially more complicated and unworkable as you think through the ramifications. Stories aren't true, in the way that "Danny broke his knuckle against the wall" is true. Stories aren't facts, but the links we make between observations as we articulate the world to ourselves and to others, and good stories are only as good as the artistry running through them. If a story has a happy ending it is because a poet wrote one out and then lived it out, choosing her lines to chime with the rhyme in the beat of the metre.

YHWH's boast isn't fair, but it is the case – far more so than Ezekiel's rose-tinted optimism. The powers are morally ambivalent, as nature made them: YHWH Elohim the Definer, breaking the world into chunks; El Shadday the Sustainer, racing across the aeons, predator pursuing prey and pursued by hunger; YHWH the Tribalist, jostling at the frontiers of the mega-self. YHWH's curse across the generations describes the situation when the powers control us. The prophets imagine what we can be when we control the powers. If a father or anyone else in a position of authority can pin the powers when they threaten to overwhelm him, and strive as a prince to direct the passions that kept his seed and clan alive since the beginning, he can loosen the chains of action and reaction and offload the burdens of his ancestors. When meaning disintegrates, in a brush with death or DMT or demons, a space opens up between the faces for new arrangements to arise.

$$\Omega$$

When not speaking for other powers, the prophets represent the voice of the Manipulator, whose executive offices are the lobes of the Logos beneath the forehead.[114] As people we ask ourselves searching moral questions that go beyond the amoral sphere of YHWH and the other powers, beyond our innate instincts and learned associations; and in the space of 'what if...?' rather than 'what is' we generate ideals for humanity to strive towards. We make choices that direct the narrative, restraining the powers where necessary. As the angel of YHWH can overrule El Shadday's impulse, so can the Manipulator overrule YHWH's emotional overreactions – if his challenge is well-worded. When the superego is being super it assumes its proper place at the top of the pyramid with its eye wide open, illuminating. Reaching beyond the known, the prophet on the mountain steadies his hand and readies his pen to take down the mega-words.

The prophetic imagination can be hyperbolic, sometimes projecting visions of terror and the destruction of the capital into the future, at other times describing wildly optimistic visions of mankind beating swords into ploughshares in some unspecified coming era.[115][116] The early prophets tend to address local problems, foreseeing the evil approaching, discerning plotlines emerging. They issue warnings advising people to mend their ways before it is too late. Later prophets picked up a wider perspective in Babylon after the edge of the tribe had been punctured by defeat and exile. They are frequently thought-provoking, but their predictions are a little more hit and miss. Nebuchadnezzar didn't destroy Tyre, despite Ezekiel's prediction.[117] The Nile never dried up, and nor was Egypt made "utterly waste and desolate".[118] YHWH could also exaggerate in the mouths of His prophets.[119] He promised that He would drive the Jebusites from the land "without fail", but when the time came "the children of Judah could not drive them out: but the Jebusites dwell with the children of Judah at Jerusalem unto this day".[120] YHWH is subject to limitations, like everything else in this world:

> And YHWH was with Judah; and he drave out the inhabitants of the mountain; but could not drive out the inhabitants of the valley, because they had chariots of iron.[121]

The emanations are neither omnipotent nor omni-anything else, like the people whose heads they inhabit, and it is probably just as well. They do their best to carry out Their threats and promises, though that is occasionally beyond even Them. I can't say I'm much better. I do my best to keep the commandments, but sometimes, if I'm all out of bagels, I think 'screw it!' and use unleavened bread to offer the sacrificial blood.

Another development in the wake of the destruction of Jerusalem was that YHWH had previously dealt with the Children of Israel collectively, using the prophet as the go-between, but with Job He targets an individual. A new name of power is introduced for the purpose:

> Now there was a day when the sons of Elohim came to present themselves before YHWH, and Satan came also among them [...] And YHWH said unto Satan, "Hast thou considered my servant Job, that there is none like him in the earth, a perfect and an upright [YSR] man, one that feareth Elohim, and escheweth evil?"[122]

Satan (literally 'the adversary') destroys Job's wealth and family with a series of disasters.[123] He afflicts him "with sore boils from the sole of his foot unto his crown", but even then Job refuses to curse YHWH, who is a part of him as much as any other, and only a fool would curse his own ringpiece when it was smelly.[124] To Job's credit, he doesn't buckle either. He is bold with YHWH, seeking to "come before him like a prince" and state his case.[125] In the final showdown he lives up to the virtuous name of *YSRAL* by maintaining his upright (*YSR*) posture:

> "Behold, He will kill me; I have no hope. Nevertheless,
> I will maintain my ways before Him."[126]

Job realised, as Frankl realised under the boot of the Nazis, that we retain a degree of freedom even in the most challenging situations. Standing firm against the terror and torment of the adversary and his master, Job's autonomy is revolutionary. It may have been too revolutionary for the KJV, which neutered him in translation of the line above, making him a paragon of faith rather than defiance:[127]

> "Though He slay me, yet will <u>I trust in Him</u> [sic]: but I
> will maintain mine own ways before Him."[128]

Job's luck reverses and his wealth is returned to him – multiplied to 14,000 sheep, 6,000 camels, 1,000 oxen, 1,000 she-asses, seven sons and three daughters. He also wins an even greater victory, because his impeccable defence proves to be a game-changer. YHWH retires from the pitch, and His whole team goes with Him. From that moment to the end of the OT, no godname says anything at all.[129]

Ω

The balance of power shifts to its extreme with Job, and echoes of his radical autonomy persist in Talmudic legends. In one tale the rabbis argued all day over the kosher status of an oven, leaving Rabbi Eliezer in a minority of one refusing to yield to the majority position.[130] Eventually a tree intervened, uprooting itself to show its support for him, but the leader of the majority insisted that "No proof can be brought from a carob tree". A river joined the protest by flowing uphill, and the walls of the debating house began to collapse in crumbling solidarity, but these unlikely partisans were also disqualified. Finally a divine voice called out in Rabbi Eliezer's favour, but "Rabbi Joshua stood up and protested":

"'The Torah is not in heaven!' [Deuteronomy 30:12].
We pay no attention to a divine voice because long ago
at Mount Sinai You wrote in your Torah at Mount Sinai,
'After the majority must one incline'. [Exodus 23:2]"

Some time later, Elijah in heaven was asked "What did the
Holy One do at that moment?":

"He laughed, saying, 'My children have defeated Me,
My children have defeated Me'."

Mankind has absolute autonomy to be pushed by the powers
or pulled by his goals, and this is our gift and our curse. We
can hold back the blind forces of domination and tribalism
in the name of the Logos, or we can form a bad consensus
among ourselves. We can even impose it upon everybody else,
sidelining and incarcerating the opposition whilst celebrating
our democratic principles. We can hang on to them until the
trees have gone and the water has flowed away, until the walls
begin to crumble.

Demokratia is 'people power' in Greek, though ballot
box democracy may not be the most efficient way to apply
it. In Hebrew, the godname YHWH Tz'vaot has a similar
etymology; *tzava* is 'a mass of persons' and YHWH is a focused
manifestation of power.[131] Translated as "the Lord of Hosts" in
the KJV, the power of the collective is mighty indeed as the
many-handed mega-mind or the lynch mob. Occasionally,
when things get really bad, the ballot box might exercise
some aspect of that power, as when Hitler took the helm of
a humiliated nation. Social forces directly affect the workings
of the human brain to induce conformity (see page 37), and
they are as dangerous and as powerful as the other powers
driving an individual. Politics is the art of manipulating these
forces. When we do not face and engage the power of other
people, and do not organise and energise the people around us
concerning the things we care about, we merely abdicate that
power to someone else more power-hungry.

Our words are things of power, both for good and for evil. They stir powerful emotions that lead people to great acts of heroism in times of crisis; witness the legendary bravery of the tommies in the trenches, flinging themselves on grenades to save their friends. All logic and the Logos aside, the front line is a place of simple dualisms: us or them and live or die. YHWH, the god of love and war, moves us emotionally and profoundly, and that makes us vulnerable to manipulation and the god of the mob. The jargon of solidarity provokes pre-rational, tribalistic sentiments, and we 'stand shoulder to shoulder' and 'support the boys' of our tribe or country, our creed or colour or class, or whatever we define as ours when we divide ourselves out. Hopelessly romantic, we are hardwired to serve our communities with selfless and ruthless obedience. Those tommies went willingly to their deaths by the million as declining empires struggled over markets. Lenin was as eloquent as Rabbi Joshua, and surpassed even Moses in thoroughness with his massacres:

> I have been wondering and concerned about the slowing of action against Kazan [...] You have a real opportunity to completely destroy a [class] enemy by artillery fire. In my view there is no need to feel sorry for cities [and their citizens], and postpone it any further, because of the necessity of merciless extermination.[132]

It wasn't a lack of principles that led to the Red Terror; the principles were formally and fastidiously laid out in the articles of working groups such as the Plenipotentiary Commission of the All-Russian Central Executive Committee of the Bolshevik Party for the Liquidation of Banditry in the Governorate of Tambov.[133] The world revolution that had seized Lenin's imagination was his guiding principle, and it justified any number of atrocities.

Bolshevism is a constellation of principles, as are Nazism and neo-conservatism, as are humanism and pacifism. Anarchy, by definition, has <u>no</u> over <u>arch</u>-ing principles, no code to defer to, no rules carved into megaliths. Nothing is fixed, and there is nothing for the mind to relax into, so the Manipulator has to assess each moral challenge in its own right and context. Associations are bound by co-operative principles that associates agree upon, and run along lines that can be rewritten, or people can disassociate and go elsewhere (but for the fact that everywhere else is controlled by the archons, for the time being). Anarchy might not solve all the problems in the world – that is a lot to ask for – but it opens up an empty space where possibilities can be experimented with. It works if it is worked at, as much as anything can work, on a small scale in the belly of the beast at least. The anarchistic Free Territory of the Ukraine ran successfully and inclusively for three years with a population of seven million, until it was crushed by Tsarists.[134] Anarchist societies were the norm for most of human history, and recent centuries provide several examples of large-scale experiments in anarchy where production and distribution, education, transport, hospitals, communications and rubbish collection all ran satisfactorily for several years.[135] They didn't collapse through mismanagement or infighting. They were crushed by nationalists, communists, fascists or flag-waving killers of some persuasion or other.

Consensus collectivism is not conducive to the ends of empire, and in the absence of any sustained challenge our war gods continue to demand feeding. The plunder goes on, from the land of milk and honey to lands of oil and money, via land grabs and gold rushes, nutmeg wars and opium wars. Slave raids are more or less consigned to history, and today labour is extracted from sweatshops in former colonies. The opiate supply is controlled by patent lawyers and regulatory bureaus rather than Her Majesty's Royal Navy, but despite more efficient methods it is business as usual as the spirit of the frontier expands into the Amazon and the Arctic circle. The powers don't go away when we imagine that we have outgrown them. According to mythologist Joseph Campbell, they merely become more destructive:

> A devil is a god who has not been recognized. That is to say, it is a power in you to which you have not given expression, and you push it back. And then, like all repressed energy, it builds up and becomes completely dangerous to the position you're trying to hold.[136]

Today's prophets speak the language of statistics, with looming environmental and financial catastrophes to match anything in the Bible. Their info-charts alert us to the errors of our ways, but our rulers are in denial as in the days of Judah, maintaining economic principles through crash after crash as the seas rise. Policy makers are bound to the Market by a thousand schemes, and the Market is a power most fickle, pouring out abundance and destitution by turns. Its covenants and trade contracts are discussed in secret meetings, its engines too big to fail or jail, its wrath placated with sacrifices like any other power, with 12-figure financial bail-outs and 6-figure body counts in the pursuit of disposable minerals.[137] "The thing proceedeth from economic necessity," cry the operatives at the International Monetary Fund, "we cannot speak unto thee bad or good". And yet, it is the prophet's duty to stand up for himself and his people, even when he has no hope. Doing battle with the idols and abominations around him, and with the powers within him, he discovers new sides to himself.

The subsystems of the brain interact to shape our worlds, first between our ears and then before our eyes, driven by the powers and guided by the conscience. "Who is in charge?" asked Frankl, "The car, the engine, the steering wheel? Or the driver?"[138] YHWH Elohim the Definer squeezes shapes out of the ground, builds up a man and animates him. El Shadday the Sustainer protects and increases him. YHWH the Tribalist integrates him into a greater whole. The serpent raises questions and objections. But Eve picked the fruit. Powers and angels spoke to Abraham, but Abraham bound his son, and Abraham released him. YHWH spoke to the stuttering goatherd, saying "go, and I will be with thy mouth, and teach thee what thou shalt say"; so Moses went and Moses spoke, and Moses climbed Mount Sinai and wrote down the mega-words.[139]

The Manipulator combines letters and words to make names and meaning, transcribing possibilities into rhyme and reason, foreseeing the evil ahead and forging the future. Taking responsibility for his responses, and mastering the powers of perception, of obedience, and of resistance, he becomes a power in his own right, "as the gods" but "knowing good and evil". His is the power of the word and the last word, for he can inhibit the other powers and force something of his own creation into the world. In the revelation on the mountain between heaven and earth in our heads, the whisperer is at our heels and the pen is in our hands. With all that power between our fingers, will we write a story or a law code?

THE BRICKS OF BABYLON

N ANOTHER BEGINNING, everything that had been remembered stepped off the Ark, and Noah's family and furry friends began multiplying enthusiastically:

AND THE WHOLE EARTH WAS OF ONE LANGUAGE, AND OF ONE SPEECH. AND IT CAME TO PASS, AS THEY JOURNEYED FROM THE EAST, THAT THEY FOUND A PLAIN IN THE LAND OF SHINAR; AND THEY DWELT THERE. AND THEY SAID ONE TO ANOTHER, "GO TO, LET US MAKE BRICK, AND BURN THEM THOROUGHLY."

AND THEY HAD BRICK FOR STONE, AND SLIME HAD THEY FOR MORTAR. AND THEY SAID, "GO TO, LET US BUILD US A CITY AND A TOWER..."[1]

Legend recalls that even pregnant women were forced to build, and the sick were cursed for their uselessness.[2] As the tower grew it took ever more effort to carry masonry to the top, and after a time people would weep over a falling brick, but not for a falling person. The building had become more precious than the builders, and there was no end in sight.

"...WHOSE TOP MAY REACH UNTO HEAVEN..."

A 91-meter brick ziggurat rose to dominate the skyline of ancient Babylon and crumbled, but the Hebrew word *levenah* (brick) also describes a slab for inscribing information.[3] Hundreds of thousands of clay tiles have survived, pressed with cuneiform script and fired to fix credit notes, political treaties and other contracts beyond argument.[4] Among them are copies of one of the world's oldest law codes, composed by King Hammurabi of Babylon in the 18th century BC, and it was also engraved into an obelisk that stood in the Great Ziggurat. Today the Hammurabi Code stands in the Louvre among the loot of Napoleon, another conqueror with a law code and a complex. Bastard sons of the Babylonian god-king have claimed jurisdiction over territories across the planet, wherever generals have invaded, wherever presidents have presided laying down new laws upon old with slime between them.

"...AND LET US MAKE A NAME [SM], LEST WE

*BE SCATTERED ABROAD
UPON THE FACE OF THE
WHOLE EARTH.* "[5]

The Lord God YHWH Elohim forms clay into living, fluid beings; the lords of men fixed clay into brick and burned it thoroughly. In Babel they were eager for something that would retain its integrity, and keep them from being scattered to the winds of an uncertain world, but a structure too rigid strangles the life growing within; Milgram's nightmare begins, and people start dropping from the scaffolding. *Solve et coagula.* That which comes together shatters apart, thank the Lord, who visited Babel to spread confusion and diversity.[6]

"GO TO, LET US GO DOWN…"[7]

…said YHWH (to someone or other)…

*"…AND THERE CONFOUND
THEIR LANGUAGE,
THAT THEY MAY NOT
UNDERSTAND ONE
ANOTHER'S SPEECH."
So YHWH SCATTERED
THEM ABROAD FROM
THENCE UPON THE FACE
OF ALL THE EARTH: AND
THEY LEFT OFF TO BUILD
THE CITY…*

In Akkadian, the language of Babylon, *bab ili* is 'the gate of gods'.[8] The Hebrews saw things differently, and cursed Babel with a pun:

...THEREFORE IS THE NAME OF IT CALLED BABEL [BBL]; BECAUSE YHWH DID THERE CONFOUND [BLL] THE LANGUAGE OF ALL THE EARTH...

The name Babylon has been synonymous with corruption for millennia, and is shouted at the police even today, because names stick. Things change, events slip by and meaning slides; but names stick, and laws stick. What's in a law, that represents nothing that exists or could exist, and yet is made with pretensions at eternity? A law of nature can't be broken, whereas civil laws exist by virtue of the fact that they can be. Master physicists distil out elegant natural laws from a mass of data, such as $E=mc^2$; lawmakers do the opposite, spawning complexity. With 37,000 acts, 13,000 court verdicts and 52,000 international standards the last time I checked, translated into 24 tongues and fully understood by no one, the Tower of Brussels continues to grow even as the foundations are breaking up, confounded as in the days of Babel.[9] On the Eve of the feast of St. John the Baptist 2016, a week ago at the time of writing, half of the UK enraged the other half by electing to leave the European Union, as polling stations flooded, as lightning raked the city and a fire engine crashed into a bus.[10] With a tax code of 6,000 pages administered from offices registered in Panama, the city of London is no less confounded.[11] [12] Structures founded upon contradiction rise precariously towards the heavens, casting long shadows; but brick is brittle, and what doesn't bend must break.

...AND FROM THENCE DID YHWH SCATTER THEM ABROAD UPON THE FACE OF ALL THE EARTH.

Ω

DEUTERANARCHY

How do you say, "We are wise, and the Torah of YHWH is with us"? But, behold, the false pen of the scribes has worked falsely.[1]

- Jeremiah 8:8

N THE BEGINNING it isn't obvious where the Israelites come from. Meticulously kept historical records from the Egyptian libraries mention no great flight of slaves or series of plagues, and archaeological digs at sites from the stories of the wilderness have turned up nothing to suggest Israelite encampments.[2][3] The liberator of the tribe was adopted as a baby from a casket on the Nile, and it seems that something of the story was adopted too because Osiris was also found in a casket on the Nile.[4] Snakes hissed in Sumerian gardens.[5] An Assyrian god warned a man to build a boat for the coming flood.[6] Even the name 'Hebrew' may be adopted, from Akkadian, where *habaru* means 'to migrate'.[7]

People called *habiru/hapiru/apiru* are mentioned across the Middle East, starting from before the date given for Abraham's birth, in Mesopotamian, Sumerian, Hittite and Egyptian inscriptions.[8][9][10] They shared neither ethnicity nor language, nor any obvious cultural traits such as given names; they used names that were common in their home cities.[11] They are reported as slaves, labourers, outlaws, mercenaries and dependants of the temple, and invariably in a derogatory manner (as migrants on welfare are in some sections of the media today). At this point in history they may be better described as a social class rather than a nation.

In the cities of the ancient world, when crop failures or other pressures meant that the poorest of the poor could no longer support themselves, one of their few options was to unite under a charismatic leader and strike out to live by plunder. Moses' stories evoke such a leader, emerging from obscurity in a time of locust swarms and cattle plagues, leading the downtrodden to freedom by way of pillage.[12] Whoever they were to begin with, by the 15th century BC Habiru groups are reported in the politically volatile zone of Canaan, between the Assyrian and Egyptian empires, sometimes serving as mercenaries for client kings loyal to one or other emperor.[13] They supported local independence movements in the late 14th century BC, as noted in letters fired into clay and sent by King Abdi-Heba to his overlord in Egypt:

> All the lands are at peace with one another, but I am at war with them [...] They [the Habiru] have given my enemies food, oil and any other requirement. So may Pharaoh provide archers.[14]

The archers were never dispatched, and Abdi-Heba's mountain stronghold fell; today it is called Jerusalem.[15] One archaeologist sums up the evidence from the late 13th century:

> There was no sign of violent invasion or even the infiltration of a clearly defined ethnic group. Instead, it seemed to be a revolution in lifestyle. In the formerly

sparsely populated highlands from the Judean hills in
the south to the hills of Samaria in the north, far from
the Canaanite cities that were in the process of collapse
and disintegration, about 250 hilltop communities
suddenly sprang up. Here were the first Israelites.[16]

The Children of Israel were like Israel himself, a story that
caught on and survived while other cultures were buried beneath
the sand, their stories buried in footnotes. Tales percolated
around family hearths and sacrificial fires in the hilltops,
absorbing the distilled wisdom of lifetimes as they were retold.
It is thought that legends Abraham became known for were
native to Shechem, whereas Isaac's were from Beersheba and
Jacob's from Bethel.[17] They were drawn through the land with
the wanderings of minstrels, and weaved together into oral
cycles for many generations before they were written down.

As legendary time fades into history there are twelve(ish)
Jewish(ish) tribes living in the land, worshipping a variety of
godforms, with snake gods at Shechem and the cult of the bull
at Bethlehem, and "Yahweh […] and his Asherah" among the
pantheon.[18] [19] YHWH left His consort Asherah for a solo career
that would bring the tribes together into a commonwealth, with
common stories, common ancestors and communal festivals
throughout the year. That lore and Logos also separated them
from other cultures, with rituals like circumcision and taboos
against eating the staple food of the pig-rearing heathens of
Canaan.[20] Pig bones disappear from the archaeological record
of the highlands in the 12th century BC.[21]

Community leaders in the commonwealth were elders and
heroes, the women as well as men remembered as the judges.
Despite the name, the judges didn't oversee lawcourts; they
used their judgement to dispense advice. They had the wisdom
of their oral traditions to consult, along with their incenses and
their divinatory devices, and they were thought to be divinely
inspired, for "when YHWH raised them up judges, then YHWH
was with the judge".[22] None of the stories recalling the period

mention a law code, nor any authority to make general demands upon the behaviour of the population:[23]

> In those days there was no king in Israel: every man did
> that which was right in his own eyes.[24]

Those days came to an end in the late 11th century, when Saul became the first king of an expanding kingdom. "They have rejected me, that I should not reign over them," moaned YHWH, jealous as ever, warning that the royal house would grow corrupt (he was right, of course).[25] The Children of Israel became subjects subject to the king's orders, but still there was no law code. Problems in the community were resolved by the community, and when difficult cases were referred to the king he was expected to apply his wisdom, not bylaws. Solomon famously resolved a dispute by offering to divide a contested baby between two women with his sword.[26]

The first centuries of the monarchy were theologically promiscuous times. Hundreds of idols have been discovered from the time of the first temple, half of them in Jerusalem itself near the temple mount.[27] Saul's son was called Eshbaal (Ba'al exists), his grandson was Meribaal (Ba'al rewards).[28] When the songs and stories of the Israelites began to be crystallized out of the oral tradition into letters, probably under David the second king or Solomon the third, the writers assumed a plurality of gods.[29] In Psalm 86, for example,

> Among the gods (elohim) there is none like unto thee,
> Adonai.[30]

Many centuries later the name Adonai would be adopted as a euphemism for YHWH, to avoid uttering the terrible name when reading the scroll aloud, and this is still the case today.[31] Back in the day, however, it was a distinct godname in its own right, the best of all the gods according to the Psalmist. This type of theology is called monolatry. It is a kind of monogamous paganism where only one god is worshipped, fundamentally different to monotheism where only one god exists.

Along with the Psalms, stories about great men and the gods that inspired them were collected together into a document that scholars call the Jahwist.[32] It is the foundational layer of the Bible, making up the bulk of Genesis and the first half of Exodus, and its theology is consistently monolatristic. "Against all the gods of Egypt I will execute judgement," boasts YHWH, and after the escape Jethro comments, "Now I know that YHWH is greater than all gods".[33] This YHWH was a tribal god, not a universal god; other tribes had their abominations to worship and their pigs to eat. YHWH was also not much of a lawgiver, stipulating no general commandments beyond food taboos and ritual norms. Jahwist morality is framed in terms of narrative, where "whoso sheddeth man's blood, by man shall his blood be shed".[34] This reliance on fate, rather than temporal authority and law, resembles other poetic world scriptures such as the *Tao Te Ching*:

> Killing itself should be the province of the great executioner alone.
>
> Trying to take his place and kill is like cutting wood in the place of the master carpenter:
>
> The odds are you'll hurt your own hand.[35]

The Jahwist document has been broken up with material from later centuries, including layers of law and priestcraft that stand out in embarrassing aspect compared to the mastery of older work. What remains is, to my mind, the work of unfathomably skilled poets, with advanced techniques of inspiration and penetrating insight into the secrets of mind and cosmos. They are the literary equivalents of the pyramid builders who worked with pinpoint accuracy to raise structures rich in secret ratios and perfect alignments.[36] [37]

The kings of Judah prospered 3,000 years ago, in the days when a royal dowry could be paid in the foreskins of Philistines slain.[38] The kingdom expanded until Solomon "passed all the kings of the land in riches", collecting 25 tons of gold per year from the provinces, resting his slippers on a golden footstool, tended by "700 wives, princesses, and 300 concubines" from the cities under his dominion.[39][40][41] When the old oligarch died, the northern tribes begged his heir King Rehoboam to lower their taxes. His advisors gave counsel:

> "Thus shalt thou say unto them, 'My little finger shall be thicker than my father's loins. For whereas my father put a heavy yoke upon you, I will put more to your yoke: my father chastised you with whips, but I will chastise you with scorpions.'"[42]

This was advice fit for a king like King Rehoboam, and he responded accordingly; so "Israel rebelled against the house of David".[43] As with the Boston Tea Party 27 centuries later, the tax revolt rapidly developed into a war of independence. The Holy Land was divided for over two centuries, during which time the northern kingdom, called Israel, produced a text to rival the southern kingdom of Judah's Jahwist.[44] It draws on different oral traditions, and has its own angle on the same episodes. Though the documents were later woven together, the different styles of the Hebrew betray their diverse origins, as do other details; the action happens in buildings rather than tents, for example, with gates and "the stranger that is within thy gates".[45] Again the poetry is exquisite, but its style is more refined and philosophical, with sublime meditations like the encounter between Moses and I AM THAT I AM (see page 147).[46] Its deity is more detached, working behind the scenes. He is referred to as Elohim until the chapter where YHWH is introduced to Moses, so this document is called the Elohist.

It appears that the Elohist's Isaac gets it in the neck, poor chap, and that's the end of him; but fortunately for Isaac the Jahwist's YHWH likes to intervene, and the story of His intervention with a ram caught in a thicket made it into the final cut.[47] All the Jahwist miracles are well-timed naturalistic events like this, as well as pestilences, earthquakes, and strong east winds. Elohist miracles are different, going beyond the natural into the supernatural, with Moses producing water from a rock, for example, and his rod turning into a snake (travellers' tales from early last century report snake-charmers in Cairo performing a similar trick, alongside speculation that the snakes had been hypnotized rigid beforehand.)[48] [49]

Ω

With a powerful rival in the south, the northern kingdom sought alliances with its neighbours. Suzerain treaties were commonly struck between greater kings (suzerains) and lesser kings, pressed into a pair of clay tablets that were fired and divided between the parties. They followed a standard format, and that format seems to have influenced a couple of chapters of the Elohist. It begins with the name and title of the suzerain, and the history between the parties. Next, the terms of the contract are listed. Finally come the blessings to result if the agreement is honoured, and the curses to befall the party that breaks it.[50]

Both the Jahwist and the Elohist contribute stories of a covenant between Moses and YHWH, but only the Elohist version follows the format of a suzerainty treaty. It begins with the standard three-part introduction of name, title and historical summary:

> "I am YHWH [1] thy God [2], which have brought thee
> out of the land of Egypt, out of the house of bondage
> [3]."[51]

The terms that follow are the ethical Decatesseranom, commonly called "the ten [sic] commandments", with blessings and curses appended to the end of some of them.[52] The first section is about man's relationship with God, as was the covenant with Noah, the covenant with Abraham, and the Jahwist covenant with Moses. The second section is different. It is a series of civil laws concerned with relationships between people, about honouring parents, murder, adultery, theft and lying in court. These laws resemble nothing in the Jahwist, where justice is left to fate and the poetry of the cosmos, but they all have close analogues in the Hammurabi Code.[53] Whether the Decatesseranom is derived from Hammurabi, or from another related law code, is not clear. What is clear is that civil law is a completely new addition to the Israelite corpus, written in a new literary style and reflecting new political contingencies. The final section goes beyond Hammurabi's concern with property, hybridizing it with the native religious obsession with taboo to prohibit coveting, and thereby instigate a program of mind control.

War had split the tribes and war would bring them together again, in 722 BC when the northern kingdom was destroyed by Assyria. The ten(ish) tribes were scattered and lost, and a flood of refugees arrived in Jerusalem bearing books. It seems that the Elohist and Jahwist documents were combined at this time, and the resulting hybrid posed a problem to the Jerusalem priesthood.

The Israelite priests were Levites, a special caste and perhaps the only tribe with some connection to Egypt. They alone took Egyptian names, they performed the rite of circumcision as practised among Egyptian nobles, and they mixed the psychedelic secrets known to the Egyptian apothecaries, so it seems that if an exodus happened to anyone it happened to them.[54 55 56] Their oral traditions traced their lineage back to Aaron, the original High Priest, which gave them special status as ritualists for hire and allowed them to live from tithes in a more-or-less mutually beneficial spiritual protection racket. Political developments shifted the balance, however, as political power began to concentrate under a king in the capital, and the Jerusalem priesthood grew rich and influential alongside him. Feuds that festered were written into Elohist legends that arrived with the refugees, slating Aaron and fingering him as the idolater responsible for the Golden Calf. It seems that these insults were retained when the texts were combined.[57]

The Jerusalem priesthood responded by writing their own scroll that retold the entire history of the Children of Israel, threading the Levite clan into legend with genealogies begetting their way back to illustrious ancestors.[58] It also inserts priests into day-to-day affairs wherever possible. To resolve a case of suspected adultery, for example, a priest would take some dust from the floor of the Tabernacle (which was off-limits to non-Levites), and mix it with water for the accused to drink:

> Then it shall come to pass, that if she be defiled, and have done trespass against her husband, that the water that causeth the curse shall enter into her, and become bitter, and her belly shall swell, and her womb shall rot.[59]

A cynic might wonder what other powders the master herbalists might have mixed into the dust behind the veil of the ancient laboratory . It would surely have looked impressive when a priest announced the dishonour of the accused and her womb answered promptly by aborting.

The Priestly document would end up alongside the hybrid Jahwist-Elohist text, making up most of Leviticus and Numbers and contributing verses elsewhere.[60] It is dated to anywhere between the 8th and 6th centuries BC, and may have been added to at various points over that period. Some or maybe all of the sources contain material from different centuries, and debate continues over dates, details and attributions of verses, how many writers contributed to each source, what agendas they represented, and the influence of the redactors that edited it all together. The Priestly text is particularly eclectic, including genealogies that read like the phone book, an assembly guide for a flat-pack Tabernacle, and also the sublime poetry of Genesis 1.[61] That chapter's linguistic and thematic similarities to the Babylonian creation story of *Enuma Elish* suggest that they both arise from an oral composition in an older language that may date back to the Bronze Age or earlier.[62] Another Priestly addition is the name of El Shadday.[63] The Jahwist originally marked Abraham's covenant using the godname YHWH Yireh, where *yireh* is connected to 'seeing', with a nuance of watching out or seeing to things.[64] The *Strong's Concordance* biblical dictionary translates it as "Jehovah will see (to it)", with the same soft and spiky nuance of El Shadday (see page 101).[65]

Like a Spanish colonial cathedral built on the ruins of an Inca temple, the Priestly account has its own majesty and beauty, but on close inspection the workmanship is vastly inferior to that of the foundations. Still, the priests possessed profound knowledge about the nature of the powers, as one might imagine given their position and the neuro-techniques they employed. They had a great deal of influence over the lives of their charges, especially with their new document. They also had plenty of freedom to decide how they would wield their power.

Ω

As Assyria was laying waste to the northern kingdom of Israel, King Hezekiah was busy smashing the shrines of his own kingdom of Judah in a brutal religious reformation.[66] Things slid backwards over the next few generations, but his great-grandson King Josiah restarted the campaign in 621 BC with a new trick up his sleeve:[67]

> The High Priest said unto Shaphan the scribe, "I have found the Book of the Law in the House of YHWH."[68]

One might imagine that finding the law of the prophet of YHWH in the Temple of YHWH would have been no great surprise, but apparently the High Priest was astonished. King Josiah "rent his clothes", and then began a massacre that obliterated the religious traditions of the countryside, beginning with the priests who burned incense to idols.[69] [70] He destroyed shrines to Ba'al, to the sun and the moon, and "the high places [...] which Solomon the king of Israel had builded for Ashtoreth the abomination of the Zidonians, and for Chemosh the abomination of the Moabites, and for Milcom the abomination of the children of Ammon." Ashtoreth is YHWH's old flame Asherah, now recast as the abominable ex.

> And he slew all the priests [...] and filled their places with the bones of men [...] And all the abominations that were spied in the land of Judah and in Jerusalem, did Josiah put away, that he might perform the words of the law which were written in the book.[71]

It isn't known what laws "the Book of the Law" contained, but since it necessitated the destruction of all the "high places" in the land except the Jerusalem temple, it seems that it included Deuteronomy's command to maintain only one specified holy place:

> "Thither shall ye bring all that I command you; your burnt offerings, and your sacrifices, your tithes [...] Take heed to thyself that thou offer not thy burnt offerings in every place that thou seest."[72]

If Moses uttered that decree then the first three kings were entirely ignorant of it; they sacrificed at various shrines and no one rebuked them, nor did the ground swallow them up.[73] Deuteronomy commands that "thou mayest not eat within thy gates the tithe of thy corn, or of thy wine, or of thy oil, or the firstlings of thy herds or of thy flock"; all of this would have to be blessed and tithed (i.e. taxed) at the Jerusalem temple first.[74] The scheme centralized the cult and the economy, ensuring that a constant stream of economic resources would flow into the capital. A comparable centralizing tendency has re-emerged in the modern era, with international standards and free trade legislation imposed upon local economies, allowing multinationals with their own tax arrangements to pool resources and redistribute them around the globe.

Deuteronomy's laws focus on many areas of concern to a centralized ruling class, such as property, debt, witness testimony and assault:

> When men strive together one with another, and the
> wife of the one draweth near for to deliver her husband
> out of the hand of him that smiteth him, and putteth
> forth her hand, and taketh him by the secrets: then thou
> shalt cut off her hand, thine eye shall not pity her.[75]

Assault is of concern to everyone, of course, because no man wants his secrets seized; but note that this is not Bonnie and Clyde tag-teaming someone. She is defending her husband, trying to deliver him from a beating in progress, and she would lose her hand for her fidelity.

Laws are made to formalize and standardize behaviour, taking from the Manipulator the problem of choosing appropriate responses to situations, and giving it to the Categorizer to perform automatically. Laws define chunks of life in terms of 'what', cutting away the 'why', the troubling questions that separate humans from other apes, and this necessarily introduces biases. The assault law in Deuteronomy rules against the integrity of the family unit, and it also makes the context of the fight arbitrary. This is also the case with modern assault laws, which protect bailiffs as they evict London families on behalf of transnational property conglomerates.[76] In Bristol the law protected riot coppers defending a new Tesco that was built after 96% of polled locals opposed it.[77] Law interferes with people who organize associations at the local level to protect their own interests.

Deuteronomy consistently favours property owners over injured parties. If an ox gores someone, for example, the owner would only be culpable if (i) the beast had a history of aggression and (ii) it hadn't been tied up – so never, unless they were reckless enough to let an animal maim a second victim.[78] The Hammurabi Code made exactly the same ruling, illustrating with exactly the same example. Various biblical laws are identical to Babylonian laws in defining crimes and assigning punishments. Even the quintessential statement of

OT morality, "breach for breach, eye for eye, tooth for tooth", had a close parallel in Babylon:[79]

> If a man put out the eye of another man, his eye shall be put out [...]
>
> If he break another man's bone, his bone shall be broken.
>
> If a man knock out the teeth of his equal, his teeth shall be knocked out.[80]

Unless YHWH is borrowing Hammurabi's material, laws have been adopted in a series of waves going back centuries as the Israelite land flipped between suzerains. The Elohist contributes the ethical Decatesseranom, and "eye for eye" is from the Priestly account. The largest chunk of law was imported with the last of the sources, the Deuteronomist, which makes up the whole of Deuteronomy and a few lines elsewhere.[81]

Like a Roman settlement built on more ancient ruins, with exquisitely carved prehistoric blocks scavenged and jammed into shabby fortress walls, the juxtaposition of styles in the OT highlights the poverty of the Deuteronomist's construction. The books following Deuteronomy (Joshua, Judges, Samuel and Kings) make up the so-called 'Deuteronomistic History', and were written as part of the same project.[82] They revise Israelite history according to the assumption that everything that ever went wrong was because of the idolatrous traditions of the land – not, say, because of the rapacious greed of the royal house. We see something similar in the politics of austerity today, where slipping standards in UK schools are blamed on "the shackles of local bureaucracy", rather than 25% cuts to education following an economic crash caused by colossal greed and fiscal mismanagement by central government.[83]

Deuteronomy and the Deuteronomistic History offer a fascinating insight into the politics of control, written down plainly in an era when spin doctors spun simpler webs. There's no memorable poetry to recommend these books; their function is purely to justify Josiah's reforms. Where they touch upon spiritual matters it is usually to prohibit traditional practices, condemning one "that useth divination, or an observer of times, or an enchanter, or a witch, or a charmer, or a consulter with familiar spirits, or a wizard, or a necromancer".[84] Regarding the wise and good and not remotely pagan King Solomon, the First Book of Kings explains his uncharacteristic plunge into abomination as the result of dementia and bad women:

> For it came to pass, when Solomon was old, that his
> wives turned away his heart after other gods.[85]

According to the Deuteronomistic History, the very existence of Moses' law had been completely forgotten about until the High Priest rediscovered it in the temple (down the back of the sofa when he was looking for his *kaneh bosem*, no doubt).[86] Josiah's Stalinist-style reign of terror is glorified as "that which was right in the sight of YHWH"; but if so then His good will didn't last long.[87] Josiah was killed by an Egyptian arrow, and his successor was deposed by Egypt. The next was an Egyptian vassal, who was killed when the ascendant empire of Babylonia invaded, and the king after him was deposed within months.[88] Nebuchadnezzar chose the following king, who rebelled after nine years, so his overlord had his children murdered in front of him and then had him blinded, bringing the Israelite monarchy to a gruesome end a mere 35 years after the reformation. Jerusalem was razed to the ground, and the urban intelligentsia were carried off to Babylon.[89] When Nebuchadnezzar's choice of governor was assassinated a few months after his appointment, most of the remaining population fled to Egypt for fear of reprisals. "Ye-eah we wept when we remembered Zion" sang the exiles "by the rivers of Babylon," in a psalm that was deeply moving even before it was a disco ballad.[90] "How shall we sing the Lord's song in a strange land?" they asked, and indeed they could not. The Israelites had to change their tune.

Ω

The exiles grew old and raised children in the shadow of the Great Ziggurat of Babylon. With the temple destroyed, text became the highest authority, and rabbis in Babylon argued over the implications of verses, noting their decisions for posterity in rulings that are collected in the Talmud and remain binding today. This is the root of 'rabbinical' Judaism and the tradition of legal expertise that would become the Pharisee movement. Things changed radically again around half a century later in 539 BC, just as the original exiles were dying off and memories of Zion were becoming legends of Zion, when Babylon was subjugated by Cyrus the Great of Persia in the greatest conquest the world had ever seen. The captives were liberated, and a portion would be sent back to Jerusalem.

The Israelites were exposed to Zoroastrian ideas for the first time with the conquest, beginning a complex interaction that would develop over centuries. Little is known about how much Cyrus himself was inspired by Zoroastrianism, which was one of many religions syncretized together in his empire. Though ideas that appear in scripture written during and shortly after the exile suggest a Zoroastrian influence, they were not adopted wholesale.[91] Isaiah 45, for example, has YHWH announcing that "I form the light, and create darkness: I make peace, and create evil", which appears to be a direct rejection of Zoroastrian dualism:[92] [93]

> The Origins are two: the Creator and the Destroyer. The Creator is Ohrmazd [Ahura Mazda], from whom all goodness and all light emanates. The Destroyer is the wicked evil Spirit, who is all badness and full of death, wicked and deceiving.[94]

The trouble-making character of Satan first appears as a title in Babylon, and the character is most developed in the Book of Job. His name means 'adversary', though he was not an adversary to YHWH; he was an adversary to Job, but acting in that function as a servant of YHWH and with His permission.[95] The character may have been imported in a modified form. It was not until the 1ˢᵗ century AD and the NT that Satan was rolled into a Zoroastrian-looking amalgamation of everything awful, as "that old serpent, called the Devil, and Satan, which deceiveth the whole world".[96]

In Zoroastrianism, two great moral antipoles are arranged against each other with their armies of angels and demons in a kind of cosmic chess game. They are set to collide in the battle at the end of the world, and everything will come out in the wash afterwards when all the well-behaved folk of history will be resurrected in paradise. This final curtain is called 'the apocalypse' today in vulgar parlance, but it is much different to our neuro-apocalypse, where the curtain lifts for an individual. It is also larger than the kind of community-wide apocalypses which will be the subject of *Apocalypses Past, Present and Personal*. Zoroaster's catastrophic crescendo is a universal event, and while it may be the inevitable last step of a logical progression that begins with a perfectly dualistic cosmology, nothing so global or final is found in pre-exile books of the Bible. There the action was limited to a few thousand miles by the Mediterranean, and the worst the future might hold was pestilence and the sack of the capital. Noah's flood, for example, is not conceived of on a planetary scale; it covered the *eretz*, which is more often translated as 'land' than 'earth'.[97] There was no difference between 'land' and 'earth' in Hebrew, and perhaps no difference in the minds of the people who first spoke it, who lived and died in a landscape that was self-contained except for the occasional caravan rolling through.

The Book of Daniel was the first to feature a global final judgement and resurrection, and it was compiled in around the 3ʳᵈ or 2ⁿᵈ century BC under a Persian dynasty that was more uniformly Zoroastrian than Cyrus'.[98][99] Daniel is also the first to name angels.[100] Rabbis in Babylon developed a hierarchy of angels and demons with close similarities to Zoroastrian entities.[101] One Iranianist describes how,

> Zoroaster was thus the first to teach the doctrines of an individual judgment, Heaven and Hell, the future resurrection of the body, the general Last Judgment, and life everlasting for the reunited soul and body. These doctrines were to become familiar articles of faith to much of mankind, through borrowings by Judaism, Christianity and Islam; yet it is in Zoroastrianism itself that they have their fullest logical coherence.[102]

The revelation of Zoroaster may have been logically coherent in its original language of Avestan, being an Indo-European language like Greek and English that snaps neatly into dualisms.[103] Hebrew doesn't fold that way, however, and the original YHWH was never so categorical about morality. His concern was the good of the tribe, not an ideal of 'goodness'.

The cosmology may be poorly matched with older books of the Bible, but the Israelites were in a new world. While YHWH had served them well for centuries as the toughest of the tribal gods, things changed forever when the columns of His temple were pulled asunder by worshippers of Marduk. Horizons expanded in Babylon, and traditional Yahwism didn't have much left to offer. Something bigger than YHWH and Marduk combined would have made much more sense, a new and improved, broader but shallower monotheistic mega-god in command of the whole world (if still predisposed towards the Israelites). New code was written and old code updated to accommodate the upgrade, with some of the more flagrant monolatristic flourishes edited out. The "divine sons" referring to the gods of different nations were cut from Deuteronomy, as we know from more ancient versions found in the Dead Sea caves.[104] YHWH 2.0 could be served by people from other nations, and so late versions of Jeremiah upgraded Nebuchadnezzar II to the rank of YHWH's "servant", in an edit that sits incongruously alongside the slander he receives elsewhere.[105] Even the hallowed title of Messiah, once reserved for the House of David, was given to a heathen ruler – and without a drop of oil spilled:

> "Thus saith YHWH to his anointed [*mashiyach*], to Cyrus, whose right hand I have holden, to subdue nations before him [...] For Jacob my servant's sake, and Israel mine elect, I have even called thee by thy name: I have titled thee, though thou hast not known me."[106]

Small blasphemies aside, it made political as well as theological sense for the exiles to humour Cyrus with a title, because it was by his leave that they would go free:

> Thus says Cyrus king of Persia, "All the kingdoms of the earth has YHWH the God of heaven given me, and He has appointed me to build a temple for Him at Jerusalem [...] Whoever there is among you of all His people, his God be with him, and let him go up to Jerusalem, which is in Judah, and build the house of YHWH, the God of Israel (He is Elohim)."[107]

The Babylon-born Jews who went met a rural population that had been practising their cults for a couple of generations unmolested by monarchs. Scholars disagree about which lost tribe, displaced population or mixture the Samaritans were, but their bible (which is still used by the few hundred that survive today) has many differences to the normal version. They accepted only Moses as a prophet, and rejected the doctrine of resurrection.[108] Though they offered to help rebuild the temple, their gesture was rejected:

> "Ye have nothing to do with us to build an house unto our God, but we ourselves together will build unto YHWH, God of Israel, *as King Cyrus the king of Persia hath commanded us.*" [outraged italics mine][109]

Instructions given by Cyrus, and preserved in the Bible in his mother tongue of Aramaic, specify the exact dimensions of the temple and format of its rites.[110] The returnees informed Persia that the Samaritans would be troublesome subjects who would raise walls and resist taxes; and meanwhile they secured their own exemptions from "toll, tribute or custom" for "the priests and Levites [...] or ministers of this house of God".[111] The High Priest took charge of the treasury, and a new clerical class was created that would be responsible for tax collection and law.[112] The law code would be approved by the emperor as part of a drive to standardize law across Persian territories. It would be administered in Aramaic, the language of the Imperial court.[113] [114]

Running on the new programming language, YHWH 2.0 was compatible with the Persian mainframe; but it would take generations to debug the old system. The following century, "a ready scribe in the law of Moses" by the name of Ezra was sent "to teach in Israel statutes and judgments [...] [to] them that know them not".[115] Raised and trained at the Persian court, his task was sweetened with "all the silver and gold that thou canst find in all the province of Babylon":[116]

> "And whosoever will not do the law of thy God, *and the law of the king*, let judgment be executed speedily upon him, whether it be unto death, or to banishment, or to confiscation of goods, or to imprisonment." [outraged italics mine][117]

The king was the Persian emperor, of course; Cyrus had forbidden the restoration of the Israelite monarchy.[118] His officer Ezra the Scribe is an exalted figure in Jewish history, and likely the redactor who compiled the sources and tweaked them into something like the final form of the OT.[119] He is traditionally held to be the source of the standard formula of Jewish blessings, which are said after meals and when washing the hands, when seeing a rainbow or a strange animal, and at many more rare and routine moments during the day.[120] All of these prayers begin by namechecking the new mega-god:

> Blessed art Thou, YHWH our Elohim, King of the Universe...

After Agent Ezra came Agent Nehemiah. He was formerly the personal cup-bearer of the emperor, a most intimate servant in a time of intrigue and poisoning, and he likely lost his nuts for the privilege.[121][122] Though castration is neither cool nor kosher, it was obligatory for court attendants like Nehemiah, who had access to the king's harem, and the first Greek OT describes him as "a eunuch".[123] Mighty with another man's chutzpah, Nehemiah the Nutless followed Ezra with a contingent of his master's troops to help fortify Jerusalem.[124] Things had become cosy between political and divine powers under the wing of Persia, after a fraught relationship during the monarchy. Along with imperial law, the cult adopted the emperor of a mega-state spanning nations, races and languages, a mega-god to match his megalomania, and a Messiah complex that would carry over into Christianity and Islam (with the character of the Mahdi).

Scholars disagree over how great the influence of Zoroaster was in the changes that occurred in Babylon. It may be that similar philosophies arose organically and somewhat independently in two religions developing in the same cultural environment, along with almost identical rites of purification and criteria for distinguishing between clean and unclean animals.[125] [126] Whatever their origin, the new doctrines remained unpopular in the Holy Land. In the 1st century AD, the Sadducees still rejected resurrection and the angels, and they made up the majority of the political class in Judea.[127][128] And yet, it was the Habiru-Babylo biblico-rabbinical religion that would survive the turmoils at the beginning of the common era, when Jerusalem was sacked again and the people scattered.

Ω

In the beginning, in the head, where the gods were created, it was enough to appease the powers with daily rituals and seasonal festivals, with blessings at the local shrine to spiritualize the fruits of the field. Things changed in the Promised Land as kings and empires jostled, as treaties were made and tribute was paid. Relationships with the powers driving us and the people around us came to be mediated more and more by authorities further and further away with ever more complex law codes.

In the time of the judges the day ended when the third star could be seen, and the month was over at the first sliver of the new moon. The new moon had to be reported by several witnesses of sound mind and good standing, not any old moon-gazing lunatic, but if testimonies matched up then signal fires were lit to spread the news of the new month and keep everyone in rhythm.[129] The year ended twelve moons after it had started, unless the barley needed more time to ripen, in which case a leap month was inserted. In this way, the lunar year was kept in phase with the slightly longer solar year.

Final decisions on the calendar rested with the judges, and they also handled moral challenges, keeping behviour in order as they kept time in order – with observation and discussion when things were drifting out of phase with custom. If several witnesses of sound mind were raising an issue, and if their testimonies agreed, then it was down to the judges to apply their good judgement. They weren't a caste apart like the Levites, and nor did they speak in strange tongues like the officials appointed by Persia, or like the jargon-spouting justices of the Supreme Court today. They were ordinary members of society distinguished only by their wisdom or their heroism. They were also engaged in tribal life and immediately answerable to the community, unlike leaders today who periodically put on a circus to dazzle voters. The judges had their insights and their incenses, and the resources of the community to draw upon, but they didn't have a law code. Lashes or execution would have been among their options, along with reparations, community service, counselling, threats, or a quiet word with any number of people; but all that could have been decided at the time and in context, in conversation between relevant parties and people well-versed in life and its stories.

Anyone could have been a guardian of the peace in a time before crime, when theft and assault were not felonies but social problems. Sexual violence was not unlawful; it was a public health issue, as it is in many primate societies.[130] The sons of Abraham have been persecuting sex workers ever since Josiah "brake down the houses of the sodomites that were by the house of YHWH" during his reforms, and it is bad news for all concerned as countries that limit access to prostitutes have higher incidences of rape.[131][132]

Perhaps justice under the judges would have been served unfairly sometimes, perhaps even as often as it is today. Maybe in superstitious times an unpopular old spinster might have been drowned when a plague struck the date crop; but is that much worse than Monsanto's indiscriminately insecticidal and currently legal solution? Life without law, with people pursuing their interests as they saw fit, could be a beautifully integrated super-organism or a cauldron of paranoid intrigue. It would depend entirely on the conversations unfolding, but as nasty as things became, at least decisions would remain specific to a given context, not generalized as categories and cemented into legislation. When one in three defendants in the dock in the UK has at least 15 previous offences, is our judiciary serving its citizens, including its criminals, any better than the open-source justice model of 3000 years ago?[133] How long would the people in a more organically managed moral system have endured a society that produced an abundance of serial thieves and rapists, before organizing themselves to tackle the problem?

Far from the signal fires of the Holy Land, the exiles in Babylon began to order the calendar not by observation but with a formula specifying the length of each month and where the leap years would fall in each 19 year period.[134] This kept things cycling neatly, if not perfectly, drifting out of phase at a rate of around half a second per month. Ordering human affairs according to formulas is a more complex matter. In the time of Noah there was only one law, but when someone thrust ten or so laws into the unlikely hands of Moses it began a process without end. Rabbi Simlai derived 613 laws from the Bible, and rabbinical rulings continued to proliferate over the centuries and down to the present as more and more situations arose and were pinned down, as ever more aspects of life were outsourced to the Categorizer:[135]

> See *Minchas Yitzchak* 6:38:3 that after producing a urine sample, the blessing of *Asher Yatzar* is said. It does not matter that it was induced and not completely natural.[136]

Ω

Back in ancient Palestine, governance passed from Persian to Greek to Ptolemaic to Seleucid to Maccabeean and then to Roman control over the next few centuries; and then stories began circulating about a holy man stirring up trouble with the Pharisees. Jesus' ministry lasted three years from his baptism to his death, which is only slightly longer than Sid Vicious's musical career. There were a few tours that hardly anyone saw and all agreed were legendary. There were clashes with the authorities, charges of obscenity and violent public disorder. When a life of confrontation was spectacularly cut short, a legend was born that would change the world forever.

Anarchy in Judea between the Romans, the Pharisees and the Sadducees was a more delicate matter than Anarchy in the UK in 1976, and yet the Galilean preacher gave rabble-rousing speeches and openly resisted the law. He defended those who committed the capital offence of harvesting on the Sabbath, by saying that "the Sabbath was made for man, not man for the Sabbath".[137] He put another capital crime back into context by inviting "he that is without sin" to cast the first stone at a woman accused of adultery. His suggestion punctured a lazy dichotomy, dissipating the power of a mob united in judgemental righteousness, using reason and reflection to break the group up into individuals examining their own lives.[138]

The parables Jesus tells almost invariably ask the listener to think carefully, and often about the morality as opposed to the legality of their actions. Jesus also resurrects the aesthetic of the Jahwist, where retribution is left to fate and "all they that take the sword shall perish with the sword".[139] The Pharisees multiplied the law, but Jesus distilled it down to two principles encapsulating his teaching on spiritual and social behaviour: love God and love your neighbour.[140] Despite all his anti-authoritarianism, however, he was careful to say "think not that I am come to destroy the law [...] but to fulfil/complete" – because Jesus was a better artist than Sid:[141] [142]

> "Ye have heard that it hath been said, 'An eye for an eye, and a tooth for a tooth.' But I say unto you, that ye resist not evil: but whosoever shall smite thee on thy right cheek, turn to him the other also..."[143]

"Turn the other cheek" is invariably spun as a call for a kind of aloof masochism, but observe closely. The passage describes a strike on "thy right cheek", and if the attacker is right-handed that means either a roundhouse punch or a back-handed slap. Given that Judea was a long way from Shaolin, it is presumably the backhander, which was how Roman men and men schooled in Roman ways disciplined their slaves, their wives and other subordinates. The violence is symbolic, damaging only the pride. The strike is first and foremost a sign, and it indicates the direction of the hierarchy. Turning the left cheek is also a sign, and it means that the hierarchy does not apply. It brings the confrontation into a new context, as an interaction between two thinking individuals rather than members of nations or classes acting according to custom. It also forces the oppressor's hand. He must either back down, or make good on his signage with a real act of aggression, fist-to-face and man-to-man this time, and that might have repercussions more concrete than symbology. At the very least it demands that he reflect carefully upon his next move. If the backhander was out of order in the first place, the assailant would have to take himself outside the protection of the law to escalate, as unprovoked violence was a crime in both Roman and Jewish law.[144]

This brilliant provocation means that the law would be fulfilled, just as Jesus promised, but in favour of the rebel taking charge of it rather than the oppressor who habitually relies on it. In certain situations, an activist facing a line of coppers or a civil rights movement vying with the state can gain an advantage by nonviolently goading an oppressor after a careless act of overkill. In 1989, tens of thousands of Leipzigers defied the Stasi by illegally assembling just days after beatings were administered at a similar demonstration in Berlin. They were joined by hundreds of thousands, and the police were in no position to escalate. The limits of the power of the state had been defined, and the Berlin wall would fall within a month.

Our Lord of Discord continues with a reference to another law, this time from Deuteronomy.

> "…And if any man will sue thee at the law, and take away thy coat, let him have thy cloke also…"[145]

The law in question addresses a man who had taken a man's final possession (the coat off his back) as a pledge in lieu of money owed. It decrees that the coat must be restored to him at sundown "that he may sleep in his garment, and bless you: and it shall be righteousness to you before YHWH your God."[146] Rather than waiting patiently for small acts of righteousness before a deified bank-manager, the Redeemer suggests that the debtor give up his undergarment to his creditor as well. A naked man is not in breach of Jewish law, which makes no particular demand about clothing outside of prayer time; but looking upon nakedness is the sin that caused Ham to be cursed.[147] With a simple gesture, the shame of debt slavery is transmuted into the shame of the society that looks on and sanctions it.

> "…And whosoever shall compel thee to go a mile, go with him twain."[148]

Going the extra mile was not originally a trite call to cajole unenthusiastic people into working harder; it was a way of messing with Roman occupiers. Soldiers were legally empowered to force Judeans to carry packs, and it seems that the custom was to demand no more than a distance of one mile.[149] A Judean going a second mile could wrong-foot his oppressor, putting him the uncomfortable position of having to ask something of someone beneath him. Interrupting the routine business of oppression might force the soldier to think of the Judean as something more complex than a packhorse.[150]

With the other cheek, the other mile and the other garment, the master Manipulator pushes laws to logical extremes and flips the hierarchy. He introduces his guide to intelligent resistance with the word *anthistemi*, which is translated as "ye resist not evil"; but the Greek is more nuanced than that. *Anti* is 'against' and *histemi* is 'stand/stand up/rear up/make firm/ be steadfast'.[151] *Anthistemi* does not caution against resistance per se, but the kind of head-to-head, tooth-for-tooth redemptive violence that goes back to Babylon, and was first adopted in a completely different political situation. Jesus explicitly attacks the eyes and teeth of Hammurabi in this passage, because that strategy is a poor one when your enemy has more teeth than you.[152] On a political level, "do not rear up against evil" applies to the type of revolt seen in 66 AD, around the time that these verses were composed, when the People's Front of Judea attacked and wiped out the Roman garrison.[153] The military response from Rome left 100,000 dead or sold into slavery, and was the beginning of the second exile.[154]

Solve et coagula. Stories blended and coagulated where Habiru migrants aggregated, later to be dispersed through the Diaspora where the Hebrews wandered. The Jesus story joined the melting pot of the Hellenistic world, where Jews and Arabs were mixing with Egyptians, Ethiopians, Romans and wise men of the Orient bearing spices. Different groups took the tale in different directions, writing scriptures representing a broad range of ideas, where the favoured apostle might be Mary Magdalene or even Judas, where the serpent could be Sophia herself, "the wisest of all".[155] [156]

The only detailed record of the broad spectrum of early 'Christian' movements is a five volume polemic by Bishop Irenaeus called *On the Detection and Overthrow of the So-Called Gnosis*. The heretics it documents use practices to attain knowledge (*gnosis*) directly, without the need for intermediaries. Some Gnostic circles would wait in silence until someone felt moved to speak, as Quakers do today.[157] Others would choose their prayer leader by lot. In one group, the initiate would be told, "Behold, grace (*charis*) has descended upon thee; open thy mouth and prophesy!"[158] *Charis* is the root of the word 'charisma', but it means more than that. It is an invisible manifestation of divinity that confers spiritual powers to speak with divine authority, to reveal the hidden and cast out sickness. Gnostics were leaving things in the ethereal hands of the Holy Spirit, waiting for inspiration to seize them, taking instructions from visions and voices while lampooning the human authorities that sought to govern them. In the Apocalypse of Peter:[159]

> There shall be others of those who are outside our number who name themselves bishop and also deacons, as if they have received their authority from God. They bend themselves under the judgment of the leaders. Those people are dry canals.[160]

Some scriptures questioned authority all the way up to YHWH Himself, who punished Adam in envy and sent the flood in spite. He was the Demiurge, who demands you "serve Him in fear and slavery all the days of your life", who rules a world where a perfectly innocent man was tortured to death.[161] He was Yaldabaoth, Child of Chaos, emerging limited and ignorant into finity to patrol its edges.[162] [163] Some schools characterized Him as evil, others merely as foolish, but they tended to make a clear distinction between Him and God the

Father of the Gospels.[164] Gnostic texts also proposed feminine powers beyond the Demiurge, including Sophia and the Holy Spirit. The Virgin Birth was not principally a bloody affair in a stable, from a Gnostic perspective. It was the miracle of creation from the feminine power of the Holy Spirit, an immaculate conception in the absence of a fertilizing seed. The Gospel of Philip lampoons the orthodox position:

> Some said, "Mary conceived by the Holy Spirit." They
> are in error. They do not know what they are saying.
> When did a woman ever conceive by a woman?[165]

The Gospel of Mary is a positively feminist book, not only because it makes Jesus' favourite apostle a woman, but also because it directly attacks patriarchy, with Jesus appearing in a vision to tell Mary Magdalene "do not give a law like the lawgiver lest you be constrained by it."[166]

Invisible anarchists and uppity women were among many Gnostic motifs that were not conducive to the ambitions of an expanding empire, so Irenaeus selected which texts would end up in the official canon, as other censors of scripture had done before him. He crafted the messy mop of Jewish-Christian apocalypses into a neat side-parting that would be easier to control, trimming away the lunatic fringe. The very picture of a paternalist protecting his flock, Irenaeus introduced his book with a display of kindly authority, asking "What inexperienced person can with ease detect the presence of brass when it has been mixed up with silver?"[167] As Bishop of Lyon on the main road into Gaul, he oversaw the communication and administration hub of the western empire, so his censored bible would be broadcast across Christendom as it expanded.[168] Anarchy and resistance were cut out.[169] Slavery was retained, along with capitulation to masters "even if they are cruel. Because God is pleased when, conscious of His will, you patiently endure unjust treatment."[170]

Some lines in the new canon facilitated the free expression of imperial power, others militated against rival powers: spiritual presences, disembodied visions and voices. Stories where Christ left no footprints on the sand were out, along with most other stories alluding to a non-material level of reality. Stories where doubting Thomas' hand passes through Christ Arisen were out, and only John's account was included, which doesn't say whether he touched something or not.[171] Church Fathers helpfully declared that he did, despite the fact that the previous verse has Christ walking through a wall, and you don't do that kind of thing in my flat unless you are without a body. Never mind, the mystery was sealed with the Creed, fixing "resurrection in the flesh" (i.e. not in spirit) as an article of faith to be affirmed weekly and questioned on pain of eternal pain. A dream or vision of Christ returning in spirit (i.e. not 'in the flesh') could be a dangerous heresy to admit to, especially if he gave the wrong advice.

Manifestations of charisma at the periphery of the empire were policed by political powers at the centre, and the Holy Spirit was focused through the consecrated hands of an all-male priesthood unsullied by the stain of intimate relations with women. Gnostic groups were stamped out in the 3rd and 4th centuries, and their texts were destroyed (though some were rediscovered in 1945, having been buried in earthenware jars for the interim).[172] In the writings of Paul, upon which the Roman church was built, faith was key to salvation, unlike the Gnostics who favoured knowledge and the Jews who prioritized deeds. Paul addressed the problem of unauthorized prophesy directly:

> If any man think himself to be a prophet, or spiritual,
> let him acknowledge that the things that I write unto
> you are the commandments of the Lord.[173]

Enthusiasts are difficult to control if they are crackling with charisma, convinced that their practices give them direct access to the truth without the mediation of appointed intermediaries. That remains the case today in the science lab today as the battle over the liminal zone of the known continues, and he who pays the piper prints the peer-reviewed paper. As revealed in *Science Revealed*, the most severe scientific censorship of the 20th century focused on the very areas identified by Irenaeus in the 4th century: invisible powers, altered states, the significance of personal experiment where it conflicts with dogma, and matters of authority. His assertion that "it is impossible for anyone to heal the sick if he has no knowledge of the disease of the patients" would not be out of place in a British Medical Association pamphlet.[174]

Solve et coagula; the saviour is corrupted. Rome was Christianized, and a Latinized and polarized Habiru-Babylo bible was reborn Caesarean, laying down the law in Roman letters and cutting up complexity into category. Emperors and the King of the Universe ruled together with the collusion of the clerical class, collecting souls and taxes, surveilling the population through the confessional, accessing the innocence of children from their very first days. In medieval church lore the three wise men of the Orient became three kings, as political power eclipsed wisdom as witness to Christ. Exalting lords and blessing swords, the church legitimized the state's monopoly on power, and also promised an eternity of violence in Hell for the disobedient. Helplessness was fetishized in church iconography, with the baby Jesus, the crucified Jesus, the corpse of Jesus in his mother's arms. The Messiah was whipped and humiliated down the centuries and along church walls through the stations of the cross. Worshippers in the nave continue to behold icons of resignation in every direction as they sing state-approved affirmations of the status quo. A 19th century riff on this perennial theme is *All Things Bright and Beautiful*:

> ...all creatures great and small,
> All things wise and wonderful, the Lord God made them all.
> The rich man in his castle, the poor man at his gate,
> God made them high and lowly and ordered their estate.

Medieval Christians were generally illiterate in their mother tongues, and ignorant of Latin, so what could they have known of the Good News beyond sermonizing and iconography? Latin remained the *lingua franca* of power in law and religion. The categories were and still are defined in Latin in professional fields with designs on omniscience, omnipotence, and omnipresence: the plasmas and placebos of medicine, legions and lieutenants in the military, and debts and deficits in finance. Only with the Reformation and the development of the printing press were some of these hierarchies of power upset, and then charismatics emerged from the Dark Ages once again with gleaming eyes and mouths praising God and freedom in the vernacular.[175] Quakers quaked. Diggers dug. Ranters ranted and Anabaptists rioted, while Rosicrucians and other itinerate initiates spread their heretical experiments in empiricism throughout Europe (more on that wave of novelty in the next book).

Solve et coagula; the salvaged is co-opted again. The heirs of the Protestant Reformation became imperialists in their own right, and today One Nation Under God has military bases spanning the world. Outside of the Bible Belt, Christian scripture doesn't directly influence politics much, and Christian institutions have less power to compel and to punish these days; but culture does not escape millennia of moral and cosmological manipulation unscathed. The emasculated version of "turn the other cheek" has escaped into the secular world as a cornerstone of civil society. More fundamentally, we have been talking about (big G) GOOD and (ghoulish font) EVIL for thousands of years, and this dichotomy has set the terms of the debate – even of all debates. One survey found that 76% of English people believe in good and evil.[176] In TV interviews, people at all points of the political spectrum seem incapable of talking about terrorism without condemning it as 'evil'. Jihadis banging on about America "the Great Satan" are singing from the same hymn sheet, and plenty of people seem to think that drones are evil, or Rupert Murdoch is evil, or their ex-husband is evil. Dualism doesn't solve any of these problems; it just saves us from having to think too deeply about causes, and dodges the troubling questions that separate us from other apes. Evil doesn't require a cause, it simply is. According to Zoroaster and the heirs to his cosmology, Evil will be resolved once and for all by the vigilance and valour of the Good. This cosmology gives rise to the kind of crusader rhetoric common to evangelical Christians and evangelical atheists alike.

A sharp division in morality leads to much that is abhorrent and oxymoronic. One example is the mass-incarceration in the Land of the Free, a country which hosts nearly a quarter of the world's prison population, and where one in 36 of its adult citizens is under correctional supervision (often with voting rights curtailed).[177] Correctional facilities are supposed to make Bad people Good, as the name suggests, but the majority reoffend because the whole idea is simplistic nonsense. Prison cells are the dungeons of a fantasy world inhabited by hordes of orc and knights in shining riot gear. Law has more to do with power than morality. From courtroom theatrics up to multi-bloc trade pacts, the rituals of law are conducted in a formalized jargon that is as foreign to most people as Aramaic was in Jerusalem at the beginning of Persian rule. Law continues to do what the Hammurabi Code was originally intended to do, which is to protect people with property from the problems of inequality. And God forbid you should think about your neighbour getting more ass than you.

Ω

Towers rose and fell over the millennia as crusades swished around the globe, and through it all the Jews kept the ancient texts as they kept the commandments, while Christians kept the faith. Jews wandered between territories, persecuted by law and pogrom, writing between cultures and leaving gifts of wisdom behind – the Kabbalah of Luria, the philosophy of Maimonides, the groundbreaking works of Spinoza, Freud and

300

Einstein. Jews existed on the edge of empire, often as merchants trading between them, money-lenders financing kings where Christians were forbidden to, and also serving kings and sultans as physicians. They remained exposed to the wrath of their neighbours whenever plagues or acts of espionage required a scapegoat, but as brutal as the superstitious Middle Ages were, they were surpassed with the rise of the modern nation state. The French Revolution severed the head from the body politic amid the thud and the blood of the guillotine, and mechanized killing has remained the hallmark of the nation state ever since. Nationalism grew as Bretons, Parisians and others began to identify as French nationals. The young state sought enemies abroad with the Napoleonic wars, and at home with the aliens amongst them, including Jews and Gypsies. Anti-semitism grew alongside nationalism in France and England, and elsewhere as the 19th century wore on and Germany and Italy also unified.

In the new political climate, 'the Jewish question' (i.e. what to do with a people that refuses to assimilate) became a hot topic. The atheist Jew Theodore Herzl answered it with a Jewish version of nationalism, rejecting the traditional Talmudic prohibitions against founding a homeland and ending the exile "ahead of time".[178] There had been small settlements of religious Jews in Palestine since antiquity, but a mass migration had never happened because the Talmud prohibits going to the Holy Land *en masse* "like a wall".[179 180] Secular Jews only began to arrive in Palestine at the end of the 19th century, and rabbis across the Diaspora were horrified. Missionary schemes to encourage an observant lifestyle failed. According to one prominent Hasidic leader, Zionism made "nationalism a substitute for the Torah and the commandments".[181] At the turn of the 20th century, the Chief Rabbi of Jerusalem described a "fearful danger looming on the horizon of Judaism".[182] He was my great great great great uncle:

> The rabbanim should get together and excommunicate the Zionists from the Jewish people. They should forbid their bread, their wine, and intermarriage with

them, just as Chazal did to the Kuthites. I am certain
that if we do not take this step, the Jewish people will
eventually regret it.

In the 20th century, the engines of murder span faster than
ever, and the Jewish death count approached unprecedented
levels. Maybe the twisted logic of trauma explains why one
Zionist leader toured Palestine with an SS commander in
1933, and why another introduced an embargo on food aid to
Polish Jews.[183] [184] Maybe it explains why the Jewish Agency
consistently scuppered initiatives to help European Jews
fleeing the Nazi ovens to anywhere except Palestine (because
"one cow in Palestine was worth more than all the Jews in
Poland", according to one executive).[185] The Lord of Hosts
took up arms to defend the new dichotomy when paramilitary
Zionist forces emerged in the 1930s, with veterans of the
British Army's Jewish Brigade taking a leadership role. This
is in breach of another Talmudic prohibition, on waging war
against sovereign states.[186] One unit called Haganah routinely
tortured and even assassinated religious Jews.[187] Haganah also
authorised the bombing of the King David Hotel by its sister
organisation Irgun (initially called Haganah Beyt), though later
denouncing this act of terrorism that killed 91 people.[188] Even
the Zionist newspaper *Hatsofeh* decried Irgun as an "evil gang
of fascists".[189] Another paramilitary unit called Lehi sought
treaties with Hitler and Mussolini to assist in the mission of
forming a "new totalitarian Hebrew republic".[190] Haganah,
Lehi and Irgun were combined into the Israeli Defence Force,
which continues to kill civilians and seize land today, while
beating religious Jews who oppose it.[191] [192] Lehi members were
given military honours and a special Lehi ribbon by the Israeli
government in 1980.[193]

As in the days of Cyrus, the Jewish narrative was broken
in the catharsis of war and genocide and exile, and reset again
under the auspices of an emerging superpower. Israel is NATO's
closest ally in the Middle East, and the imperial overlord

funding fortified walls built in the Promised Land. Although "the Jewish state" remains something of a kosher pork pie for some orthodox groups, the majority of traditionally-minded European Jews were exterminated by fascists, and most of the rest came round, as is often the case when the God-fearing have something more concrete to fear than God.[194] [195] [196] Today the boot is on the other foot, with boots on the ground in occupied territories in the day-to-day horror of state politics after 2,000 years out of the game. In the most awful sense, the Children of Israel have remained true to the prophecy to be "a light unto the nations", by illuminating the inviolable relationship between statehood, violence and oppression.[197]

The irony is that the story of Israel commemorates a supplanter who mastered the forces of destruction to make peace with the brother he had wronged. The name of *YSRAL* evokes well-directed and justly applied power, and has long been a popular boy's name in the Jewish community. Muslims throughout their history have likewise chosen the name Jihad for their sons, a word which means 'struggle' in Arabic and also evokes the noble and divine striving at the heart of our humanity. The nuances of both of these names changed radically when the struggle was dragged from divine poetry into the dirty politics of the Caliphate and the "Jewish state".[198] [199]

In the beginning there was a story written down in a time before crime, when legal categories hadn't set yet and all the best people heard voices. Different powers interact at every level, beginning in the head between the temples and rolling out into history, with tribes fighting and scribes writing, with priests and kings politicking through the trials and triumphs of the Children of Israel. Different faces of the text and commentaries record the revelations, explanations and political machinations of a story mutating over 3,000 years. Corrupted and censored, like the journals in the libraries and the memories in our heads, the Bible and its commentaries remain an archive of the best and worst that the human mind can conceive of, with letter-crunching wordplay so brilliantly complex as to suggest divine or mega-savant intelligence alongside passages that are illuminating in the brazen effrontery of their politics. It brings together the two conflicting forces of the human condition, which are not good and evil but *solve et coagula*, softening and hardening of the clay of experience, building up and breaking down the walls in the head and the body politic. And throughout the text there are keys to secret locks in the crannies of the mind where the categories don't quite tessellate.

> Wherefore I gave them also statutes that were not good, and judgments whereby they should not live; And I polluted them in their own gifts, in that they caused to pass through the fire all that openeth the womb, that I might make them desolate, to the end that they might know that I am YHWH.[200]

Beneath the layers of text are old and amoral gods, resplendent in mind-blowing poetry. Mankind was and is created by the forces of the universe, made in the image of the powers, and those powers have no moral component to them. Their laws are not directives about what to do with your genitals; they are the formulas of nature, and gravity pulls down saints just as hard as it pulls down sinners. If you want morality and fairness in life you'll have to make a story yourself, and enchant it with meaning.

If micro-managing your behaviour in the privacy of your toilet brings you closer to God then that's fine by me, but law begat law in the Holy See and the Houses of Parliament, with bulls, bills and bylaws rewritten and redacted, compounding iniquity unto the hundredth generation and the Tax Codes of the nations.[201] If you feel that you require an omnipresent policeman to micromanage your affairs and keep you on the straight and narrow, it is probably best for everyone concerned that you hang onto your mega-god or your mega-state, and consult your mega-nom whenever you feel like killing someone or dissing your mum. Personally I'm a Logos man, in an infinitely complex world, and I prefer to talk to myself. For my tastes, a lawmaker god at the head of an army of functionaries enforcing the tyranny of the category is not a fit object of worship. It is an idol made in the image of our most childish conceits, where people can't be left alone in case they make a mess.

More laws may alter some facets of how stock transactions are handled and property is allocated; but so would anarchy, and in a more joined-up manner. I would cast my vote for a government that addressed pressing matters of international politics by firing up giant incense burners in the chambers of parliament and tossing divinatory dice – at the very least it would make Prime Minister's Question Time more entertaining. Failing that, I'm sceptical that regulating something or other or switching ministers can salvage our precarious situation. In a way, our current moment is even more terrifying than the crises of the past, because our states have made an enemy of the planet itself. Are the prophets of Zoroaster going to have the final say, running their self-fulfilling prophecy of doom and dualism until the final curtain? Or can we read the stories we are living through with a little more nuance?

Perhaps anarchists should not preempt the end of their exile from a stateless state of being, and avoid the kind of overlarge projects that tend to end in massacres. In the meantime, however, until the wheels come off completely, anarchists can open up spaces for experiments. Maybe migrants and others suffering on the fringes of collapsing power blocks will once again be the ones to survive uncertainty and lay the foundations of a radically new culture. There is always an apocalyptic element to moments of extreme novelty in history, along with the promise of unimaginable new vistas as the cracks open up in the brickwork.

In [the] beginning was the Word.

And at the end is [the] Apocalypse.

Ω

LIVE AND LET LEVITICUS

N (THE) BEGINNING was the Word, and nothing was articulated without it. We arrange and engage the world through our arrangements, through dynamic mind-frames of words weighted and memories fabricated, with abstractions at every level and infinity on all sides. Lines lay possibilities over the thoughtscape, threading together sense and semantics, metre and plot. We order chaos into coherence. And we can question our orders.

In the beginning is apocalypse, where iteration and inflection erupt unbidden, overwhelming in the babbling of the youngest and the pens of the ancients. Minds are mercifully changeable and poetry is elastic, but once upon a time rhyme was sullied with reason, and words were written down fixed, bricks upon bricks building towers in time with pretentions at eternity. Chunks coagulate in print, 'order' sticks to 'law and', 'do not step on' to 'on the grass'. Details that don't fit are lost to the edge. Compacted philosophies in holy books, rulebooks and textbooks float cumbersomely through neural networks, streams of consciousness jam up and stagnate, gathering parasites and festering itches, seeding diseases. We are saved from monoculture of the mind by the forked tongue that divides out, by different interpretations channelling the stream in different directions – but all statements impose limits, as the word conceals while it reveals. A master who has reached the limits of his field keeps inquiring, compelled to know and attend the birth of a new order. Rules don't bend, but they break and must be broken if we are to overcome our limitations, both as individuals and as communities.

Words born in sin and into sin are imbibed at the breast and stained from the very beginning. Even the mega-words of millennial poetic traditions have been sullied beyond recognition by their contact with the prose profanity of politics. Words of power have become crusades and curses, pearls trampled underfoot. Unuttered, a new order frames a question, and starts a conversation that can undermine towers of assumption.

The perfect Word is born immaculate into opposition, setting this against that. Tempted by his shadow and rejected by the people of a city marked for destruction, the Word rages against limitation and is sacrificed to the plotline at the summit of the hill outside the old city, reunited with his father beyond the contradictions. "The stone that the builder refused," sang the Psalmist (and the Masons, and the Wailers), "shall be the head corner-stone" – after it is worked to perfection and set at the apex of an arch to hold opposing forces in balance.[1] The arch-builder is the *archi-tect* of New Jerusalem, his arch constructed on a frame built by the master carpenter. With the work complete the frame is obsolete, and so too the artisan broken and pinned upon it.

In the head are created Powers irrational and vital, driving us to love and war and neurosis. We have bowed down to them and sacrificed to them, and we have tried to pretend they don't exist – but we can't hide from what's in our heads, as Adam discovered. We can only harness them, perceiving their movements, recognising their forms, guiding and goading them with what we have discovered. You are heavens and you are earth, between fluid and fixed and release and control, between the poles and the temples and the towers as the tales unfold. Without YHWH Elohim there would be nothing to do and nothing to be done. Without El Shadday there would be nothing driving the plot, without YHWH nothing holding it together, without the serpent no hope of breaking it apart.[2] Behind the scenes and the good cop bad cop routines, something is manipulating dualisms through the cycles of nature and empire and chaos and crystallisation, the magic in the mud propelling intelligence in a seasick spiral toward mind unlimited. The Son of Man slips around the law and between the worlds at the edge of the possible, between I AM and I WILL BE, between past imperfect and future perfect, present continuous. His ally slithers through the branches, inquiring into the shady canopy above, skin-shedding and shape-shifting, questions cutting through assumptions, refutations sharp as razors. What is true? What are we capable of? What are we waiting for?

"Ye shall not surely die [...] and ye shall be as gods."[3]

'Surely not?' thinks Adam, ashamed of the magick in his naked wand. And in which case, probably not.

But what if?

Ω

ILLUSTRATIONS

Ambigraph did the cover art,

And the two-headed snake at the very start.

The illuminated letter man

Is the luminous Loren Fetterman

NOTES

Notes for chapter 1: Japanese Whispers

1   *Apocalypse Delayed: The Story of Jehovah's Witnesses* Penton, J. M. (Toronto: 1997), introduction.

2   *Jesus in the Gospels and Acts: Introducing the New Testament* Scholz, D. J. (Wonona, MN: 2009) p. 227

3   Galatians 5:22 (NWT)

4   *Letter XXII to Eustochium* St. Jerome

5   Matthew 13:49

6   See, for example, the Gezer Calendar, in *The Paleo-Hebrew Gezer Agricultural Calendar or Almanac translated into Mycenaean Linear B* Vallance, R. Retreived on 11 September 2016 from https://www.academia.edu/12678574/The_Paleo-Hebrew_Gezer_Agricultural_Calendar_or_Almanac_translated_into_Mycenaean_Linear_B

7   *The Journey from Texts to Translations: The Origin and Development of the Bible* Wegner, P. D. (Michigan: 1999) p. 167

8   *The Introduction to the Commentary on the Torah* Nachmanides

9   *Bamidbar Rabbah* 13:15

10 *Strong's Expanded Exhaustive Concordance of the Bible* Strong, J. (Nashville: 2009) Dictionary, H3045

11 *God is a Verb* Cooper, D. (Riverhead: 1997) p. 66

12 הָעוּנְת in Hebrew. Retrieved on 27 November 2015 from www.morfix.co.il/הָעְ%D6%BCוּנ%D6%BCת

13 *The Holy Bible: Containing the Old and New Testaments*, Vol. 1 Clarke, A. (New York: 1837) p. 2

14 Cooper, p. 56

15 *Tao Te Ching*, chapter 1 (Lin Yutang trans.)

16 *The Zohar*, vol. 1 (Matt, D. C. trans.) (California: 2004) p. 6, footnote 62

17 *The Zohar*, pp. 154 & 165, footnote 463

18 1 Kings 11:5, 33, 23:13

19 *Commentary on the Torah* Nachmanides (Chavel, C. B. trans.) (New York: 1976), Vol. 1, Genesis, introduction

20 *Eruvim* 13b

21 *The Septuagint*, Goldsonm, Y. 12 December 2014, *Jewish World* Retrieved Jan 4 2015 from www.jewishworldreview.com/jewish/jhistory11.php3

22 Vatican confirms excommunication for US dissident group *Catholic World News* 7 December 2006 Retrieved on 26 September 2015 from www.catholicculture.org/news/features/index.cfm?recnum=48072&repos=4&subrepos=1&search id=1559657

311

23 *Hellas: A Lyrical Drama*, Vol. 7 Shelley, P. B. (London: 1821) p. viii

24 *Is God Transgender* Samethaug, M, *New York Times* 12 August 2016 Retrieved on 20 August 2016 from http://www.nytimes.com/2016/08/13/opinion/is-god-transgender.html?action=click&pgtype=Homepage&clickSource=sto ry-heading&module=opinion-c-col-right-region&region=opinion-c-col-right-region&WT.nav=opinion-c-col-right-region&_r=0

25 *Rio Olympics 2016: Caster Semenya's history-making could spell the end* Fordyce, T. BBC Website, Retrieved on 20 August 2106 from http://www.bbc.co.uk/sport/olympics/37102204

26 John 1:1

27 *The Visions Seminars*, Vol. 1, Jung, C. G., in Abridged Version of *Interpretation of Visions* (Zurich: 1976) p. 156

28 Psalm 37:11

29 Numbers 31:15

30 Psalm 22:26

31 *The Mutilation of Mark's Gospel* Croy, N. C. (Nashville: 2003) pp. 18-42

32 *Studying the Ancient Israelites: A Guide to Sources and Methods* Matthews, V. H., (Nottingham: 2007) p. 108

Notes for chapter 2: The Monkey Nut

1 *The Stimulus and Anatomy of the Visual System. Experiencing Sensation and Perception* Krantz, *John* H. (1 October 2012) Pearson Education.

2 *Color Appearance Models*. Fairchild, M. (Massachusetts: 1998), p. 7

3 *Diagnostic and Statistical Manual of Mental Disorders* (3rd ed) American Psychiatric Association, Washington DC (1980).

4 *Visual Hallucinations During Prolonged Blindfolding in Sighted Subjects* Merabet, L. B. et al. *Journal of Neuro-Ophthalmology* 24(2) pp. 109-113, June 2004

5 *Seeing big things: Overestimation of heights is greater for real objects than for objects in pictures* Yang, T. L. *Perception*, Vol. 1 28(4) pp. 445 – 467

6 *On Creative, Psychotic and Ecstatic States Fischer, R. in Art Interpretation and Art Therapy, Psychiatry and Art*, Vol. 2, pp. 33-65, Proc. 5th International Colloquium of the Society of Psychopathology of Expression (Los Angeles: 1968)

7 *Effects of group pressure upon the modification and distortion of judgment* Asch, S. E. (Pittsburgh: 1951) in Groups, Leadership and Men H. Guetzkow (ed.)

8 *Neurobiological Correlates of Social Conformity and Independence During Mental Rotation* Berns, G. et al *Biol. Psychiatry* 2005;58: pp. 245-253

9 *Gorillas in our midst: sustained inattentional blindness for dynamic events* Simons, D. J. & Chabris C. F., in *Perception*, 1999, Vol. 28, pp. 1059-1074

10 *Failure to detect changes to people in a real-world interaction* Simons, D. J., & Levin, D. T. in *Psychonomic Bulletin and Review* (1998) 5(4), pp. 644-649

11   *Inattentional Blindness: An Overview* Mack, A. & Rock, I. Psyche, 5(3), May: 1999

12   *Sights unseen: Research on a phenomenon known as inattentional blindness suggests that unless we pay close attention, we can miss even the most conspicuous events* Carpenter, S. *American Psychological Association Magazine*, April 2001, Vol 32, No. 4 p. 54

13   *Ghrelin Enhances Olfactory Sensitivity and Exploratory Sniffing in Rodents and Humans* Tong, J. et al *The Journal of Neuroscience*, April 13, 2011, 31(15) pp. 5841–5846

14   *Memory* Loftus, E. (Addison-Wesley Publishing: 1980) pp. 135-44

15   *The Future of Memory: Remembering, Imagining, and the Brain* Schacter, D. L.et al. *Neurone* 76, November 21, 2012

16   *Who am I?* Radiolab Retrieved on 7 March 2016 from www.radiolab.org/story/91496-who-am-i/

17   *Creating False Memories* Loftus, E. F. *Scientific American* September 1997, vol 277 no. 3 pp. 70-75

18   *The Anatomy of Self: The Individual Versus Society* Doi, T. (New York: 1986)

19   *The Geography of Thought: How Asians and Westerners think differently... and Why* Nisbett, R. E. (New York: 2004) p. 93

20   Nisbett, pp. 89-92

21   *Dark, cold and hungry, but full of mutual trust: Manners among the 2011 Great East Japan Earthquake victims* Abe, T. et al *Psychology in Russia: State of the Art* Vol 7, 1 (2014)

22   *Room 101* (2001) Season 6 Episode 10

23   Nisbett, p. 60

24   Nisbett, pp. 81-82

25   Nisbett, pp. 81-82

26   Nisbett, p. 150

27   *Styles of reasoning in Japan and the United States: Logic of education in two cultures* Watanabe, M. (1998) Paper presented at the American Sociological Association, San Francisco, CA.

28   Nisbett, p. 97

29   Nisbett, p. 108

30   Nisbett, p. 195

31   Nisbett, p. 225

32   Intelligence: Maze-solving by an amoeboid organizm Nakagaki et al. Nature 407, 470 (28 September 2000)

33   *Amoebae anticipate periodic events.* Saigusa, T. et al *Phys Rev* Lett. 2008 Jan 11;100(1):018101.

34   *Lao Tzu: Tao Te Ching 175+ Translations of Chapter 1* Bureau of Public Secrets Retrieved 12 January 2015 from www.bopsecrets.org/gateway/passages/tao-te-ching.htm

35   *Functional magnetic resonance imaging (fMRI) changes and saliva production associated with acupuncture at LI-2 acupuncture point: a randomized controlled study* Deng, G Complement Altern Med. 2008; 8: 37.

36 *On the chemical correlation of the functions of the body* Starling, E. H. (1905) The Croonian Lectures. I. *Lancet* 166: pp. 339–341.

37 *The genius of China: 3,000 years of science, discovery & invention* Temple, R (2007). (3rd ed.). London: Andre Deutsch. pp. 141–145.

38 *The Endocrinologist*, Issue 115, Spring 2015, p. 6

39 *Do Antidepressants Work?* Hendriksen, E. *Scientific American* August 27, 2014

40 *Joseph Needham on Chinese Astronomy*, Cullen, C. *Past and Present*, No. 87. (May 1980), pp. 39-53

41 *Grammatical Man: Information, Entropy, Language and Life. The Story of the Modern Revolution in Human Thought* Campbell, J. (Middlesex 1984) p. 248

42 *Freedom of speech and freedom of silence: An analysis of talking as a cultural practice* Kim, H. S., & Markus, H. R. (2002). In R. Shweder, M. Minow, & H. R. Markus (eds.), *Engaging cultural differences: The multicultural challenge in liberal democracies* (New York: 2002) pp. 432–452

43 *Chronology of Science* Rezende, L. (New York: 2006) p, 33

44 Nisbett, p. 228

45 Nisbett, p. 118-119

46 *We talk therefore we think? A Cultural Analysis of the Effect of Talking on Thinking* Kim, H. S. *Journal of Personality and Social Psychology* 2002, Vol. 83, No. 4, pp. 828-842

47 *Who Wrote the Bible?* Friedman, R. E. (New York: 1997)

48 Genesis:17

49 Exodus 32:14

50 Exodus 14:21

51 John 10:30 (Young's Literal Translation)

52 Sefer Yetzirah, chapter 4, part 2

53 Retrieved on 21 December from www.2letterlookup.com

54 *Gesenius' Hebrew-Chaldee Lexicon*, DBR, meaning 4

55 Strong's, H1696

56 *Tractate Baba Metzia* 59a

57 *The Sound of the One Hand* Hoffmann, Y. (New York: 1975) p. 114

Notes for chapter 3: Gene(mu)sis

1 Exodus 12:15

2 *The Science of God: The Convergence of Scientific and Biblical Wisdom* Schroeder, G. L. (New York: 2009) p. 102

3 *Photius, Biography of Pythagoras, Pythagoras Sourcebook and Library* Guthrie, K. S. Section 14, p. 155

NOTES

Notes for chapter 4: Behind the Word

1   *Tractatus Logico-Philosophicus* Wittgenstein, L. (Ogden, C. K. trans.) (London: 1922) 5.6

2   Strong's, H1696

3   *Tractatus*, 1

4   *A Lecture on Ethics* Wittgenstein, L. (1929), p. 40.

5   *Wittgenstein* Bartley, W. W., (Quartet: 1977) pp. 107, 198

6   *Wittgenstein, Russell and the Problem of the Rhinoceros* McDonald J. F. in *The Southern Journal of Philosophy* (1993) Vol. 31, No. 4

7   *Tractatus,* 1

8   *Tractatus*, 1

9   *Wittgenstein: The Way Out of the Fly-bottle* Schroeder, S. (Cambridge: 2006) p. 1

10 *Bertrand Russell: The Spirit of Solitude*, 1872-1921 Monk, R. Vol. 1, (New York: 1996) p. 252

11 *Going around the Vienna Circle: Wittgenstein and Verification* Hymers, M. *Philosophical Investigations* 28:3 July 2005

12 *Wittgenstein's Poker* Edmonds, D. *The Guardian* 21 November 2001

13 *Ludwig Wittgenstein: A Memoir* Malcolm, N. (Oxford: 2001) pp. 58.

14 *Tractatus,* 5.6

15 *Born on a Blue Day: Inside the Extraordinary Mind of an Autistic Savant - A Memoir* Tammet, D (Free Press: 2006)

16 *Word-taste synaesthesia Tasting names, places and Anne Boleyn*. BBC News Retreived on 11 October 2015 from www.youtube.com/watch?v=ENLcrbby-70

17 *Frequent association of autism spectrum disorder in patients with childhood onset epilepsy* Matsuo, M.,et al *Brain Dev.* 2010; 32 pp. 759–763

18 *Frequent association of autism spectrum disorder in patients with childhood onset epilepsy* Matsuo, M., et al. Brain Dev. 2010; 32 pp. 759–763

19 Impers. noncom, Marcleo

20 *A Genius Explains* Johnson, R. *The Guardian* 12 February 2005

21 *Academic achievement in high functioning autistic individuals* Minshew, N. J. et al. *Journal of Clinical and Experimental Neuropsychology* (1994). 16(2), pp. 261–270.

22 *Born on a Blue Day: The Gift of an Extraordinary Mind* Tammet, D. (London: 2007) p. 2

23 *Animals in Translation: Using the Mysteries of Autism to Decode Animal Behaviour* Grandin, T. and Johnson, C. (London: 2005). p. 295

24 *How does visual thinking work in the mind of a person with autism? A personal account* Grandin, T. in *Philosophical Transactions of The Royal Society B Biological Sciences* 364(1522) pp. 1437-42

25 Hermelin, p. 43

26 Hermelin, p. 40

27 *The Reason I Jump* Naoki Higashida & David Mitchell Sceptre (2007) p. 91-92

28 *Borges and Memory: Encounters with the Human Brain* Quiroga, R. Q. (Massachustetts: 2012) p. 106

29 Hermelin, pp. 44-45

30 *Are people with autism and Asperger Syndrome faster than normal on the Embedded Figures Test?* Jolliffe, T. & Baron-Cohen, S. *Journal of Child Psychology and Psychiatry* 1997, 38, pp. 527-534

31 *Susceptibility to the Shepard illusion in participants with autism: reduced top-down influences within perception?* Mitchell, P. et al *Autism Research* Vol. 3 (3), June 2010, pp. 113–119

32 Hermelin, p. 25

33 Hermelin, p. 109

34 *Autistic teen's 20-point night touches all* ESPN. 2006-02-24.

35 *Are you smarter than a 5-year-old chimp?* Ritter, M. NBC News. Retrieved on 1 March 2016 from www.nbcnews.com/id/22080399/ns/technology_and_science-science/t/are-you-smarter--year-old-chimp/#.VtXA71I1VE0

36 *How does visual thinking work in the mind of a person with autism? A personal account* Grandin, T. in *Philosophical Transactions of The Royal Society B Biological Sciences* 364(1522) p. 1438

37 *Brain Hyperconnectivity in Children with Autism and its Links to Social Deficits* Supekar, K. *Cell Reorts* Vol. 5, Issue 3, pp. 738–747, 14 November 2013

38 *Prosopagnosia: Face Blindness after Brain Injury* The Brain Injury Association factsheet. Retrieved on 5 March 2016 from www.headway.org.uk/media/2816/prosopagnosia-face-blindness-after-brain-injury.pdf

39 Wisconsin Medical Society website

40 The Musical Genius Docufilm TV

41 Hermelin, p. 160

42 *Neural Correlates of Natural Human Echolocation in Early and Late Blind Echolocation Experts* Thaler, L. et al (2011) *PLoS ONE* 6(5): e20162.

43 *The Musical Genius* Docufilm TV - 18:13

44 *Born on a Blue Day: The Gift of an Extraordinary Mind* Tammet, D. (London: 2007) p. 193

45 *The Boy With The Incredible Brain* Extraordinary People Aired on 23 May 2005

46 *The Reason I Jump* Higashida, N. & Mitchell, D. (New York: 2007) question 42

47 Hermelin, p. 30

48 *Autism: functional brain mapping of exceptional calendar capacity* Boddaert, N. et al *The British Journal of Psychiatry* June 2005, 187 (1) pp. 83-86

49 *The Reason I Jump* Higashida, N. & Mitchell, D. (New York: 2007) p. 59

50 Retrieved on 25 December 2015 from http://autismfamily.com/early-signs-of-autism-stacking-blocks-no-eye-contact.html

51 *The Inner Savant* Smolka, J & Fox, D. S. Discover Magazine February 01, 2002

316

NOTES

52   *Origin of maximal symmetry breaking in even PT-symmetric lattices* Joglekar, Y. N. & Barnett, J. L. *Phys. Rev. A* 84, 024103 30/8/2011

53   *Enhancing Creative Behavioral Expressions in School Systems: The Need for Educational Reform and a Center for Creativity* Kader, S. A. Doctoral Thesis, Pennsylvania State University, 2008 p. 78

54   *Einstein: A Life* Brian, D. (New York: 1995) pp. 60-61

55   *Albert Einstein's dyslexia and the significance of Brodmann Area 39 of his left cerebral cortex.* Kantha, S. S. *Med Hypoth.* 1992;37:119–122.

56   Quoted in Meta*phors and Action Schemes: Some Themes in Intellectual History* Schwarz, R. L. (Bucknell: 1997) pp. 235

57   Retrieved on 25 February 2016 from www.autismweb.com/forum/viewtopic. php?t=3896

58   *The Autistic Spectrum* Wing, L. (revised edition) (London: 2002)

59   *The Relationship Between Subthreshold Autistic Traits, Ambiguous Figure Perception and Divergent Thinking* Best, C. et al *Journal of Autism and Developmental Disorders* pp. 1-10

60   *The Inner Savant* Smolka, J & Fox, D. S. Discover Magazine Febuary 2002

61   Retrieved on 22 Febuary 2015 from http://www.petplace.com/drug-library/ methylphenidate-ritalin/page1.aspx

62   Retrieved on 25 December 2015 from www.neurodiversity.com/

63   *Embracing the Wide Sky: A Tour Across the Horizons of the Mind* Tammet, D. (London: 2009) p.78

64   *Reduced gyral window and corpus callosum size in autism: possible macroscopic correlates of a minicolumnopathy* Casanova M. F. et al, *J Autism Dev Disord.* 2009 May;39(5):751-64.

65   *Kim Peek: The Real Rain Man* Wisconsin Medical Society. Retrieved on 4 June 2015 from https://www.wisconsinmedicalsociety.org/professional/savant-syndrome/profiles-and-videos/profiles/kim-peek-the-real-rain-man/

66   *Disrupted neural synchronization in toddlers with autism.* Dinstein, I. et al *Neuron* 2011; 70: 1218–1225

67   *Brain Hyperconnectivity in Children with Autism and its Links to Social Deficits* Supekar, K. et al *Cell Reports* 14 November 2013 Vol. 5: Is. 3, pp.738–747

68   *Loss of mTOR-Dependent Macroautophagy Causes Autistic-like Synaptic Pruning Deficits* Tang, G. et al. *Neuron* Vol. 83 (5) , pp. 1131–1143, 3 September 2014

69   *Autism may involve disordered white matter in the brain* Science News 5 December 2011 Retrieved on 3 June 2015 from http://www.sciencedaily.com/ releases/2011/12/111205140517.htm

70   *The Master and His Emissary: The Divided Brain and the Making of the Western World* McGilchrist, I. (Yale: 2009) pp. 8-10

71   *Kim Peek, Inspiration for 'Rain Man,' Dies at 58* Weber, B. *New York Times*, December 26, 2009. Retrieved on August 4 2015 from http://www.nytimes. com/2009/12/27/us/27peek.html?pagewanted=all&_r=0

72 *Synchronicity: An Acausal Connecting Principle* Jung, C. G. (Princeton, N. J.: 1969) pp. 109–110

73 *The Inner Savant*, in *Discover Magazine* (published online February 1, 2002)

74 *Acquired Savant Syndrome in Frontotemporal Dementia* Takahata, K. et al in *Japanese Society of Neurology Journal* 2010;50:1017

75 *The Inner Savant* February 1, 2002 *Discover Magazine* Retrieved on 5 September 2015 from http://discovermagazine.com/2002/feb/featsavant/

76 *Ingenious Minds* Discovery Communications (2010-2011)

77 It's a joke. 'nads. Gettit?

78 Jake: Math prodigy proud of his Autism *60 Minutes* Textor, K. CBS News, Jan 17 2012

79 *The Reason I Jump* Higashida, N. & Mitchell, D. (New York: 2007) p. 79

80 *Thus Spake Zarathustra* Nietzsche, F (Thomas Common trans.) quote from the introduction by his sister.

81 *Phaedrus* Plato, quoted in *A History of Ancient Philosophy II: Plato and Aristotle* Reale, G. (New York: 1990) p. 131

82 *It's No Delusion: Evolution May Favor Schizophrenia Genes* Swaminathan, N. *Scientific American* September 6, 2007

83 *Nikola Tesla: A Spark of Genius* Dommermuth-Costa, C. (Minneapolis: 1994) p. 128

84 *Tesla: Man Out of Time* Cheney, M. (New York: 1981) p. 1

85 *A Portrait of Sir Isaac Newton* Manuel, F. (Cambridge, MA: 1968)

86 Data extrapolated by *BP or not BP*, from *Ice melt, sea level rise and superstorms: evidence from paleoclimate data, climate modeling, and modern observations that 2° C global warming could be dangerous* Hansen, *J. Atmos. Chem. Phys.*, 2016, 16, pp. 3761–3812

87 *Newton set 2060 for end of world The Telegraph* 22 February 2003

88 *Religiousness and Obsessive-Compulsive Cognitions and Symptoms in an Italian Population* Sica, C. et al, *Behaviour, Research and Therapy*, 40 (7) (2002), pp. 813-23

89 *A Portrait of Sir Isaac Newton* Manuel, F. (Cambridge, MA: 1968) p. 380

90 *Isaac Newton's Freemasonry: The Alchemy of Science and Mysticism* Bauer, A. (Rochester: 2007), chap. 3

91 *University of California San Francisco Magazine*, Vol. 11, p. 126

92 Daniel 10:16

93 Genesis 15:12

94 *Localizing and Lateralizing features of auras and seizures* Foldvary-Schaefer, N. & Unnwonqse, K. (2011). *Epilepsy Behavior* 20: pp. 160-166

95 1 Samuel 28

96 Epilepsy Foundation forums, retrieved on 1 December 2014 from www.epilepsy.com/node/975314 (edited for clarity)

97   Epilepsy Foundation forums

98   *The prevalence of voice-hearers in the general population: A literature review* Beavan, V. et al (2011). *Journal of Mental Health*, 20(3), 281-292.

99   *The Fortean Times*, November 2007, p. 41

100 *Mentalizing Deficits Constrain Belief in a Personal God* Norenzayan A, et al (2012). PLoS ONE 7(5)

101 *Hyper-religiosity associated with focal temporal lobe atrophy* Chan, D. et al., 2009

102 *Neural correlates of a mystical experience in Carmelite nuns* Beauregard, M & Paquette, V. *Neuroscience Letters* 405 (2006) pp. 186–190

103 *The Tyrany of Treatment: Samuel Johnson, his Friends, and Georgian Medicine* (McEnroe, N. & Simon, R. eds) (London: 2002) p. 12, 15

104 *Loving Dr. Johnson* Deutsch, H. (Chicago: 2005) p. 273 footnote 96

105 *The Prayers of Dr. Samuel Johnson* (New York: 1902) Prayer XXIX

106 *1755: Johnson's Dictionary* British Library website. Retrieved on 23 June 2016 from www.bl.uk/learning/langlit/dic/johnson/1755johnsonsdictionary.html

107 *Tic Tips: Strategies to help you manage your Tourette Syndrome* Retreived on 23 June 2106 from http://www.tourettes-action.org.uk/storage/downloads/1374586633_Tic-tips---managing-your-TS.pdf

108 *Long Division and Thatcher* Touretteshero website. Retrieved on 23 June 2016 from http://www.tourettehero.com/2010/01/05/long-division-and-thatcher/

109 *The Sky Gets Told* Touretteshero website. Retrieved on 23 June 2016 from www.touretteshero.com/2015/12/07/the-sky-gets-told/

110 *Hypergraphia for Poetry in an Epileptic Patient* Mendez, M. F. (letter) *The Journal of Neuropsychiatry and Clinical Neurosciences*, 17(4), pp. 560–561

111 *Robert Anton Wilson: Life and Times* (Audio) 26 Apr 2013 Retrieved on August 8 2015 from www.youtube.com/watch?v=TtMCFq7_CbE

112 *The Geschwind syndrome*. Benson D. F., *Adv Neurol*. 1991; 55: pp. 411-21

113 *Compulsive versifying after treatment of transient epileptic amnesia* Woollacott, I. O. C. et al, *Neurocase* 26 August 2014

114 *Absence seizures: Symptoms, diagnosis and treatment* Retrieved on August 8 2015 from www.webmd.boots.com/a-to-z-guides/absence-seizure-symptoms

115 Genesis 5:24

116 *Temporal lobe epilepsy and Dostoyevsky seizures: Neuropathology and Spirituality* Coles, A. Royal College of Psychiatrists website. Retrieved on 29 June 2016 from www.rcpsych.ac.uk/pdf/Alasdair%20Coles%20Temporal%20lobe%20epilepsy%20and%20Dostoyevsky%20seizures.pdf

Notes for chapter 5: In the /b/ginning

1   *Sefer Yetzirah*, short Version, (Kaplan A. trans.) 2.2 Retrieved on 25 September 2015 from www.psyche.com/psyche/txt/kaplan_sy_short.html

2   *Genesis Rabbah* 1:10

3   *Genesis Rabbah* 1:10

4   Exodus 21

5   Exodus 21:28, 35

6   McGilchrist, p. 276

7   *Dendritic right/left asymmetries in the neurones of the human hippocampal formation: a quantitative Golgi study* Sa, M. J. et al. *Arq. Neuro-Psiquiatr.* 2007, vol.65, n.4b, pp. 1105-1113

8   http://www.sciencedirect.com/science/article/pii/S0093934X0200531X

9   *Sefer Yetzirah*, chapter 3

10 *A Critical Edition of the Midrash Aleph Beth with an English Translation, Commentary and Introduction*, Middeton, D. F. (Edinburgh: 1988), p. 99

11 The word 'wind' here is usually translated as 'spirit.'

12 Retrieved on 18 Novemeber 2015 from Hebrew online dictionary at www. morfix.co.il/העונת

13 Newborns' cry melody is shaped by their native language Mampe, B. et al Current Biology, 5 November 2009

14 *Sefer Yetzirah*, chapter 2

15 *First Years: Professional Development through Distance Education.* Retrieved on 1 January 2015 from http://firstyears.org/miles/chart.pdf

16 Baby Centre homepage. Retrieved on 17 September 2015 from www.babycentre. co.uk/x1048875/when-will-my-baby-talk

17 *Ancient Hebrew Dictionary* Benner, J. A. (Virtualbookworm: 2009) p. 113

18 Retrieved on 14 January 2016 from www.2letterlookup.com

19 Retrieved on 14 January 2016 from www.2letterlookup.com

20 *The development of phonology* Grunwell, P. (1981) First Language pp. 161-191.

21 *When are speech sounds learned?* Sander, E. (1972). *Journal of Speech and Hearing Disorders*, 37, pp. 55-63.

22 *The Emergence of the Sounds of Speech in Infancy* Oller, D.K. Chapter 6. In G. Yeni-Komshian, J.F. Kavanagh, & C.A. Ferguson (eds.), Child Phonology: Vol. 1. Production. (New York: 1980). pp.93-112

23 *Developmental milestones: sight* Retrieved on 13 December 2015 from www. babycentre.co.uk/a6508/developmental-milestones-sight

24 *First Language Acquisition: Method, Description and Explanation* Ingram, D. (Cambridge: 1989) p. 373

25   Retrieved on 18 November 2015 from www.whattoexpect.com/first-year/month-by-month/your-child-month-5.aspx

26   *Sefer Yetzirah*, chapter 5

27   *The Ancient Hebrew Lexicon of the Bible* Benner, J. A. (College Station, Texas: 2005) p. 24

28   Benner, p. 25

29   Genesis 2:19

30   *The Hebrew Letters: Channels of Creative Consciousness* Rabbi Ginsburg, Y. (Jerusalem: 1990) p. 154

31   Strong's, H3334, H3335

32   Exodus 13:9

33   Daniel 2:21-22

34   *Ages and Stages Summary: Language Development 0-5 years* Bowen, C. (1998). Retrieved from http://www.speech-language-therapy.com/ on 5 April 2015

35   *First Years: Professional Development through Distance Education* Retrieved on Jan 1st, 2015, in the beginning, from http://firstyears.org/miles/chart.pdf

36   Retrieved on 13th February 2016 from http://www.essentialbaby.com.au/forums/index.php?/topic/956206-does-your-toddler-refer-to-themselves-in-the-3rd-person/

37   *Return of the Candy Witch: Individual differences in acceptance and stability of belief in a novel fantastical being* Boerger, E. A. et al *Br J Dev Psychol*. 2009 Nov; 27(Pt 4): pp. 953–970.

38   *Neuropsychology of prefrontal cortex* Siddiqui, S. V. *Indian J Psychiatry*. 2008 Jul-Sep; 50(3): pp. 202–208

39   Exodus 6:3

40   Strong's, H7706

41   Matthew 4:16 (immediately after Satan's tests the people saw "great light")

42   *The Alef-Beit: Jewish Thought Revealed through the Hebrew Letters* Rabbi Ginsburgh, Y. (New Jersey: 1995) p. 316

43   *Sefer Yetzirah: The Book of Creation in Theory and Practice* Kaplan, A. (Boston: 1997) p. xxi (And Hayri Pottah is Harry Potter, silly!) There are differing theories on Abracadabra. If it is Aramaic then it was borrowed from Hebrew: aramaicnt.org/2014/01/29/abracadabra-is-not-aramaic/

Notes for chapter 6: Numb3rs

1   *The Principles of Psychology* James, W. (New York: 1950), chapter 3

2   *The neuropsychiatry of paranormal experiences.* Persinger, M. A. *The Journal of Neuropsychiatry and Clinical Neurosciences*, Vol 13(4), 2001, pp. 515-523

3   *Learning and Memory: The Brain in Action* Sprenger, M. (Alexandria: 1999) p. 2

4   Introduction to Physiological Psychology Thompson, R. F. (New York: 1975) p. 162

5   McGilchrist, p. 35

6   *Capacity Limits of Information Processing in the Brain* Marois, R. Phi Kappa Phi Forum, Vol. 85, No. 1 , Spring 2005

7   *A Course in Classical Physics 3: Electromagnetism* Bettini, A. (Switzerland: 2016) p. vi

8   pers. comm. The unnamed source

9   *Searching for God in the Brain* Bello, D. in *Scientific American* 1 October 2007

10   *Why We Believe What We Believe: Uncovering Our Biological Need for meaning, Spirituality, and Truth* Newberg, A. & Waldman, M. R. (New York: 2006) p. 176

11   *Parietal Cortex Mediates Conscious Perception of Illusory Gestalt* Zaretskaya, N. et al *The Journal of Neuroscience*, 9 January 2013, 33(2): 523-531

12   *A deficit of spatial remapping in constructional apraxia after right-hemisphere stroke* Russell, C. et al (April 2010). *Brain* 133 (Pt 4) pp. 1239–51

13   *The Reason I Jump* Higashida, N. & Mitchell, D. (New York: 2007) pp. 91-92

14   *Neuropsychiatry, Neuropsychology, Clinical Neuroscience* Joseph, R. Parietal Area 5 (New York: 2000)

15   *A deficit of spatial remapping in constructional apraxia after right-hemisphere stroke* Russell, C. et al (April 2010). *Brain* 133 (Pt 4) pp. 1239–51

16   *Sound lateralisation in patients with left or right cerebral hemispheric lesions: relation with unilateral visuospatial neglect* Tanaka H et al. *J Neurol Neurosurg Psychiatry* 1999; 67: pp. 481–6.

17   *Parietal Cortex Mediates Conscious Perception of Illusory Gestalt* Zaretskaya, N. et al *The Journal of Neuroscience*, 9 January 2013, 33(2) pp. 523-531

18   *Perceiving in Depth* Vol. 3: Other Mechanisms of Depth Perception Howard, I. P. (Oxford: 2012) p. 218

19   *Brain activity during driving with distraction: an immersive fMRI study* Schweizer, T. A. et al. *Front Hum Neurosci.* (2013); 7 p. 53.

20   *In Search of the Self: A Positron Emission Tomography Study* Craik, F. I. M. et al *Psychological Science* vol. 10, no. 1 January 1999

21   *New Introductory Lectures on Psychoanalysis* Freud, S. (New York: 1933) p. 73

22   *The Reason I Jump* Naoki Higashida & David Mitchell Sceptre (2007) p. 123-124

23   John 8:58

24   McGilchrist, p. 70

25   *Differential Contribution of Right and Left Temporo-Occipital and Anterior Temporal Lesions to Face Recognition Disorders* Gainotti, G. & Marra, C. *Front Hum Neurosci.* 2011; 5: 55

26   *Solving deductive-reasoning problems after unilateral temporal lobectomy* Read, D. (1981) *Brain and Language*, 12:116-127.

27 *Nonverbal auditory agnosia with lesion to Wernicke's area* Saygin, A. P. et al
    Neuropsychologia. 2010 Jan; 48(1): pp. 107–113.

28 *Acquired Speech and Language Disorders: A Neuroanatomical and Functional
    Neurological Approach* (2nd ed.) Murdoch, E. M. (Singapore: 2010) p. 240

29 *On the preservation of word order in aphasia* Bates, E. A. et al(1988). *Brain and
    Language*, 33, pp. 323-364.

30 *Sign language aphasia* Poizner, H. et al in *Handbook of Neuropsychology* Boller,
    F. & Grafman, J. (eds.) (Amsterdam: 1989) pp. 157-172

31 Strong's, H8034

32 *A History of Greek Philosophy: Volume 1, The Earlier Presocratics and the
    Pythagoreans* Guthrie, W. K. C. (Cambridge: 2000) p. 490

33 *Color categories: Evidence for the cultural relativity hypothesis* Roberson, D. et
    al *Cognitive Psychology*, 2005, 50(4), pp. 378-411

34 *Russian blues reveal effects of language on color discrimination* Winawer, J. et
    al *Proc Natl Acad Sci USA*. 8 May 2007; 104(19): pp. 7780–7785

35 *In Search of the Self: A Positron Emission Tomography Study* Craik, F. I. M et al
    Psychological Science vol. 10, no. 1 January 1999

36 *Objects automatically potentiate action: an fMRI study of implicit processing*
    Grezes, J. *European Journal of Neuroscience*, 2003, Vol. 17, pp. 2735–2740

37 *Impulsivity and risk-taking behavior in focal frontal lobe lesions* Floden, D. et al,
    Neuropsychologia, Vol. 46, Issue 1, 2008, pp. 213–223

38 McGilchrist, p. 41

39 McGilchrist, p. 90

40 *Neuropsychology of prefrontal cortex* Siddiqui, S. V. et al *Indian J Psychiatry*
    2008 Jul-Sep; 50(3): 202–208

41 *Damage to the prefrontal cortex increases utilitarian moral judgements* Koenig,
    M. et al *Nature* 446, pp. 908-911, 19 April 2007

42 *"Altruistic" behavior in Rhesus Monkeys* Masserman, J. H. et al *The American
    Journal of Psychiatry* Vol 121. Dec. 1964. 584-585.

43 *Emotional reactions of rats to the pain of others* Church, R. M. J Comp Physiol
    Psychol. 1959 Apr;52(2) pp. 132-4.

44 *Functions of the frontal cortex of the rat: A comparative review* Kolb, B. Brain
    Research Reviews, Vol. 8, (1), November 1984, pp. 65–98

45 *Effects of focal brain lesions on visual problem-solving* Laurie A. Miller, L. A. &
    Tippett, L. J. *Neuropsychologia* Vol. 34 (5), May 1996, pp. 387–398

46 Centre for Neuro Skills website. Retrieved on 27 April 2015 from www.
    neuroskills.com/brain-injury/frontal-lobes.php

47 *The Lives of the Brain: Human Evolution and the Organ of Mind* Allen, J. S.
    (London: 2009) p. 103

48 McGilchrist, p. 58

49   *A neuropsychological test of belief and doubt: damage to ventromedial prefrontal cortex increases credulity for misleading advertising* Asp, E. et al. *Front. Neurosci.*, 9 July 2012

50   *Neuropsychology of prefrontal cortex* Siddiqui, S. V. et al *Indian J Psychiatry.* 2008 Jul-Sep; 50(3) pp. 202–208.

51   Centre for Neuro Skills website, frontal lobes page. Retrieved on 4 June 2015 from www.neuroskills.com/brain-injury/frontal-lobes.php.

52   *What are the effects of alcohol on the brain?* Dekker, A. *Scientific American* 26 July 1999

53   *Brain damage and addictive behavior: a neuropsychological and electroencephalogram investigation with pathologic gamblers.* Regard, M. et al. *Cogn Behav Neurol.* 2003 Mar;16(1) pp. 47-53

54   McGilchrist, p. 59

55   *50 Ideas You Really Need to Know: The Human Brain* Costanti, M. (London: 2013) p. 70

56   *Neuroscientist Explains The Similarities Between The Brains Of Praying Nuns And Psychedelic Drug Users* Buxton, R. 28 May 2015 Retrieved on 19 November 2015 from www.huffingtonpost.com/2015/05/28/psychedelic-drug-brain-effects_n_7455368.html

57   *Tic Tips: Strategies to help you manage your Tourette Syndrome* Retreived on 23 June 2106 from http://www.tourettes-action.org.uk/storage/downloads/1374586633_Tic-tips---managing-your-TS.pdf

58   *The Man Who Mistook His Wife For a Hat* Sacks, O. (New York: 1985) pp. 95-6

59   *Compensatory Neural Reorganization in Tourette Syndrome* Jackson, S. R. et al. *Current Biology* , Vol. 21 , Issue 7, pp. 580-585

60   *Randomized Trial of Behavior Therapy for Adults With Tourette Syndrome* Wilhelm, S. et al. *Archives of General Psychiatry*, 2012; 69 (8): p. 795

61   *Cage fighter says Tourette's is no disadvantage* AFP 3 November 2014 Retrieved on 24 June 2016 from www.yahoo.com/news/cage-fighter-says-tourettes-no-154106147.html?ref=gs

62   Sherdog website. Retrieved on 24 June 2016 from www.sherdog.com/fighter/Amir-Khan-124985

63   *Americans in the Premier League: why have Numbers dropped recently?* Carlisle, J. Retrieved on 24 June 2016 from www.espnfc.com/blog/espn-fc-united-blog/68/post/2331121/americans-in-the-premier-league----why-have-numbers-dropped-recently

64   *Who, what, why: Could Tourette's syndrome make a goalkeeper better?* 2 July 2014 www.bbc.co.uk/news/blogs-magazine-monitor-28128439

65   McGilchrist, p. 12

66   *Language disorders (aphasia).* Goodglass, H., & Geschwind, N. in *Handbook of Perception* (Vol. 7). E. C. Carterette & M. Friedman (eds.) (New York: 1976).

67   *Dendritic right/left asymmetries in the neurones of the human hippocampal formation: a quantitative Golgi study.* Sa, M. J et al. *Arq. Neuro-Psiquiatr.* 2007, vol.65, n.4b, pp. 1105-1113

68 *Hemispheric Differences in Layer III Pyramidal Neurons of the Anterior Language Area* Hayes, T. L & Lewis, D. A *Arch Neurol.* May 1993, Vol 50, No. 5 pp. 501-505.

69 *Mapping Human Cortical Areas in vivo Based on Myelin Content as Revealed by T1- and T2-weighted MRI* Glasser, M. F. & Van Essen. D. C. *J Neurosci.* 2011 Aug 10; 31(32): pp. 11597–11616.

70 McGilchrist, pp. 26

71 McGilchrist, pp. 65

72 McGilchrist, pp. 49-52

73 *Jill Bolte Taylor's Powerful Stroke of Insight* TED talk. Retrieved on 12 August 2016 from www.ted.com/talks/jill_bolte_taylor_s_powerful_stroke_of_insight/transcript

74 *The Cambridge Handbook of Creativity* (Kaufman, J. C. & Sternberg, R. J. eds) (Cambridge: 2010) pp. 413-446

75 *Encyclopedia of the Neurological Sciences* Aminoff, M. J & Daroff, R. B. (Boston: 2003) p. 396

76 *Pigeons' Discrimination of Paintings by Monet and Picasso* Watanabe, S. et al *Journal of the Experimental Analysis of Behavior* Vol. 63, Issue 2, pp. 165–174, March 1995

77 *Music discriminations by carp (Cyprinus carpio)* Chase, A. R. *Animal Learning & Behavior* November 2001, Vol. 29, Issue 4, pp. 336–353

78 McGilchrist, p. 86

79 *Alcoholics Anonymous: the story of how many thousands of men and women have recovered from alcoholism* Bill W. (June 2001) chapter 5

80 *Relative Efficacy of Mindfulness-Based Relapse Prevention, Standard Relapse Prevention, and Treatment as Usual for Substance Use Disorders: A Randomized Clinical Trial* Bowen, S. et al. *JAMA Psychiatry.* 2014;71(5) pp. 547-556

81 *Harvard University Gazette* 18 April 2002

82 *Exaggerated Heart Rate Oscillations During Two Meditation Techniques* Peng, C. K et al. in *International Journal of Cardiology* (1990)70:pp. 101-107

83 *Heart rate dynamics during three forms of meditation* Peng C.-K. in *International Journal of Cardiology* vol. 95 (2004) pp. 19-27

84 *Learned Control of Single Motor Units* Basmajian V.J. in *Biofeedback: Theory and Research* Schwartz, G. E, & Beatty, J. (New York: 1977)

85 *Neuroscientist Explains The Similarities Between The Brains Of Praying Nuns And Psychedelic Drug Users* Buxton, R. 28 May 2015 Retrieved on 19 November 2015 from www.huffingtonpost.com/2015/05/28/psychedelic-drug-brain-effects_n_7455368.html

86 *Kohlbergian moral perspective responses, EEG coherence and the Transcendental Meditation and TM Sidhi program* Nidich, S. I. et al in *Journal of Moral Education* Vol. 12, 3, October 1983, pp. 166-73

87 *Seventeenth-Century Quaker Sought Redress by Undressing* Berry, M. *Geneology Magazine* Retrieved on 5 August 2015 from www.genealogymagazine.com/quakers.html

88   *On Religion and Politics: Noam Chomsky interviewed by Amina Chaudary Islamica Magazine*, Issue 19, April-May, 2007

89   *Stanford Encyclopedia of Philosophy*: William of Ockham entry. Retrieved on 13 December 2015 from http://plato.stanford.edu/entries/ockham/

90   Retrieved on 5 March 2015 from http://www.savetibet.org/resources/fact-sheets/self-immolations-by-tibetans/

91   *Stanford Encyclopedia of Philosophy*: William Godwin entry. Retrieved on 8 August 2015 from http://plato.stanford.edu/entries/godwin/

92   *Enquiry Concerning Political Justice and Its Influence on Morals and Happiness* Godwin, Vol. 1 W. (London: 1798) p. 290

93   *Essays Never Before Published* Godwin, W. (London: 2013) pp. 84-85

94   *Code of Canon Law*, (1983) Part 3, Section 1, canon 573

95   *New school dharma, McMindfulness, and the politics of Buddhist insight: a talk with Jay Michaelson* Expanding Mind podcast. Retrieved on 5 September 2015 from http://expandingmind.podbean.com/2014/03/17/expanding-mind-evolving-dharma-031714/

96   *What God does to your brain* Smith, J. L. *The Telegraph*, 20 June 2014. Retrieved on 13 September 2015 from www.telegraph.co.uk/culture/books/10914137/What-God-does-to-your-brain.html

97   *What God does to your brain* Smith, J. L. *The Telegraph*, 20 June 2014. Retrieved on 13 September 2015 from www.telegraph.co.uk/culture/books/10914137/What-God-does-to-your-brain.html

98   *Long-Term Enhancement of Brain Function and Cognition Using Cognitive Training and Brain Stimulation* Snowball, A et al. (2013). *Current Biology* Vol. 23, Issue 11, pp. 987–992

99   *Savant-like skills exposed in normal people by suppressing the left fronto-temporal lobe* Snyder, A. W. *Journal of Integrative Neuroscience*, Vol. 2, No. 2, (2003) pp. 149-158

100   *Sean Paul's songs sparked woman's seizures* Mental Health on NBC News, 17 January 2008, Retrieved on March 5 2015 from www.nbcnews.com/id/22718183/ns/health-mental_health/t/sean-pauls-songs-sparked-womans-seizures/#.VPh-dimxzW4

101   *Woman has seizures every time she hears a Ne-yo song*, SWNS TV 12 November 2014

102   *Aura of mystery* Dolgin, E *Nature Medicine* 19, 1083–1085 (2013)

103   *Symptomatology of temporal lobe epilepsy* Neppe, V. M. SA *Medical Journal*, 5 December, 1981, pp. 902-907.

104   *Epilepsy: A Comprehensive Review* Sharma, S., Dixit, V. *International Journal of Pharmacological Research & Review*, (2013) 2(12) pp. 61-80.

105   *Drunken Glory* Vice Documentary Retrieved on 5 September 2015 from www.vice.com/en_uk/video/drunken-glory-full-length

106   He was reading from *The Jesus Sutras: Rediscovering the Lost Scrolls of Taoist Christianity* Palmer, M. (New York: 2001)

107 *The neuropsychiatry of paranormal experiences* Persinger, M. A. *The Journal of Neuropsychiatry & Clinical Neurosciences* (2001) 13 (4): 515–524.

108 *Neuropsychological Bases of God Beliefs*, Persinger, M. A. (New York: 1987)

109 *Remote viewing with the artist Ingo Swann: neuropsychological profile, lectroencephalographic correlates, magnetic resonance imaging (MRI), and possible mechanisms* Persinger, M. A. Percept Mot Skills. 2002 Jun 94 (3 Pt 1) pp, 927-49

110 *God on the Brain, BBC Horizon documentary*, aired 17 April 2003 Retrieved on 20 January 2015 from www.bbc.co.uk/science/horizon/2003/godonbraintrans. shtml

111 *God on the Brain*, BBC Horizon documentary, aired 17 April 2003

112 *God on the Brain*, BBC Horizon documentary, aired 17 April 2003

113 Doing what the mob do: priming effects on conformity Pendry, L. & Carrick, R. *European Journal of Social Psychology* 2001 January/February 31 (1) pp. 83–92

114 *The relation between perception and behavior, or how to win a game of trivial pursuit* Dijksterhuis, A. & van Knippenberg, A. *J Pers Soc Psychol.* 1998 April 74(4) pp. 865-77.

115 Exodus 8:1

116 Exodus 11:10

117 *Anomalous Events That Can Shake One's Skepticism to the Core* Shermer, M. *Scientific American* Sep 16, 2014 Retrieved on 14 June 2015 from http://www.scientificamerican.com/article/anomalous-events-that-can-shake-one-s-skepticism-to-the-core/

118 *Results of the National Demonstration Project to Reduce Violent Crime and Improve Governmental Effectiveness in Washington, D.C.* Hagelin, J. S. et al. in *Social Indicators Research* 47, (1999) pp. 153-201

119 Princeton website Retrieved on 31st October 2015 from www.princeton. edu/~pear/press-statement.html

120 *Offline: What is medicine's 5 sigma?* Horton, R. *The Lancet*, Vol. 385, No. 9976, p. 1380, 11 April 2015

121 *We found only one-third of published psychology research is reliable – now what?* Villiger, M. 27 August 2015. Retrieved on 24 September 2015 from theconversation.com/we-found-only-one-third-of-published-psychology-research-is-reliable-now-what-46596

122 *Earth Lights Revelation: UFOs and Mystery Lightform Phenomena* Devereux, P. *The Earth's Secret Energy Force* (London: 1990)

123 *Possible Effect of Geomagnetic Fluctuations on the Timing of Epileptic Seizures* Spottiswoode, S. J. P. et al. http://www.jsasoc.com

124 *Geophysical variables and behavior: XXIX. Intense paranormal experiences occur during days of quiet global geomagnetic activity* Persinger, M. A. *Perceptual and Motor Skills* 61 (1985), pp.320-322.

125 *Dr. Michael Persinger, interview* 3 Retrieved on February 28 2015 from www.youtube.com/watch?v=6iNyHiItCmk

126 *Psychedelics and Religious Experience* Watts, A. *The California Law Review*, Vol. 56, No. 1, Jan. 1968, pp. 74-85

127 *The Psychedelic State Induced by Ayahuasca Modulates the Activity and Connectivity of the Default Mode Network* Palhano-Fontes, F. et al. *PLoS ONE* 10.2 (2015)

128 *Neuroscientist Explains The Similarities Between The Brains Of Praying Nuns And Psychedelic Drug Users* Buxton, R. 28 May 2015 Retrieved on 19 November 2015 from www.huffingtonpost.com/2015/05/28/psychedelic-drug-brain-effects_n_7455368.html

Notes for chapter 7: Eve's Apple and Adam's Nostril

1   *The Collected Works of Oscar Wilde* Wilde, O. (London: 2007) p. 1043

2   Genesis 1

3   Daniel 2:22

4   Genesis 30:22

5   Genesis 5:24, 6:9, 20:3, 30:22

6   Genesis 3:8

7   Genesis 1:1 etc.

8   Genesis 2:7 (with extra nutritional optional articles, and 'clay' rather than 'dust', which makes more sense given its malleability)

9   Strong's, H5731

10 Strong's, H6335

11 Strong's, H6376, H1521, H2313

12 Strong's, H2342

13 Strong's, H3568

14 Strong's, H804, H833

15 *Pigeons' Discrimination of Paintings by Monet and Picasso* Watanabe, S. et al *Journal of the Experimental Analysis of Behavior* Vol. 63, Issue 2, March 1995 pp. 165–174

16 *Music discriminations by carp (Cyprinus carpio)* Chase, A. R. *Animal Learning & Behavior November* 2001, Vol. 29, Issue 4, pp. 336–353

17 Genesis 2:19

18 *The neuropsychiatry of paranormal experiences* Persinger, M. A. *The Journal of Neuropsychiatry & Clinical Neurosciences* (2001) 13 (4): 515–524.

19 *Experimental facilitation of the sensed presence is predicted by the specific patterns of the applied magnetic fields, not by suggestibility: re-analyses of 19 experiments* St-Pierre L. S. & Persinger M. A. *Int J Neurosci.* 2006 Sep;116(9), pp. 1079-96.

20 Genesis 2:18

NOTES

21 Genesis 1:29 (modified KJV)

22 Genesis 1:29 (NIV), 2:17

23 Genesis 3: 4-5

24 Genesis 3:7

25 Genesis 3:7

26 Genesis 3:13 Alternative translation from *God is a Verb* Cooper, D (Riverhead: 1997) p. 66

27 Genesis 3

28 Jeremiah 24:2

29 Strong's, H5172

30 *Gesenius' Hebrew-Chaldee Lexicon*: entry for 'nachash'

31 Jeremiah 4:6

32 *Answer to Job* Jung, C. G. (Princeton, N. J.: 2011). para. 560

33 Exodus 32:9-14

34 Genesis 6:6, Exodus 32:14, 2 Samuel 24:16, 1 Chronicles 21:15, Jeremiah 26:19, Jonah 3:10

35 Isaiah 45:7

36 Genesis 24:50

37 Genesis 25: 31-34

38 Genesis 27:11-29

39 Genesis 12: 14-16

40 Proverbs 14:18

41 *Encyclopedia Judaica* 1906: Masorah Retrieved on 9 May 2015 from http://jewishencyclopedia.com/articles/3268-bible-texts

42 *What's Bothering Rashi: A Guide to In-Depth Analysis of his Torah Commentary* Bonchek, A (Jerusalem: 2001) p. 70

43 *Tikkune Soferim: "Scribal Emendations"* Tzipor, M. Department of Bible. Retrieved on 14 December 2015 from www.biu.ac.il/JH/Parasha/eng/behaalot/tzip.html

44 *Tikkunei Soferim, an Analysis of a Masoretic Phenomenon* Lieberman, A. Footnote 2, in *Hakirah* Vol. 5 (Fall 2007)

45 Proverbs 22:3

46 *On The Origin of the World* (Bethge H-G & Layton, B. trans.) in *The Nag Hammadi Library* Kuhmann, R. C. p. 357 Retrieved on 30 December 2015 from www.kuhmann.com/poetry/The%20Nag%20Hammadi%20Library.pdf

47 *The Testimony of Truth* (Giversen, S. and Pearson, B. A. trans.) Retrieved on 30 December 2015 from www.bibliotecapleyades.net/nag_hammadi/testruth.htm

48 Genesis 1:29

49 *The Everlasting Gospel* in *Blake: Complete Writings* (Keynes, G. ed) (London: 1971), from *Supplementary Passages*, version 2, pp. 758-759

Notes for chapter 8: The Monkey Wrench

1   *The Ecstatic Adventure: Reports of Chemical Explorations of the Inner World* (Metzner, R. ed.) (New York: 1968) forward.

2   *The Principles of Psychology* James, W. (New York: 1950), p. 183

3   John 10:25-33, modified from 'my' to 'the'

4   John 10:34

5   Psalm 82:6-8 The translations invariably read "Arise, O God", not gods, but grammatically it is not. It seems reasonable to interpret elohim as "all" the god-men to whom elohim refered in the previous verse

6   *I AM THAT I AM* 23 December 1998 Retrieved on 5 October 2015 from http://lists.ibiblio.org/pipermail/b-hebrew/1998-December/000793.html

7   *Targum Onkelos to* Exodus Drazin, I. (Denver: 1990) p. 59

8   *The Pentateuch and Haftorahs* (Hertz, J.H., ed.) (Soncino: 1956) p. 215

9   *Georg Cantor and the Battle for Transfinite Set Theory* Dauben, J. W. Department of History, Herbert H. Lehman College, CUNY p. 8 Retrieved on March 1 2015 from http://heavysideindustries.com/wp-content/uploads/2011/08/Dauben-Cantor.pdf

10 *Faith and Heresy* Agushevits, R. (New Jersey: 2006), p. xiv

11 *Ludwig Wittgenstein: The Duty of Genius* Monk, R. (London: 1990) p. 439

12 *Wittgenstein: the philosophical investigations: a collection of critical essays* Pitcher, G. (New York: 1966) part I, pp.66-67

13 *Genesis Rabbah* 1:10

14 *Infinity and the Mind: The Science and Philosophy of the Infinite* Rucker, R. (Princeton: 1995) p. 191

15 Exodus 3:11-14 (no 'Certainly' in the Hebrew)

16 *The Wisdom of the Christian Mystics* Freke, T. (Boston: 1998) p. 26

17 *Meditation and Kabbalah* Kaplan, A. (New York: 1985), p. 305

18 Exodus 7:1

19 *Magic mushrooms' effects illuminated in brain imaging studies* Wong, S. 24 January 2012 Retrieved on 5 March 2016 from www3.imperial.ac.uk/newsandeventspggrp/imperialcollege/newssummary/news_24-1-2012-10-39-58

20 *Psychedelic chemical subdues brain activity* Costandi, M. *Nature* 23 January 2012

21 *Anterior Cingulate Cortex: Unique Role in Cognition and Emotion* Stevens, F. L. *J Neuropsychiatry Clin Neurosci* 23:2, Spring 2011

22 *A Developmental fMRI Study of the Stroop Color-Word Task* Adleman, N. E. et al *NeuroImage* 16, 61–75 (2002)

23 *The role of the anterior cingulate cortex in the counting Stroop task* Hayward, G. *Experimental Brain Research* February 2004, Vol. 154, 3, pp. 355-358

24 *The Road to Eleusis: Unveiling the Secret of the Mysteries*, Wasson, G. et al, chapter 1, p. 6

25 *Tractate Eruvin* 13b

26 *Prefrontal and anterior cingulate cortex abnormalities in Tourette Syndrome: evidence from voxel-based morphometry and magnetization transfer imaging* Müller-Vahl, K. R. et al BMC *Neuroscience*, 2009, 10: 47

27 *A Primary Role for Nucleus Accumbens and Related Limbic Network in Vocal Tics* McCairn, K. W. *Neuron*, 20 January 2016 Vol. 89, 2, pp. 300–307

28 McGilchrist, p. 125

29 *Brains on LSD*, Expanding Mind podcast, 03 December 2015. Retrieved on 01 June 2015 from http://expandingmind.podbean.com/e/brains-on-lsd-031215/

30 *The Ketamine Model of the Near Death Experience: A central role for the NMDA Receptor* Jansen, K. L. R. (1997) in *Journal of Near-Death Studies* Vol. 16, No.1

31 *Ketamine: Dreams and Realities* Jansen, K. (MAPS 2004) pp. 114, 123

32 *Excitatory Actions of NMDA Receptor Antagonists in Rat Entorhinal Cortex and Cultured Entorhinal Cortical Neurons* Väisänen, J. *Neuropsychopharmacology* (1999) 21, pp. 137–146

33 If I could remember the wit that came out with that I'd cite him

34 *Subjective Effects of Nitrous Oxide* James, W. *Mind*. 1882; Vol. 7

35 *Subjective Effects of Nitrous Oxide* James, W. *Mind*. 1882; Vol. 7

36 *The Gnostic Gospels* Pagels, E. (New York: 1979) chapter 2

37 *The Psychedelic State Induced by Ayahuasca Modulates the Activity and Connectivity of the Default Mode Network* Palhano-Fontes, F. et al. *PLoS ONE* 10.2 (2015)

38 *Decreto de Serviço da doutrina do Santo Daime*, Serra, R. I. Retrieved on 19 November 2015 from http://afamiliajuramidam.org/liturgia/decreto_de_servico.htm

39 *Eu Vim da Minha Armada*, Mestre Irineu Hymn no. 86

40 *Ayahuasca enhances creative divergent thinking while decreasing conventional convergent thinking* Kuypers, K. P. C. et al., *Psychopharmacology (Berl)*. July 2016

41 *The American Trip: Set, Setting, and Psychedelics in 20th Century Psychology* Hartogsohn, I. *MAPS Bulletin* Special Edition Spring 2013

42 *The safety and efficacy of ±3,4-methylenedioxymethamphetamine-assisted psychotherapy in subjects with chronic, treatment-resistant posttraumatic stress disorder: the first randomized controlled pilot study* Mithoefer, M. C. et al *J Psychopharmacol* April 2011 vol. 25 no. 4 pp. 439-452

43 *Durability of improvement in post-traumatic stress disorder symptoms and absence of harmful effects or drug dependency after 3,4-methylenedioxymethamphetamine-assisted psychotherapy: a prospective long-term follow-up study* Michael, M. C. et al *J Psychopharmacol* January 2013 vol. 27 no. 1 28-39

44   pers. comm Rick Doblin, director of MAPS

45   *Subjective Theories about (Self-)Treatment with Ayahuasca* Schmid J. T. et al, Anthropology of Consciousness Vol. 21, Issue 2, Fall 2010, pp, 188–204,

46   *The View of Life Influences of Ayahuasca Experiences* Lavonius, J. Presentation at AYA2014 Retrieved on April 23 2015 from www.aya2014.com/en/videos-2/

47   *Great scientific news on ayahuasca's therapeutic potentials* Labate, B. Retrieved on 7 June 2016 from www.bialabate.net/news/scientific-breaking-ground-news-regarding-ayahuascas-therapeutic-potentials

48   *Dad uses CANNABIS OIL to treat 3-year-old daughter;s EPILEPSY after she suffered 50 seizures a day* Lubin, B *Mirror* Online, 5 February 2016 Retrieved on 7 June 2016 from www.mirror.co.uk/lifestyle/health/dad-uses-cannabis-oil-treat-7317695

49   *Cannabidiol Displays Antiepileptiform and Antiseizure Properties In Vitro and In Vivo* Jones N. A. et al. *The Journal of Pharmacology and Experimental Therapeutics* 2010; 332 (2): pp. 569-577.

50   *Response of cluster headache to psilocybin and LSD* Sewell, R. A. et al in *Neurology* June 2006;66; pp. 1920-192

51   *Science Revealed* by me

52   *The powerful placebo* Beecher, H. K. *JAMA*. 1955;159: pp. 1602-1606.

53   *The Placebo Effect: History, Biology, and Ethics* Lemoine, P. Retrieved on 7 June 2016 from www.medscape.com/viewarticle/852144

54   *The Incorporation of Umbanda by Santo Daime* Marques, A. A. Jr. (Thornton, D. trans.) Retrieved on 7 June 2016 from www.neip.info/upd_blob/0001/1281. pdf

55   *Cosmic Trigger:Final Secret of the Illuminati* Wilson, R. A. (Scotsdale, AZ: 1977)

Notes for chapter 9: Exodrugs

1   If you want to pay for this crock of shit, this is the URL: http://www.tektonics. org/ezine/eblock0716/howdy.html
    However, I have also archived it on my website, www.nemusend.co.uk

2   *Sacred Weeds: Blue Water Lilly / Ancient Egypt.* Channel 4 TV Pt1/6

3   *The Book of the Dead* (Wallis Budge, E. A. trans.) The chapter of Making the Transformation into the Lotus

4   *Garden of Eden: The Shamanic Use of Psychoactive Flora and Fauna, and the Study of Consciousness* Voogelbreinder, S. (2009) p. 247

5   *The Long Trip: A Prehistory of Psychedelia* Devereux, P. (New York: 1997), p. 88

6   *Biblical Entheogens: a Speculative Hypothesis* Shanon, B. in *Time and Mind: The Journal of Archaeology Consciousness and Culture* March, 2008 1 (1): pp. 51–74

7   *Ars Quatuor Coronatorum* Songhurst, W. J.

8   *NMT: A Spatial Hallucinogen with Therapeutic Applications* Talk given at
     Breaking Convention by Nen, retrieved from https://vimeo.com/76519380 on
     February 19 2015

9   *The Book of the Dead* (Wallis Budge, E. A. trans.) The Solar Litany

10   *Cunningham's Encyclopedia of Magical Herbs* Cunningham, S. (Llewellyn
     e-book 2012)

11   *Dictionary of Symbols*. Chevalier, J. et al (New York: 1996)

12   Exodus 26:15

13   *Transcultural use of narcotic water lilies in ancient Egyptian and Maya drug
     ritual* Emboden, W. A. *Journal of Ethnopharmacology* Vol. 3, 1, January 1981,
     pp. 39-83

14   *Monkey* chap. 11-12

15   *The Aeneid* Homer, 9:83-102

16   *Indigenous Australian Stories and Sea-Level Change* Reid, N. et al in *Indigenous
     Languages and their Value to the Community* (Heinrich, P. & Ostler, N. eds.)
     Proceedings of the 18th Foundation for Endangered Languages conference,
     Okinawa, Japan, 2014

17   McGilchrist, p. 105

18   *Rig Veda*: Soma, book 9

19   *The Tawny One: Soma, Haoma, and Ayahuasca* Clark, M. (forthcoming) See
     video at AYA2014 - *Matthew* Clark. The botanical identity of the soma/haoma
     plant ICEERS Ayahuasca conference video. Retrieved on 5 September 2015
     from www.aya2014.com/en/videos-2/
     Also see his forthcoming book, chapter 5

20   *Haoma and Harmaline. The Botanical Identity of the Indo-Iranian Sacred
     Hallucinogen 'Soma' and its Legacy in Religion, Language, and Middle Eastern
     Folklore* Flattery, D. S., & Schwartz, M. (California: 1989) vol. 21

21   *Cannabis and the Soma Solution* Bennett, C. (Chicago: 2010)

22   *Soma: Divine Mushroom of Immortality* Wasson, R. G. (Harcourt: 1972)

23   *The Tawny One: Soma, Haoma, and Ayahuasca* Clark, M. (forthcoming) See
     video at AYA2014 - *Matthew* Clark. The botanical identity of the soma/haoma
     plant ICEERS Ayahuasca conference video. Retrieved on 5 September 2015
     from www.aya2014.com/en/videos-2/

24   *Nymphaea cults in ancient Egypt and the New World: a lesson in empirical
     pharmacology* Bertol, E. *Journal of the Royal Society of Medicine* February
     2004 Vol. 97, 2 pp. 84-85

25   *Homeric Hymn to Demeter* (Nagy, G. trans.)

26   *The Road to Eleusis: Unveiling the Secret of the Mysteries* Wasson, G. et al
     (Berkely: 2008) p. 27

27   *Dirges* Pindar, Fragment 137 in *The Odes of Pindar, including the principal
     fragments* Sandys, J. E. (London: 1915)

28 *The Road to Eleusis: Unveiling the Secret of the Mysteries* Wasson, G. et al (Berkely: 2008) p. 68

29 *The Road to Eleusis: Unveiling the Secret of the Mysteries* Wasson, G. et al (Berkely: 2008) p. 43

30 *LSD and Ololiuhqui Postscriptum: The Secret of the Eleusinian Mysteries Revealed* in *Pharmacotheon: Entheogenic Drugs, Their Plant Sources and History* Ott, J. (California: 1993)

31 *Food of the Gods* Terence McKenna (New York: 1992) chap. 8

32 *The Archeology of the New Testament: The Mediterranean World of the Early Christain Apostles* Finegan, J. (New York: 2015) p. 143

33 *Cannabis and the Soma Solution* Bennett, C. (Chicago: 2010) p. 470-488

34 *Animals and Psychedelics: The Natural World and the Instinct to Alter Consciousness* Samorini, G. (Park Street Press: 2000), p. 57

35 *Peculiar Potions*, from the BBC series *Weird Nature*

36 *Intoxication: The Universal Drive for Mind-Altering Substances* Siegel, R. K. (Vermont: 2005), p. 50

37 *Dogs Licking Cane Toads Prompt Vests To Warn Pet Owners* Gates, S. *Huffington Post* 17 December 2013

38 *Stoned wallabies make crop circles* BBC News. Retrieved on 9 August 2016 from http://news.bbc.co.uk/1/hi/8118257.stm

39 *Intoxication: The Universal Drive for Mind-Altering Substances* Siegel, R. K. (Vermont: 2005), p. 128

40 Strong's, H1730

41 *The Encyclopedia of Psychoactive Plants: Ethnopharmacology and Its Applications* Rätsch, C. (Rochester: 2005)

42 Strong's, H1736

43 *Pathogenetic materia medica* Enz, E. E. (Kansas City: 1911) p. 249

44 *Wars of the Jews* Josephus Book VII, 6.3 in The Works of Flavius Josephus (Whiston, W. trans) (1737)

45 Genesis 30:14-15

46 Matthew 2:11

47 *Sacred Signs* Guardini, R. (Branham, G. trans) (St. Louis: 1956) Section on incense

48 *Identification of dehydroabietc acid from Boswellia thurifera resin as a positive GABA$_A$ receptor modulator* Rueda, D. C. et al *Fitoterapia* Vol. 99, December 2014, pp. 28–34

49 *Incensole acetate, an incense component, elicits psychoactivity by activating TRPV3 channels in the brain* Moussaieff, A. et al August 2008 *The FASEB Journal* Vol. 22 no. 8 pp. 3024-3034

50 *Anticonvulsant effect of Boswellia serrata by modulation of endogenous biomarkers* Ziyaurrahman, A. R. & Patel, J. *Der Pharmacia Lettre*, 2012, 4 (4): pp. 1308-1325 Scholar Research Library

51 *De Materia Medica* Dioscorides (Osbaldeston, T. A. & Wood, R. trans) Book 1: Aromata, 68:3

52 *Analgesic effects of myrrh* Dolara, P. *Nature* 379, 29 (04 January 1996)

53 *Fulgentius the Mythographer* (Whitebread, L. G. trans.) (Ohio: 1971) p. 92

54 Proverbs 7:16-18

55 *Characterisation of the action on central opioid receptors of furanoeudesma-1,3-diene, a sesquiterpene extracted from myrrh* Dolora, P. et al (1996) Phytotherapy Research, Vol. 10, pp. S81-S83, ISN:0951-418X

56 Mark 15:23

57 Song of Songs 4:13-14 (giving camphire its more common name)

58 Strong's, H7218

59 *How an ounce of saffron is more expensive than gold* Daily Mail online (I know, sorry. I could have got it from *Business Insider*, but it said that gold was a bit more expensive, I guess it depends who is selling) Retreived on 6 September 2015 from www.dailymail.co.uk/news/article-2823029/How-ounce-saffron-expensive-gold-Cultivation-exotic-spice-returns-Essex-time-200-years. html#ixzz3kuolMA7M

60 *Comparison of the anti-inflammatory and anti-nociceptive effects of three medicinal plants known as "Snow Lotus" herb in traditional Uighur and Tibetan medicines* Yi, T. et al *J Ethnopharmacol.* 2010 Mar 24;128(2):405-11.

61 *Protective effect of safranal on pentylenetetrazol-induced seizures in the rat: Involvement of GABAergic and opioids systems* Hosseinzadeh, H. & Sadeghnia, H. R. *Phytomedicine* Vol. 14, Issue 4, 10 April 2007, pp. 256–262

62 *The Encyclopedia of Psychoactive Plants: Ethnopharmacology and Its Applications* Rätsch, C. (Vermont: 1998)

63 *Effects of the active constituents of Crocus sativus L., crocins, in an animal model of anxiety* Pitsikas, N et al. *Phytomedicine* Vol. 15, Issue 12, December 2008, pp. 1135–1139

64 *Celestial Botany: Entheogenic Traces in Islamic Mysiticism* Dannaway, F. R., quoting Saso, Michael J., 1990.

65 *Comparative study on the effect of cinnamon and clove extracts and their main components on different types of ATPases* Usta, J. et al. *Hum Exp Toxicol.* 2003 Jul;22(7) pp. 355-62

66 *Psychobiological Assessment of Smoke of Agarwood (Aquilaria spp.) in Male Rats* Miraghaee, S. S. et al. *Journal of Applied Biological Sciences* 5 (2): 45-53, 2011

67 John 12:3-5

68 *Effects of Nardostachys jatamansi on Biogenic Amines and Inhibitory Amino Acids in the Rat Brain* Prabhu, V. & Karanth K. S. *Planta Med* 1994; 60(2): pp. 114-117

69 Strong's, H7070

70 *Early Diffusion and Folk Uses of Hemp* Benet, S. in *Cannabis and Culture*, Rubin, Vera & Comitas, Lambros (eds.) 1975, pp. 39-49

71   Strong's, H1314

72   *Early Diffusion and Folk Uses of Hemp* in *Cannabis and Culture*, Rubin, Vera & Comitas, Lambros, (eds.) 1975. pp. 39-49

73   Herodotus, Book 4 (G. Rawlinson trans.), 74-75

74   *Scythian gold vessels used in 'hemp rituals'* Archaeology News Network

Retrieved on May 28 2015 from http://archaeologynewsnetwork.blogspot. co.uk/2015/05/scythian-gold-vessels-used-in-hemp.html#.VWcNeusxmU0

75   *Aimless Wandering: Chuang Tzu's Chaos Linguistics* Hakim Bey, Fringeware Review, issue 10 (1996)

76   *Scythian gold vessels used in 'hemp rituals'* Archaeology News Network

Retrieved on May 28 2015 from http://archaeologynewsnetwork.blogspot. co.uk/2015/05/scythian-gold-vessels-used-in-hemp.html#.VWcNeusxmU0

77   *Cannabis and the Soma Solution* Bennett, C. (Chicago: 2010) p. 356

78   *First identification of drugs in Egyptian mummies* Balababova, S. F et al. (1992). *Naturwissenschaften* 79:358.

79   Jeremiah 6:20

80   *Cannabis: The Genus Cannabis* Brown, D. T. (ed) (Taylor and Francis e-library: 2003), p. 3

81   *Cannabis and the Soma Solution* Bennett, C. (Chicago: 2010) p. 351

82   *Meditation and Kabbalah* Kaplan, A. (Rowman & Littlefield: 1982), p. 156

83   *Melatonin, serotonin, and tryptamine in some egyptian food and medicinal plants* Badria, F. *J Med Food*. 2002 Fall;5(3):pp. 153-7.

84   Retrieved on 3 June 2015 from http://www.entheogen-network.com/forums/ viewtopic.php?f=10&t=5698&start=20#p42383

85   Exodus 30:22-25 (one *hiyn* is about six litres)

86   Strong's, H1969

87   *The Seven Books of Paulus Aegineta* Vol. 3 (Francis, A. trans) (London: 1847) p. 595

88   *Gesenius' Hebrew-Chaldee Lexicon*, entry for *hin*

89   Strong's, 4886

90   *The American Heritage Dictionary* Semitic Roots Appendix II Retrieved on 6 September 2015 from https://www.ahdictionary.com/word/semitic.html

91   *Anxiolytic-like effects of inhaled linalool oxide in experimental mouse anxiety models* Souto-Maior, F. N. *Pharmacology Biochemistry and Behavior* Vol. 100, Issue 2, December 2011, pp. 259–263

92   *Estragole-induced behavioural changes in rats* Rosana M. C. et al *Phytotherapy Research* Vol. 18 (11), November 2004, pp. 921–924

93   *Cinnamon: A Multifaceted Medicinal Plant* Rao, P. V. et al *Evid Based Complement Alternat Med*. 2014; 2014: 642942.

94   *Citrus Genus Plants Contain N☐Methylated Tryptamine Derivatives and Their 5☐Hydroxylated Forms* Servillo, L. et *al J. Agric. Food Chem.* 2013, 61, pp. 5156–5162

95   *Oilahuasca: The new psychedelic frontier* Retrieved on 03 June 2015 from https://drugs-forum.com/forum/showthread.php?t=156755

96   *Oilahuasca Activation: Version 1.2397* Retrieved on 30 December 2015 from http://herbpedia.wikidot.com/oilahuasca-activation

97   *In vitro evaluation of antioxidant activity of essential oils and their components.* Dorman H. J. et al *Flavour Fragr J.* 2000;15:12-16.

98   *The Psychedelic Effects of Sweet Basil Oil (Methyl Chavicol)* Retrieved on May 2016 from http://herbs.mxf.yuku.com/topic/3784181/The-Psychedelic-Effects-of-Sweet-Basil-Oil-Methyl-Chavicol?page=6#.V91N9RSVNE0

99   *Cinnamon and Cassia: The Genus Cinnamomum* (Ravindran, P. N., Nirmal-Babu, K. & Shylaj, M. eds.) (Taylor & Francis elibrary: 2005) p. 334

100   *Anti-inflammatory effect of myristicin on RAW 264.7 macrophages stimulated with polyinosinic-polycytidylic acid* Lee J. Y. & Park, W. *Molecules* 2011;16(8): pp. 7132-42

101   *Antioxidant capacity of 26 spice extracts and characterization of their phenolic constituents* Shan, B. et al *J Agric Food Chem.* 2005;53(20):7749-7759.

102   *Extraction of essential oil and lipids from nutmeg by liquid carbon dioxide.* Spricigo C. B. et al. J *Supercritical Fluids.* 1999;15: pp. 253-259.

103   Retrieved on 10 January 2016 from www.erowid.org/experiences/exp. php?ID=83145

104   *Sexual Secrets: The Alchemy of Ecstacy* Douglas, N. & Slinger, P. (Vermont: 2000) p. 246

105   *Om Vision Synergy: Nutmeg & Myrrh* Mr. Sunday Retrieved on 3 June 2015 from https://www.erowid.org/experiences/exp.php?ID=95112

106   1 Samuel 16: 13

107   Strong's, H4899

108   Exodus 30:30

109   Exodus 30:33

110   Leviticus 10:9

111   Leviticus 10:7

112   1 Chronicles 9:17-34: *The Tabernacle and Temple Responsibilities of the Sons of Korah* Edge Induced Cohesion website, retrieved 11 December 2014: https:// edgeinducedcohesion.wordpress.com/2011/02/13/1-chronicles-9-17-34-the-Tabernacle-and-temple-responsibilities-of-the-sons-of-korah/

113   *Pharmakon: Plato, Drug Culture, and Identity in Ancient Athens* Rinella, M. A. (Plymouth: 2010) p. 8

114   *The Encyclopedia of Psychoactive Plants: Ethnopharmacology and Its Applications* Rätsch, C. (Rochester: 2005) pp. 279-280.

115 *Ancient Wine: The Search for the Origins of Viniculture* McGovern, P. E. (New Jersey: 2003) p. 132

116 Leviticus 24:6-7

117 *The Guide for the Perplexed* Moses Maimonides (Digireads: 2009) p. 367

118 *Tractate Yoma* 4

119 *Tractate Yoma* 4

120 Leviticus 24:6-7

121 *Meno* Plato (Jowett, B. trans.) Retrieved on 7 November 2015 from classics.mit. edu/Plato/meno.html

122 *Tractate Niddah* 30b

123 Psalm 99:7

124 Proverbs 27:9

125 Word of the Day / Samim Gilad, E. HaAretz, June 30 2013

126 Exodus 30:34

127 *A Natural History* Pliny the Elder, chap. 35 in *Complete Works of Pliny the Elder* (Delphi Clasics: 2015) p. 406

128 *Anticonvulsant Effect of Ferula Gummosa Root Extract against Experimental Seizures* Sayyah, M. & Mandgary, A. *Iranian Biomedical Journal* 7 (3): 139-143 (July 2003)

129 *Shir HaShirim Rabbah,* 3:4

130 *Comparison of the anti-inflammatory and anti-nociceptive effects of three medicinal plants known as "Snow Lotus" herb in traditional Uighur and Tibetan medicines* Yi, T. et al *J Ethnopharmacol.* 2010 Mar 24;128(2):405-11.

131 *Uses and Abuses of Plant-Derived Smoke* Pennacchio, M. et al (Oxford: 2010)

132 *The Standard Prayer Book Authorized English Translation* Singer, S. (New York: 1915)

133 *Comparison of different extraction methods of Pistacia lentiscus var. chia leaves: Yield, antioxidant activity and essential oil chemical composition* Bampouli, A. et al *Journal of Applied Research on Medicinal and Aromatic Plants* September 2014; 1(3).

134 *Shir HaShirim Rabbah,* 3:4

135 *Rosh Hashanah Machzor* Lustiger, A. & Taubes, M. (New York: 2007), p. 185

136 1 Chronicles 9:19

137 *Tractate Yoma* 3

138 Proverbs 27:9

139 Exodus 25-31:10

140 Leviticus 16:12

141 *The Mishna: Translated from the Hebrew with Introduction and Brief Explanatory Notes* Danby, H. (Massachusetts: 2011) p. 161

NOTES

142 *The Torah* Plaut, W. G., Bamberger & B. J., Hallo, W. W. (eds.) (New York: 1981), footnote to Gen. 6:15

143 Leviticus 16:2

144 Exodus 33:9-11

145 Daniel 11:12 (NIV)

146 Brown-Driver-Briggs (Old Testament Hebrew-English Lexicon)

147 Strong's, H3381

148 Exodus 19:20

149 Exodus 15:1

150 Numbers 16:42-46

151 *Warfare and Shamanism in Amazonia* Fausto, C. (New York: 2012) p. 147

152 *Strange fires, weird smokes and psychoactive combustibles: entheogens and incense in ancient traditions* Dannaway, F. R. *Journal of Psychoactive Drugs* 2010 Dec;42(4) pp. 485-97.

153 The Poison Garden website. Retrieved on 5 September 2015 from http://www. thepoisongarden.co.uk/atoz/hyoscyamus_niger.htm

154 Exodus 28:30

155 Leviticus 8:8

156 1 Samuel 14:41

157 *Antiquities of the Jews* Josephus, 3.7.6

158 The Poison Garden website. Retrieved on 5 September 2015 from http://www. thepoisongarden.co.uk/atoz/hyoscyamus_niger.htm

159 *Abodah Zarah*, 24

160 Strong's, H7850

161 *Tractate Sanhedrin*, 106a

162 *Biblical Entheogens: a Speculative Hypothesis* Shanon, B. in *Time and Mind: The Journal of Archaeology Consciousness and Culture* March 2008 1 (1): pp. 51–74.

163 *Haoma and Harmaline: The Botanical Identity of the Indo-Iranian Sacred Hallucinogen 'Soma' and its Legacy in Religion, Language, and Middle Eastern Folklore* Flattery, D. S & Schwartz, M. (California: 1989) p. 63

164 From Har al-Anwar ["The Heat of Light"] Vol. 62, p. 235, Hadith 5, transmitted by Firdous, quoted in Arabic on Hadith City, Retrieved on 30 December 2015 from http://www.hadithcity.com/Hadith.aspx?id=1782, translated by Sheikh Muhammad Al-Hussaini, pers. comm.

165 *Sufism and Bhakti: A Comparative Study* Md. Sirajul Islam (Washington: 2004) p. 46

166 *Life or Death by EEG* Hamlin, H. *Journal of the American Medical Association* (Oct 12,1964); p.120.

167 *Sefer HaArachim* Chabad, Osios, letter mem, p. 176, Kehot Publication Society, NY

168 *The Alef-Beit: Jewish Thought Revealed through the Hebrew Letters* Ginsberg, Y. (New Jersey: 1995) p. 196

169 Exodus 3:2

170 Strong's, H5572

171 *Biblical Entheogens: a Speculative Hypothesis* Shanon, B. in *Time and Mind: The Journal of Archaeology Consciousness and Culture* March, 2008 1 (1): pp. 51–74

172 Exodus 20:18 - Young's Literal Translation

173 *DMT and the Soul of Prophecy: A New Science of Spiritual Revelation in the Hebrew Bible* Strassman, R. (Vermont: 2014) p. 285

174 *The Immaculate Heart* De Marchi, J. (New York: 1952). p. 143

175 *Stress induced changes in whole brain indolealkylamine levels in the rat: using gas liquid chromatography-mass spectrometry* Beaton J. M. & Christian S. T. (1977) *Abstr Soc Neurosci* 4:1322

176 *Of Mice and Men: Striking similarities at the DNA level could aid research* Russell, S. *SF Gate*, December 5, 2002 Retrieved on 26 September 2015 from http://www.sfgate.com/news/article/OF-MICE-AND-MEN-Striking-similarities-at-the-2748350.php

177 Strassman, p. 241

178 Strassman, p. 260

179 Strassman, p. 101

180 Exodus 16:15 (YLT and KJV)

181 *What is it? Interpreting* Exodus *16:15* Ron, Z. *Jewish Bible Quarterly*, Vol. 38, No. 4, 2010

182 *Nature and Land in the Bible* Felix, Y. (Jerusalem: 1992) p. 46.

183 Exodus 16:14 (NIV)

184 Psalm 78:21-25

185 Exodus 16:31

186 Numbers 11:8

187 *Miracle of Manna in The Desert of Sinai, Notes of a Spring Journey from Cairo to Beersheba* Bonar, H (London: 1857). Reprinted 2005 by Adamant Media Corporation for Elibron Classics pp.146-151

188 Psalm 78:25

189 Exodus 16:12 (with my alteration of 'filled' for 'satisfied')

190 Exodus 16:19-20

191 Exodus 16:23-24 (NIV)

192 *On Ergot* Carruthers, W. in *The American Naturalist*, Vol. 9, No. 8 (Aug. 1875) pp. 450-465

193 *A Laboratory Guide to the Identification of Claviceps purpurea and Claviceps africana in Grass and Sorghum Seed Samples* Alderman, S. (Oregon Department of Agriculture: 1999)

194 *Midrash Mekilta* Exodus 16:1

195 They first find water at Elim, at an oasis (Exodus 15:27), and then they travel to the wilderness of Sin (Exodus 16:1). While there is no oasis mentioned at Sin, they clearly have no trouble finding water there, as Exodus does mention any trouble finding water until the following campsite, at Rephidim (Exodus 17:1)

196 *LSD and Ololiuhqui Postscriptum: The Secret of the Eleusinian Mysteries Revealed* in *Pharmacotheon: Entheogenic Drugs, Their Plant Sources and History* Ott, J. (California: 1996)

197 Judges 1:19

198 *The Quail Epidemic of Numbers 11.31-34* Wilkinson, J. Evangelical Quarterly 71:3 (1999), 195-208

199 Numbers 26:10

200 Exodus 14:21

201 *Modelling the Hydrodynamic Situation of the* Exodus Voltzinger, N. et al (2003) *Atmospheric and Oceanic Physics*, 39, 8470;4, pp. 482-496

202 *Did Shakespeare Puff on "Noted Weed"?* Smillie, S. *National Geographic News* 1 March 2001 Retrieved on 25 September, 2015 from news.nationalgeographic. com/news/2001/03/0301_shakespeare.html

203 Retrieved on 20 August 2016 from www.2letterlookup.com: רבדמ

204 Strong's, H7793

205 Strong's, H5512. Also *Gesenius' Hebrew-Chaldee Lexicon*, where it is described as derived from a marshland, suggesting mud as much as clay.

206 Exodus 16:32

207 Exodus 16:33-34

208 *Shir HaShirim Rabbah*, 3:4

209 Hebrews 9:3

210 Genesis 37:28, 37:36 and 39:1

211 Genesis 7

212 *Catechism of the Catholic Church*, paragraph 289

213 Numbers 4:14

214 *The Original Place of the Priestly Manna Story in* Exodus *16* Baden, J., *Zeitschrift für die alttestamentliche Wissenschaft* 122 (2010): 491–504. p. 501

215 1 Chronicles 9:32

216 *Biblical Entheogens: a Speculative Hypothesis* Shanon, B. in *Time and Mind: The Journal of Archaeology Consciousness and Culture* Vol. 1, Issue 1m March 1st, 2008 pp. 51-74

217 Strong's, Numbers, G5547

218 *The Gospel of Philip* (Isenberg, W. W. trans.) Retrieved on 27 September 2015 from www.gnosis.org/naghamm/gop.html

219 Mark 6:13

220 Galatians 5:20

221 John 2

222 *Biblical Entheogens: a Speculative Hypothesis* Shanon, B. in *Time and Mind: The Journal of Archaeology Consciousness and Culture* March, 2008 1 (1): pp. 51–74.

223 *Sepher Raziel* (Peterson, J. H. ed.) (esotericarchives.com: 2006) book 2, part 2

224 *Tripping with Allah* Knight, M. M., (Berkely: 2014) pp. 43-4

225 *The Iranian Shiʿi seminary (hawza) assents: Entheogenic Shiʿi Islam and Grand Ayatollah Rohani's March 2014 fatwa in context* Azal, N. W. independent. academia.edu, Retrieved of 25 August 2016 from https://independent.academia.edu/NimaAzal

226 *Oxford Dictionary of English* Stevenson, A. ed (Oxford: 1998) p. 256

227 *Sprig of Acacia* in *Short Talk Bulletin*, Vol. X, November, 1932 No.11

228 The first part is is '*kath hemeran*', i.e. 'by day', as it is elsewhere in (e.g. Luke 9:23)

229 *Pope Benedict XVI/Cardinal Ratzinger on The Meaning of "Our Daily Bread"* Adoremus, Society for the Renewal of the Sacred Liturgy Online Edition - July - August 2007 Vol. 13, No. 5 Retrieved on 7 November 2015 from www.adoremus.org/0707BXVI_Jesus.html

230 *The Intertextual Jesus: Scripture in Q* Allison, D. C. Jr. (Harrisburg: 2000) pp. 51-52

231 2 Baruch 29:3–8

232 *The War On Drugs At A Glance* - Law Enforcement against Prohibition website. Retrieved on 2 June 2016 from www.leap.cc/for-the-media/the-war-on-drugs-at-a-glance/

Notes for chapter 10: God Against God

1 Strong's, G743

2 *The Apologists Bible Commentary - John 1*. Retrieved from www.forananswer.org/John/Jn1_1.htm on December 31st 2014, because that is what I do New Year's Eve - I read the goddam Bible, in Greek. After this, edit number a million billion, I'm going to watch the Lego movie, and then I'll probably get up in the middle of the night and do it again.

3 *The Prologue to the Fourth Gospel (John 1:1-18)* Just, F. Retrieved on 15 Septeber 2015 from catholic-resources.org/John/Outlines-Prologue.htm

4 John 8:25, 15:27 for example

5 *The Prologue to the Fourth Gospel (John 1:1-18)* Just, F. Retrieved on 15 Septeber 2015 from catholic-resources.org/John/Outlines-Prologue.htm

6 Fragment 2, Heraclitus. Quoted in *On Ancient Philosophy* Peterman, J. (Belmont: 2008) p. 42

7 Quoted by Plato in *Cratylus*, 401d

8   *Diogenes Laertius, Lives of Eminent Philosophers* (R.D. Hicks, ed.) Chapter 9, section 6

9   *Fragment 8*, in Heraclitus: Frag*ments: A Text and Translation with a Commentary* Robindon, T. M. (Toronto: 1987)

10   *Metaphysics* Aristotle book iv, pt. 7, book xi, pt. 5 etc.

11   Cate*chetical Discourses: Mystagogic* 4:22:9 Cyril of Jerusalem

12   Genesis 22

13   The Book of Job

14   John 10:30 (YLT)

15   Matthew 27:46

16   *Who Is the Heir of Divine Things* Philo in *The Works of Philo*, Vol. 2 (Yong, C. D. trans.) (Digireads: 2010) pp. 75, 81

17   Strong's, H1696

Notes for chapter 11: The Inflected Ape

1   Quoted in *Saint Augustine* Wills, G (London: 2000) p. 133

2   Quoted in *Saint Augustine* Wills, G (London: 2000) p. 139

3   *Vervet monkey alarm calls: Semantic communication in a free-ranging primate* Seyfarth, R. M. *Animal Behaviour* Vol. 28, Issue 4, November 1980, pp. 1070-1094

4   *The Sweet Stench of Success* Gordon, L. *The Independent* 12 September 1999 Retrieved on 2 October 2015 from www.independent.co.uk/arts-entertainment/the-sweet-stench-of-success-1118690.html

5   *The 66 gestures which show how chimpanzees communicate* Brooks-Pollock, T. July 2014 *The Telegrap*h 16 May 2015 Retrieved on 16 May 2015 from www.telegraph.co.uk/news/science/10945811/The-66-gestures-which-show-how-chimpanzees-communicate.html

6   The Gorilla Foundation website. www.koko.org

7   *Skinner - Operant Conditioning* McLeod, S. A. (2015). Retrieved on 9th June 2015 from www.simplypsychology.org/operant-conditioning.html

8   *Orangutan Cultures and the Evolution of Material Culture* van Schaik, C. P. *Science* 3 January 2003 vol. 299, p. 102-105

9   *Tooling through the trees: tool use by wild orangutans* Zimmer, C. *Discover Magazine*, November 1995

10   *The Biology and Evolution of Language* Lieberman, P. (Harvard: 1984) pp. 241-2

11   *Universals of Human Language* Vol 3: *Word structure* (Greenberg, J. H., Ferguson, C. A. Moravcsik, E. A. eds.) (Stanford: 1978) p. 417

12   Genesis 2:19

13   *Tool use in wild orang-utans modifies sound production: a functionally deceptive innovation?* Hardus, M. E. et al *Proceedings of the Royal Society B* October 2009 Vol. 276 Issue 1673

14   *Speaking Bonobo: Bonobos have an impressive vocabulary, especially when it comes to snacks* Raffaele, P. *Smithsonian Magazine* November 2006

Retrieved on 9 June 2015 from www.smithsonianmag.com/science-nature/speaking-bonobo-134931541/#0xwclt6JbTQdVqs6.99

15   Strong's, H8034

16   *Speaking Bonobo: Bonobos have an impressive vocabulary, especially when it comes to snacks* Raffaele, P. *Smithsonian Magazine* November 2006

Retrieved on 9 June 2015 from www.smithsonianmag.com/science-nature/speaking-bonobo-134931541/#0xwclt6JbTQdVqs6.99

17   *Who Asked the First Question? The Origins of Human Choral Singing, Intelligence, Language and Speech* Jordania, J. (Tbilisi: 2006) p. 335

18   *Orangutan Cultures and the Evolution of Material Culture* van Schaik, C. P. *Science* 3 January 2003 vol. 299, p. 102-105

19   *Culture and Cognitive Science* Prinz, J. *The Stanford Encyclopedia of Philosophy* (Winter 2011 Edition), Edward N. Zalta (ed.) Retrieved on 3 October 2015 from http://plato.stanford.edu/entries/culture-cogsci/

20   *Sumatran Orangutans Differ in Their Cultural Knowledge but Not in Their Cognitive Abilities* Gruber, T. et al 4 December 2012 Vol. 22, Issue 23, pp. 2231–2235

21   *Geographic variation in tool use on Neesia fruits in orangutans* van Schaik, C. P. & Knott, C. D. *Am J Phys Anthropol.* 2001 Apr;114(4) pp. 331-42.

22   *Colchester Zoo mandrill monkeys develop their own sign language* Tilley, C. *Colchester Daily Gazette*, 4 August 2011

23   *Orthographic Processing in Baboons (Papio papio)* Grainger, J. et al *Science* 336, 245 (2012) p. 247

24   *Language Comprehension in Ape and Child* Savage-Rumbaugh, E. S. et al *Monographs of the Society for Research in Child Development*, (1993) Vol. 58, No. 3/4, pp. 1-252

25   *Centre-embedded structures are a by-product of associative learning and working memory constraints: evidence from baboons (Papio papio)* Rey, A. et al (2012). Cognition 123, pp. 180–184.

26   *Finite models of infinite language: A connectionist approach to recursion* in *Connectionist psycholinguistics* M. H. Christiansen, & N. Chater (Eds.) (Westport: 2001) pp. 138–176.

27   *Centre-embedded structures are a by-product of associative learning and working memory constraints: evidence from baboons (Papio papio)* Rey, A. et al (2012) *Cognition* 123, pp. 180–184.

28   The Animal Communication Project website. Retrieved on 16 May 2015 from http://acp.eugraph.com/apes/

29 *The mind of an ape* Premack, D. & Premack, A. J. (1983). (New York: 1983) p. 29

30 *Who Asked the First Question? The Origins of Human Choral Singing, Intelligence, Language and Speech.* Jordania, J. (Tbilisi: 2006) p. 331

31 *The Life and Times of Leonardo* Hamlyn, P. p. 5 (*Feltham*: 1968)

32 *Being Human: Psychological and Philosophical Perspectives* Gross, R. (New York: 2013) p. 83

33 *Sex Differences in Object Manipulation in Wild Immature Chimpanzees (Pan troglodytes schweinfurthii) and Bonobos (Pan paniscus): Preparation for Tool Use?* Koops K. (2015) *PLoS ONE* 10(10)

34 *Gesture Use by Chimpanzees (Pan troglodytes): Differences Between Sexes* in *Inter- and Intra-Sexual Interactions Issue American Journal of Primatology* June 2013, Vol. 75, Issue 6, pp. 555–567

35 *Nonverbal Vocal Communication: Comparative and Developmental Approaches* Papousek, H. et al (Cambridge: 1992) p. 262

36 *Who Asked the First Question? The Origins of Human Choral Singing, Intelligence, Language and Speech.* Jordania, J. (Tbilisi: 2006) p. 341, 344

Note that not all questions in all languages use that inflection, but that infection is used in questions in all languages, including tonal languages. The final syllable of a Chinese sentence has its own tone, of course, but while its contour stays the same, the pitch of the whole syllable is still higher than in a declarative sentence. See mandarin.about.com/od/pronunciation/fl/Intonation-in-Mandarin-Chinese.htm

37 *Singing gibbons* Retrieved on October 16 2015, from www.youtube.com/watch?v=JLOn8F0p96s

38 Chinese Tongue Twister #1: Mother Rides a Horse Retrieved on 8 Novemeber 2015 from www.youtube.com/watch?v=SFwzqjfI8SM

39 *Who Asked the First Question? The Origins of Human Choral Singing, Intelligence, Language and Speech.* Jordania, J. (Tbilisi: 2006) p. 33

40 *Cultural Constraints on Grammar and Cognition in Pirahã: Another Look at the Design Features of Human Language* Everett, D. L. *Current Anthropology* Vol. 46, No. 4 (August/October 2005), pp. 621-646

41 *Yodel-Ay-Ee-Oooo: The Secret History of Yodeling Around the World* Plantenga, B. (New York: 2004)

42 *The singing origin theory of speech* Skoyles, J. R. The Evolution of Language: 3rd conference. April 3rd - 6th , 2000 Retrieved on 7 October 2015 from http://confs.infres.enst.fr//evolang/actes/_actes65.html

43 *Progress in Language* Jespersen, O. [1895] (Amsterdam: 1983) p. 365

44 *Essay on the Origin of Languages and Writings Related to Music* Rousseau, J. J. (Scott, J. T trans.). (Hanover: 2000).

45 *Left in music: Musicians' brains may use language modules listening to music* 13 August 2001 *Nature* Retrieved on 5 October 2015 from http://www.nature.com/news/1998/010816/full/news010816-4.html

46 Jordania, p. 349

47 Jordania, p. 308

48 Jordania, p. 324

49 Jordania, p. 16

50 This joke is dedicated to the magnificent Sister Rosetta Tharpe: https://www. youtube.com/watch?v=4xzr_GBa8qk&list=RD4xzr_GBa8qk

51 Comparative Anatomy of the Larynx in Man and the Chimpanzee: Implications for Language in Neanderthal Falk, D. (1975) Am. J. Phys. Anthrop., 43 (1)pp. 123-132.

52 Evolutionary and Genetic Biology of Primates, Vol. 2 *John* Buettner-Janusch (ed.) p. 218

53 There is one monkey that can escape via the trap door in the ceiling, called the capuchin, and curiously it is also almost the only New World monkey with a semi-opposable thumb.

54 *Primate Cognition* Tomasello, M. & Call, J. (Oxford: 1997) p. 82

55 *Morphological affinities of the Australopithecus afarensis hand on the basis of manual proportions and relative thumb length.* Alba, D. M. et al *J Hum Evol.* 2003 Feb;44(2):225-54.

56 McGilchrist, p. 111

57 *Gesture, Speech and Lexical Analysis: The Role of Lexical Movements in Speech Production* Rauscher, F. H. et al Psychological Science, vol. 7, no. 4, July 1996

58 McGilchrist, p. 100

59 *The humanity switch: How one gene made us brainier New Scientist* 3 May 2012 Retrieved on 9 February 2016 from www.newscientist.com/article/dn21777-the-humanity-switch-how-one-gene-made-us-brainier/

60 *Evolution of Human-Specific Neural SRGAP2 Genes by Incomplete Segmental Duplication* Dennis, M. Y. et al. *Cell*, Vol. 149 , Issue 4 , pp. 912-922

61 McGilchrist, p. 248

62 *New Hominid Ancestor Lived 3.7 Million Years Ago* Sullivan, J. *Cosmoso* 7 April 2015 Retrieved on 13 December 2015 from http://cosmoso.net/new-hominid-ancestor-lived-3-7-million-years-ago/

63 Genesis 3:7

64 *Size of sexual swellings reflects ovarian function in chimpanzees (Pan troglodytes)* Thompson, M. E. *Behav Ecol Sociobiol* (2003) 54:340–351

65 *Sexual signalling in female crested macaques and the evolution of primate fertility signals* Higham, J. P. *BMC Evolutionary Biology* 2012, 12:89

66 *Bateman Revisited: The Reproductive Tactics of Female Primates* Drea, C. M. *Integrative & Comparative Biology* vol. 45, is. 5 pp. 915-923

67 *Ovulation symptoms and signs* Retrieved on 5 October 2015 from http://infertility.answers.com/detecting-fertility/identifying-early-symptoms-to-show-you-are-ovulating

68 *Origin of Clothing: Lice Indicates Early Clothing Use by Anatomically Modern Humans in Africa* Toups, M. A. et al. *Molecular Biology and Evolution*, 2010; 28 (1): 29

69 Genesis 3:7. Or 'aprons' if you prefer, if you're a weirdo Mason or something.

70 *Lethal Wounds Suggest Spain's Pit of Bones Was a Burial Site* 27 May 2015 Retrieved on 17 January 2016 from www.archaeology.org/news/3318-150527-spain-cranium-blows

71 *Just How Much Sex Are We Talking About?* Mooney, C. *Discover Magazine* 4 June 2010 Retrieved on 5 October 2015 from http://blogs.discovermagazine.com/intersection/2010/06/04/just-how-much-sex-are-we-talking-about/#.VhG4VsvoU5M

72 *Rabbinic Fantasies: Imaginative Narratives from Classical Hebrew Literature* Stern, D. & Mirsky, M. J. (Philadelphia: 1990) pp. 183-184.

73 Genesis 3:18-19

74 Genesis 4:5-6 (NIV)

75 *Why do chimps kill each other?* Michael Balter Sciencemag.org 17 September 2014 Retrieved 12 January 2015 from http://news.sciencemag.org/plants-animals/2014/09/why-do-chimps-kill-each-other

76 *Through a Window: My Thirty Years with the Chimpanzees of Gombe* Goodall, J. (Boston: 1990) pp. 129-30

77 *Meditation on Emptiness* Hopkins, J. (Wisdom Publications: 1996) p. 438

78 *Principia Discordia, or, How I found goddess and what I did to her when I found her* Malaclypse, the Younger (Port Townsend, WA: 1990) section 3

79 Genesis 4:9

Notes for chapter 12: Lord of the Apes

1 *C. G. Jung Letters* Vol. 1 (Hull, R. F.C. trans.) (Princeton: 1992) pp. 65

2 Genesis 3:8

3 Strong's, H7307

4 Ezekiel 11:5

5 Strong's, H1980

6 Psalm 42:7

7 Isaiah 24:18

8 *2* Samuel 14:17

9 Pers comm. With Yeshiva Online, Retrieved on 20 November 2015 from http://www.yeshiva.co/ask/?id=7809

10 *Experimental facilitation of the sensed presence is predicted by the specific patterns of the applied magnetic fields, not by suggestibility: re-analyses of 19 experiments* St-Pierre L. S. & Persinger M.A. *Int J Neurosci.* 2006 Sep;116(9), pp. 1079-96.

11   *This is your brain on God* Hitt, J. *Wired Magazine*, 11 January 1999.

12   Retrieved on 25 February 2016 from www.psychforums.com/dissociative-identity/topic94279.html#p879858

13   Retrieved on 25 February 2016 from www.psychforums.com/dissociative-identity/topic94279.html

14   Retrieved on 25 February 2016 from www.psychforums.com/dissociative-identity/topic94279.html

15   Retrieved on 25 February 2016 from http://www.mind.org.uk/information-support/types-of-mental-health-problems/hearing-voices/#.V8tz2hSVNE0

16   Retrieved on 25 February 2016 from www.psychforums.com/dissociative-identity/topic94279.html

17   Retrieved on 25 February 2016 from http://www.mind.org.uk/information-support/types-of-mental-health-problems/hearing-voices/#.V8tz2hSVNE0

18   Retrieved on 24 June 2016 from www.cdc.gov/ncbddd/tourette/data.html

19   *The Reason I Jump* Higashida, N. & Mitchell, D. (New York: 2007) p. 79

20   *The Zohar* 31:236

21   Genesis 7:21

22   Genesis 8

23   Genesis 8:21

24   Genesis 9:4-6

25   *Rituals Enhance Consumption* Kathleen D. Vohs et al. *Psychological Science* September 2013 vol. 24 no. 9 pp. 1714-1721

26   *Does spirituality as a coping mechanism help or hinder coping with chronic pain?* Wachholtz, A. B. & Pearce, M. J. *Current Pain and Headache Reports* April 2009, Volume 13, Issue 2, pp. 127-132

27   *Prayer, Attachment to God, and Symptoms of Anxiety-Related Disorders among U.S. Adults* Ellison, C. G. *Sociology of Religion* 2014, 75:2 pp. 208-233

28   Genesis 17:1-8

29   Genesis 17:14

30   *Polytheism and Human Sacrifice in Early Israelite Religion Huffington Post* 11 October 2010 http://www.huffingtonpost.com/valerie-tarico/polytheism-and-human-sacr_b_777340.html

31   Genesis 22

32   Retrieved on 26 February 2016 from www.mentalhealth.org.uk/a-to-z/h/hearing-voices

33   Genesis 22:1-12

34   Genesis 18:23

35   *A History of Biblical Interpretation*, Vol. 2: *The Medieval Though the Reformation Periods* Hauser, A. J. & Watson, D. F. (Michigan: 2009) p. 213

36   Genesis 3:5

37   Genesis 32

NOTES

38 Genesis 1:22; Genesis 24:35

39 *The Name Israel in the Bible* Retrieved on 8 January 2015 from hwww.abarim-publications.com/Meaning/Israel.html

40 Strong's, H3290

41 Genesis 32:29

42 Genesis 32:32

43 Genesis 32:29-30

44 *When Fear Makes Us Superhuman: Can an extreme response to fear give us strength we would not have under normal circumstances?* Wise, J. *Scientific American* 28 December 2009

45 *Some factors modifying the expression of human strength* Ikai, M. & Steinhaus, A. H. *Journal of Applied Physiology* 1 January 1961 Vol. 16 no. 1, pp. 157-163

46 *Faced With a Crisis, Super Power Kicks In* 30 October, 2005 Minaya, M. *The Baltimore Sun* Retrieved on 23 November 2015 from articles.latimes.com/2005/oct/30/news/adna-heroics30

47 Retrieved on 26 February 2016 from http://wrongplanet.net/forums/viewtopic.php?t=153098&sid=3c3885236c57fc570e58482509ac895b

48 *Deep Survial: Who lives, Who Dies and Why* Gonzales, L. (New York: 2003) pp. 218-219

49 *Deep Survial: Who lives, Who Dies and Why* Gonzales, L. (New York: 2003) pp. 241-243

50 *2004 Tsunami: Petra Nemcova, the supermodel who survived the Boxing Day Tragedy* Sherwell, P. *The Telegraph*, 26 December 2014, Retrieved on 22 December 2015 from www.telegraph.co.uk/news/worldnews/asia/thailand/11303121/2004-Tsunami-Petra-Nemcova-the-supermodel-who-survived-the-Boxing-Day-tragedy.html

51 *Post-traumatic growth and life threatening physical illness: A systematic review of the qualitative literature* Hefferon, K. et al *British Journal of Health Psychology* (2009), 14, pp. 343–378

52 *Aleister Crowley's Illustrated Goetia: SexuaL Evocation* DuQuette, L. M. & Hyatt, C. S. (Arizona: 200) p. 24

53 *The Mind of Mahatma Gandhi* (Prabhu and Rao, eds.), (1967) pp. 33-34

54 Genesis 32:31

55 Strong's, H6215

56 *Logotherapy as a Response to the Holocaust* Bulka, R. P. *Journal of Orthodox Thought* (1975) 15 (1-2): 89-96 pp. 117

57 *Logotherapy as a Response to the Holocaust* Bulka, R. P. *Journal of Orthodox Thought* (1975) 15 (1-2): 89-96 pp. 89-95

58 *Sigmund Says: And Other Psychotherapists' Quotes* Nisenholz, B. (New York: 2006) p. 80

59 Exodus 4:10 (with more literal translation)

60   *The Stuttering Servant* Davidkin, S. 12 April, 2012 *Jewish Ideas Daily.*
     Retrieved on 22 December 2015 from www.jewishideasdaily.com/1109/features/
     the-stuttering-servant/

61   Strong's, H6189

62   *Nature and nurture in stuttering: A systematic review on the case of Moses* Leon-
     Sarmiento, F. E. et al *Neurological Sciences* 34(2) March 2012

63   Exodus 4:12

64   Exodus 6:7

65   Genesis 17

66   *Brain-wise: Studies in Neurophilosophy* Churchland, P. S. (London: 2002) p. 73

67   Genesis 17

68   *Snakes taking care of little things* ABC News. Retrieved on 14 February 2016 from
     www.abc.net.au/news/2005-09-18/snakes-taking-care-of-the-little-things/2105924

69   *How Our Brain Works: The Construction and Functionality of Your Brain
     Presented and Explained* Millers, D. A. (New York: 2010) pp. 239-240

70   Genesis 22:11

71   Exodus 34:27

72   Exodus 34:11

73   Psalm 103:8 (NIV)

74   Exodus 15:3 (NLT)

75   *Long Walk To Freedom* Mandela, N. (London: 1994), from the conclusion.

76   *Traumatic experiences in childhood and psychopathy: a study on a sample of
     violent offenders from Italy* Craparo, G. et al *Eur J Psychotraumatol.* 2013; 4

77   *Super Strength: Daughter Rescues Dad Pinned Under Car* Newcomb, A.
     ABC News Retrieved on 16 February 2016 from http://abcnews.go.com/US/
     superhero-woman-lifts-car-off-dad/story?id=16907591#.UMay9Hfeba4

78   *Polar bear no match for fearsome mother in Ivujivik: Lydia Angyiou unharmed
     after hand-to-hand street fight* February 17, 2006 Retrieved on 2 September
     2015 from www.nunatsiaqonline.ca/archives/60217/news/nunavut/60217_03.
     html

79   *The Power of Love* Lewis, H. et nuntium.

80   *Stalin: The Murderous Career of the Red Tsar* Cawthorne, N. (London: 2012)
     chapter 6

81   *Why Do Animals Sometimes Kill Their Babies?* Morell, V. *National Geographic*
28 March, 2014. Retrieved on 9 February 2016 from http://news.nationalgeographic.
     com/news/2014/03/140328-sloth-bear-zoo-infanticide-chimps-bonobos-animals/

82   Exodus 34:23

83   Exodus 12:36

84   Numbers 31

85   Genesis 2:7

86 Genesis 2:19

87 Exodus 34:13

88 *History of the Jews: From the Earliest Period to the Death of Simon the Maccabee (135 B.C.E.)* Graetz, H. (Philadelphia: 2002) p. 233

89 *The Near East, the Cradle of Western Civilization* Salem, S. I. & Salem, L. A. (San Jose: 2000) pp. 134, 162

90 Exodus 34:27-28

91 *The Indian Express* Mar 4, 1943

92 *Gandhi's Final Fast* Simeon, D. 22 March 22 2010 Retrieved on 5 October from www.gandhitopia.org/profiles/blogs/gandhis-final-fast-by-dilip

93 Exodus 34

94 Leviticus 24:17

95 *Why Everyone Should Oppose Ten Commandments In Public Schools - Especially Religious People Huffington Post* 13 May 2013, Retrieved on 31 October 2015, when I should have been out at a party in my gasmask codpiece rather than sitting in front of a computer, from www.huffingtonpost.com/paul-raushenbush/ten-commandments-public-schools_b_3266522.html

96 Exodus 2:12, 3:18, 11:2-3, Numbers 31:15-18

97 Exodus 2, Numbers 31

98 Exodus 12:35

99 Exodus 20:4

100 Exodus 32:10, 19

101 Exodus 34:17

102 Exodus 25:18

103 Genesis 2:17

104 Genesis 27:11-29

105 Genesis 25: 31-34

106 Genesis 19:8

107 Exodus 34:6-7

108 Ezekiel 18:19-20 (modified for clarity)

109 *This Be The Verse* in *Philip Larkin Poems: Selected by Martin Amis* Larkin, P.

110 *Fifth of school leavers 'illiterate and innumerate' The Telegraph*, Paton, G. Retrieved on 1 December 2015 from www.telegraph.co.uk/education/educationnews/7691919/Fifth-of-school-leavers-illiterate-and-innumerate.html

111 *The Incidence of Child Abuse in Serial Killers* Mitchell, H. & Aamodt, M. G. *Journal of Police and Criminal Psychology*, 2005, Vol. 20, No. 1

112 *The Freud Encyclopedia: Theory, Therapy, and Culture* Erwin, E. (New York: 2002) p. 447

113 *Domestic violence: the facts* Retrieved on 3 February 2016 from www.refuge.org.uk/get-help-now/what-is-domestic-violence/domestic-violence-the-facts/

114 *The Brain from Top to Bottom* Retrieved on 4 February 2016 from http://thebrain.mcgill.ca/flash/i/i_05/i_05_cr/i_05_cr_her/i_05_cr_her.html

115 Zechariah 14:1-2

116 Isaiah 2:4

117 Ezekiel 29, 30:12, 26.

118 Ezekiel 29:10

119 Josiah 15:63 neatened a little

120 Joshua 15:63

121 Judges 1:19

122 Job 1:6-8

123 Strong's, H7854

124 Job 2:7

125 Job 31:37 (NLT)

126 Job 13:15 (HNV)

127 *The New Oxford Annotated Bible with the Apocrypha* (1977), quoted in *Translation issues in Job* 13:15 Retrieved on 6 Octber 2015 from massbible.org/job-translation-question

128 Job 13:15 (KJV)

129 *Arguing with God, Talmudic Discourse, and the Jewish Countermodel: Implications for the study of Argumentation* Frank, D. A. in *Argumentation and Advocacy* 41 (Fall 2004): p. 80

130 *Tractate Baba Metzia* 59a

131 Strong's, H6635

132 *Lenin V. I., Full collection of Writings* Vol. 50. p.178. (translation pers. com by Dmitry Klochkov)

133 Retrieved on 13 April 2016 from http://military.wikia.com/wiki/Tambov_Rebellion

134 *The "Russian" Civil Wars, 1916-1926: Ten Years That Shook the World* Smele, J. (Oxford: 2015) chapter 5

135 *Rescuing Memory: the Humanist Interview with Noam Chomsky* Majfud, J28 June 2016. Retrieved on 13 July 2016 from http://thehumanist.com/magazine/july-august-2016/features/rescuing-memory

136 *Joseph Campbell, An Open Life: Joseph Campbell in Conversation with Michael Toms* (Maher, J. M & Briggs, D. eds)(New York: 1990) p. 28-29

137 Retrieved on 2 December 2015 from www.enoughproject.org/conflicts/eastern_congo

138 *What is the role of individual human beings in today's society?* TV Interview, Buenos Aires 1985. 12.25 Retrieved on 13 December 2015 from www.youtube.com/watch?v=Gc_COGWKKg8#t=798

139 Exodus 34:28

Notes for chapter 13: The Bricks of Babylon

1   Genesis 11:1-3

2   *Legends of the Jews* Ginzberg, L. Vol 1, chap. 4

3   Ezekiel 4:1

4   *Important Breakthrough in Biblical Archaeology* British Museum Press Release, Retrieved on 9 March 2015 from www.britishmuseum.org/about_us/news_and_press/press_releases/2007/biblical_archaeology_find.aspx

5   Genesis 11:1-4

6   Genesis 11:1-4

7   Genesis 11:1-4

8   *A New Testament Word Book: A Glossary* Partridge, E. (New York: 2015) p. 12

9   *Number of Laws.* Retrieved on 9 March 2015 from http://en.euabc.com/word/2152

10   *Travel disruption and floods warnings as South East hit by more rain*

23 June 2016 BBC news, Retrieved on 6 July 2016 from www.bbc.co.uk/news/uk-36603508

11   *HMRC trialling maps to decode 'galaxy' of British tax laws The Independent* 29 December 2015 Retrieved on 23 March 2016 from www.independent.co.uk/news/uk/home-news/hmrc-trialling-maps-to-decode-galaxy-of-british-tax-laws-a6790051.html

12   *A reminder that HMRC actually rents its offices from a company registered in a tax haven The Indy*, 6 April 2016 Retrieved on 14 April 20016 from http://indy100.independent.co.uk/article/a-reminder-that-hmrc-actually-rents-its-offices-from-a-company-registered-in-a-tax-haven--bJ2PgGt9eZ

Notes for chapter 14: DeuterAnarchy

1   Jeremiah 8:8 (HNV), modified to remove the work of later false pens

2   *Were Jews ever really slaves in Egypt, or is Passover a myth?* Mintz, J. *Haaretz*, 26 March, 2012, Retrieved on 7 June 2015 from www.haaretz.com/jewish-world/the-jewish-thinker/were-jews-ever-really-slaves-in-egypt-or-is-passover-a-myth-1.420844

3   *The Garden of Eden Myth: Its Pre-Biblical Origin in Mesopotamian Myths* Mattfeld, W. (2010) pp. 5-6

4   *Bible Myths and their Parallels in Other Religions* Doane, T. W. (7th ed.) (Montana: 1997) chapter 11

5   *Sumerian Mythology: A Study of Spiritual and Literary Achievement in the Third Millennium B.C.* Kramer, S. N. (Philadelphia: 1961) p. 33-34

6   *Bible Myths and their Parallels in Other Religions* Doane, T. W. (7th ed.) (Montana: 1997) chapter 2

7   *The Origin and Historical Background of Several Amarna Letters* Na'aman, N. in Bergerhof, K. et al. (eds.): UF, Vol. XI (Neukirchen: 1979), pp. 274-5

8   *Light from the Ancient Past*, Vol. 1: The Archaeological Background of the Hebrew-Christian Religion, Vol. 1. Finegan, J. (Princeton: 1969) p. 56

9   *The Ancient Near East: An Anthology of Texts and Pictures* (Pritchard, J. B. ed.) (Princeton: 1958) p. 261

10   *The Dictionary Of The Bible* Mckenzie, J. L. (New York: 1965) p. 346

11   *Bitter Lives: Israel in and out of Egypt* Redmount., C. A. in *The Oxford History of the Biblical World*, Michael D. Coogan, ed., (New York: 2001), p. 72

12   Exodus 9, 10, 12, Numbers 31

13   *The Eastern Mediterranean in the Age of Ramesses II* Van De Mieroop, M. (Oxford: 2007) p. 49

14   See Armana letters retrieved on 12 March 2016 from www.bible.ca/archeology/bible-archeology-maps-conquest-amarna-tablets-letters-akhenaten-habiru-abiru-hebrews-1404-1340bc.htm

Quotation from Amarna Letter EA 287, quoted in The Amarna Letters Moran, W. L. (Baltimore: 1992), pp. 327-28. Edited for clarity, from "all the lands are at peace [with one another], but I am at war... They [the Habiru] have given them [my enemies] food, oil and any other requirement. So may the king [Pharaoh] provide for archers."

15   *Amarna Letter EA 286*, from *A Survey of Old Testament* Archer, G. introduction (Chicago: 1985), p. 275.

16   *The Bible Unearthed: Archaeology's New Vision of Ancient Israel and the Origin of Its Sacred Texts* Finkelstein, I. & Silberman, N. A. (New York: 2001), p. 107

17   *Introduction to the Old Testament* Pfeiffer, R. H. (London: 1952) p. 155

18   *The Cult of the Bronze Serpents in Ancient Canaan and Israel* Münnich, M. in IGGUD) *Selected Essays in Jewish Studies*: Vol 1: The Bible and its World (2011) (Schwartz, B. J. ed)

19   *The Khirbet el-Kom Inscription* Shea, W. H. Vetus Testamentum 40 (1990), pp. 56–63.

20   *Ancient DNA and Population Turnover in Southern Levantine Pigs - Signature of the Sea Peoples Migration?* Meirav, M. et al. *Scientific Reports*, 2013; 3

21   *The Bible Unearthed: Archaeology's New Vision of Ancient Isreal and the Origin of its Sacred Texts* Finkelstein, I. & Silberman, N. A. (New York: 2001) p. 119

22   Judges 2:18

23   *Tractate Yoma* 21b describes the urim and thummim used until at least the time of the Temple of Solomon

24   Judges 21:25

25   1 Samuel 8:7

26   1 Kings 3:16-28

27   *The Judean Pillar-Figurines and the Archaeology of Asherah* Kletter, R. *British Archaeological Reports*, International Series S-636 (1996).

28   1 Chronicles 8:33-34

29   *Composition of the Book of Psalms.* The Columbia Electronic Encyclopedia (2013). Columbia University Press 13 Dec. 2015 Retrieved on 13 December 2015 from http://encyclopedia2.thefreedictionary.com/Composition+of+the+Book+of+*Psalm*s

30   Psalm 86

31   *Adonai* Kohler, K. *Jewish Encyclopedia 1906* Retrieved on 16 June 2016 from http://www.jewishencyclopedia.com/articles/840-adonai

32   *Who Wrote the Bible?* Friedman, R. E. (New York: 1997) p. 72

33   Exodus 12:12, 18:11

34   Genesis 9:6

35   *The Tao Te Ching of Lao Tzu* (Walker, B. B. trans.) (New York: 1985) chapter 74

36   *Torah and Mathematics: The Story of π* Ginsburgh, H. Y. Retrieved on 20 October 2015 from http://www.mywesternwall.net/wp-content/uploads/sites/4/2014/04/story-of-pi-1.pdf

37   *Moving and Lifting the Construction Blocks of the Great Pyramid* Baldridge, J. (1996) Retrieved on 13 October 2015 from www.ling.upenn.edu/~jason2/papers/pyramid.htm

38   1 Samuel 18:27

39   2 Chronicles 9:22

40   2 Chronicles 9

41   1 Kings 11:3

42   1 Kings 12:10-11

43   1 Kings 12:19

44   1 Kings 12:19

45   Exodus 20:10

46   *Who Wrote the Bible?* Friedman, R. E. (New York: 1997) p. 250

47   *The First Book of God* Yoreh, T. L. (New York: 2010) p. 67

48   *Who Wrote the Bible?* Friedman, R. E. (New York: 1997) p. 250

49   *The Old and the New Magic* Ridgley, H. (Chicago: 2006) introduction, part X.

50   *Suzerain Treaties & The Covenant Documents the Bible* Notes from lectures of Dr. Meredith Kline, presented at Westminster Theological Seminary in Escondido, California

51   Exodus 20:2

52   Exodus 20:5b-6; 7b; 12b

53   Deuteronomy 22:22 & Hammurabi Code, laws, 2, 3, 21, 22, 129, 195

54   *The* Exodus *Is Not Fiction: An interview with Richard Elliott Friedman* Reform Judaism website. Retrieved on 13 December 2015 from http://www.reformjudaism.org/exodus-not-fiction

55 *The History of Circumcision* Dunsmuir, W. D. & Gordon, E. M. January, 1999 BJU International, Volume 83, Suppl. 1: pp. 1-12, 1

56 *Ancient Egyptian Medicine* Hanafy, M. H. et al in *Urology* 1974;1 pp. 114-120

57 *Who Wrote the Bible?* Friedman, R. E. (New York: 1997) p. 251

58 *Who Wrote the Bible?* Friedman, R. E. (New York: 1997) p. 118

59 Numbers 5:27

60 *Who Wrote the Bible?* Friedman, R. E. (New York: 1997) pp. 247-255

61 *The Origins of Biblical Monotheism: Israel's Polytheistic Background and the Ugaritic Texts* Smith, M. S. (Oxford: 2001) p.167

62 *The Babylonian Genesis* Heidel, A. (London: 1951) p. 100

63 *Who Wrote the Bible?* Friedman, R. E. (New York: 1997) pp. 247

64 Strong's, H7200

65 Strong's, H3070

66 2 Chronicles 31

67 *The Non-Israelite Nations in the Book of the Twelve: Thematic Coherence and the Diachronic-Synchronic Relationship in the Minor Prophets* Timmer, D. (Boston: 2105) p. 121

68 2 Kings 22:8

69 2 Kings 22:11

70 2 Kings 23

71 2 Kings 23

72 Deuteronomy 12:11- 17 Note, there are some contradictions in this chapter that are unpicked at http://contradictionsinthebible.com/non-sacrificial-slaughter-prohibited-or-not/ Retrieved 25 October 2015.

73 *Who Wrote the Bible?* Friedman, R. E. (New York: 1997) p. 102

74 *The Book of Josiah's Reform* Malick, D. Retrieved on 20 October 2015 from https://bible.org/article/book-josiahs-reform

75 Deuteronomy 25:11-12

76 *Revealed: how developers exploit flawed planning system to minimise affordable housing The Guardian*, 25 June 2015. Retrieved on 24 June 2016 from www.theguardian.com/cities/2015/jun/25/london-developers-viability-planning-affordable-social-housing-regeneration-oliver-wainwright

77 *Bristol City council must support the community and reject Tesco* Allen, S. *The Guardian* 22 April 2011 Retrieved on 15 April 2016, from www.theguardian.com/commentisfree/2011/apr/22/bristol-riot-tesco

78 Exodus 21:28-29, 22:1, Deuteronomy 22:22, Leviticus 20:17, 24:20 & Hammurabi Code, laws 8, 129, 154, 155, 251

79 Leviticus 24:20

80 *Hammurabi Code*, laws 196-200

81 *Who Wrote the Bible?* Friedman, R. E. (New York: 1997) p. 117

NOTES

82   *Who Wrote the Bible?* Friedman, R. E. (New York: 1997) p. 117

83   Osborne to focus budget on plan to turn all English schools into academies *The Guardian* 16 March 2016

84   Deuteronomy 18:10-12

85   1 Kings 11:4

86   A-ha! I jest!

87   2 Kings 22:2

88   *Who Wrote the Bible?* Friedman, R. E. (New York: 1997) p. 98

89   2 Chronicles 35:20–27

90   Psalm 137

91   *An Introduction to the Study of Isaiah* Stromberg, J. (London:2011) p. 89

92   *An Introduction to the Study of Isaiah* Stromberg, J. (London:2011) p. 2

93   Isaiah 45:7

94   *The Wiley Blackwell Companion to Zoroastrianism* (Stausberg, M. & Vevaina, Y. S-D eds.) (Wiley Blackwell: 2015) p. 215

95   Job 1

96   Revelations 12:9

97   Strong's, H776

98   Daniel 12, Job 1. There is only one mention of 'last days' in Genesis (49:1), but it could be read 'later days', and the chapter envisions no final reckonings.

99   *An Introduction to the Study of Isaiah* Stromberg, J. (London:2011) p. 94

100 Daniel 9:21, 10:13

101 *Demons & Demonology* Jewish Virtual Library Retrieved on 15 April 2016, from www.jewishvirtuallibrary.org/jsource/Judaism/demons.html

102 *The Persian Presence in the Islamic World* (Hovannisian, R. G. & Sabagh, G. eds) (Cambridge: 1998) p. 30

103 *Introduction to Avestan* García, J. M. & de Vaan, M. P. (Leiden: 2014) p. xi

104 *The Whirlwind: Essays on Job, Hermeneutics and Theology in Memory of Jane Morse* (Stephen L. Cook, Corrine L. Patton, James W. Watts eds) (London: 2001) p. 64

105 Compare Masoretic Jeremiah 27:6 with *Septaguint* 34:6

106 Isaiah 45:1

107 Ezra 1:2-3 (HNV and Nemu)

108 *Tractate Kutim* 28. The Samaritans later adopted this belief from their Muslim neighbours.

109 Ezra 4:3

110 Ezra 6

111 Ezra 4:13

112 2 Kings 12

113 *Introduction to reading the Pentateuch* Ska, J-L. (Indiana: 2006). p. 218

114 *The Governers of Judah under the Persians* Williamson, H. G. M. *Tyndale Bulletin* 39 (1988) pp. 59-82.

115 Ezra 7:25

116 Ezra 7:16

117 Ezra 7:26

118 *Persians* Retrieved on 13 March 2016 from www.jewishvirtuallibrary.org/jsource/History/Persians.html

119 *Who Wrote the Bible? Friedman, R. E. (New York: 1997)* pp. 223-5

120 *Blessed Are You: A Comprehensive Guide to Jewish Prayer* Cohen, J. M., (New Jersey: 1993), p. 135

121 Nehemiah 2:9, Deuteronomy 23:2

122 *Tractate Shabbos* 110b–111a

123 *From Babylon to Bethlehem: The Jewish People from the Exile to the Messiah* Ellison, H. L. (Exeter: 1976) chapter 7

124 *1* Samuel 8:7

125 *Persian Religion in the Achaemenid Age* in *The Cambridge History of Judaism* I, Boyce, M. pp. 279-307.

126 *Talmud & Middle Persian Culture* Elman, Y. *Encyclopedia Judaica* 2008 Retrieved on 13 December 2015 from www.jewishvirtuallibrary.org/jsource/judaica/ejud_0002_0019_0_19548.html

127 Acts 23:8

128 *The International Standard Bible Encyclopedia*, Vol. 4 Bromiley, G. W. (Grand Rapids: 1988) p. 278

129 *History of the Calendar Jewish Encyclopedia* (1906) Retrieved on 13 December 2015 from http://jewishencyclopedia.com/articles/3920-calendar-history-of

130 *The Science of Sexism: Primate Behavior and the Culture of Sexual Coercion* Johnson, E. M. 20 July 2011 *Scientific American*. Retrieved on 18 April 2016 from http://blogs.scientificamerican.com/primate-diaries/httpblogsscientificamericancomprimate-diaries20110720science-of-sexism/

131 *Prostitution and Sex Crimes* Cundiff, K. R. 8 April 2004, Idependent Institute, Working Paper #50. Retrieved on 17 April 2016 from www.independent.org/publications/working_papers/article.asp?id=1300

132 2 Kings 23:7

133 Serious repeat offenders at record high 24 May 2012 *The Telegraph* Whitehead, T. Retrieved on 18 April 2016 from http://www.telegraph.co.uk/news/uknews/9287772/Serious-repeat-offenders-at-record-high.html

134 *Jewish Calendar is Slowly Drifting Off Track* ben Ya'aqov, M. 16 Feb 2010. Retrieved on 13 December 2015 from http://yourjerusalem.org/2010/02/jewish-calendar-is-slowly-drifting-off-track/

135 *Tractate Makkoth* 23b

136 Retrieved on 10 October 2015 from http://judaism.stackexchange.com/ questions/38524/should-one-say-asher-yatzar-when-giving-a-urine-sample

137 Mark 2:27

138 John 8:7

139 Matthew 26:52

140 Matthew 22:37-39

141 Matthew 5:17

142 Strong's, G4137

143 Matthew 5:38-42

144 *Talmud Sanhedrin* 58b, Deuteronomy 27:24

145 Matthew 5:38-42

146 Deuteronomy 24:13

147 Leviticus 18:6-18, Genesis 9:22-23, *Habakkuk* 2:15

148 Matthew 5:38-42

149 *The Love of Enemy and Nonretaliation in the New Testament* (Swartley, W. M. ed) (Louisville: 1992) p. 108

150 *Restoring the Shamed: Towards a Theology of Shame* Stockitt, R. (Oregon: 2012)

151 Strong's, G436

152 Exodus 21:23-24

153 *The Gospel of Matthew*, Duling, D. C. in *The Blackwell Companion to the New Testament* Aune, D. E. (Wiley-Blackwell: 2010) pp. 298-299

154 The Great *Revolt* Retrieved on 22 October 2015 from www.jewishvirtuallibrary. org/jsource/Judaism/revolt.html

155 *The Gospel of Judas*, published by the National Geographic Society, 2006

156 *St. Iranaeus of Lyon, Against Heresies: The Sethian-Ophites, A.D. 180* in, Barnstone, W. *The Other Bible*. San Francisco, CA., 1984. p.664

157 *Gnostic Gospels* Pagels, E. (New York: 1986) p. 60

158 *Against Heresies* Irenaeus of Lyons, 1.13.3 Retrieved on 27 October 2015 from http://www.earlychristianwritings.com/irenaeus.html

159 *Romans* 12:6

160 *The Apocalypse of Peter* (Brashler, J. & Bullard, R. A. trans.)

161 *The Apocalypse of Adam* (George W. MacRae trans.)

162 *The Pistis Sophia*

163 *Hypostasis of the Archons*

164 *The Demiurge in Valentinianism* Brons, D. The Gnostic Society Library, Retrieved on 26 November 2015 from www.gnosis.org/library/valentinus/ Demiurge.htm

165 *The Gospel of Philip* (Isenberg, W. W. trans.) Retrieved on 26 November 2015 from www.gnosis.org/naghamm/gop.html

166 *The Gospel of Mary* 4: 38

167 *Against Heresies* Irenaeus of Lyons, 1.preface.2 Retrieved on 27 October 2015 from http://www.earlychristianwritings.com/irenaeus.html

168 *Trading Gods in Northern Italy*, Humphries, M. in Helen Parkins and Christopher Smith (eds), Trade, Traders and the Ancient City (London: 1998), pp. 203-24.

169 Ephesians 6

170 1 Peter 2:18-19 NLT

171 John 20

172 *Introduction to Gnosticism: Ancient Voices*, Christian Worlds, Lewis, N. D. (Oxford: 2012)

173 *Corinthians* 14:37

174 *Against Heresies* Irenaeus of Lyons, 4.preface.2 Retrieved on 27 October 2015 from http://www.earlychristianwritings.com/irenaeus.html

175 *Money and Finance in Central Europe during the Later Middle Ages* (Zaoral, R., ed) (New York: 2016) p. 187

176 Retrieved on 9 May 2016 from https://yougov.co.uk/news/2015/11/03/do-you-believe-theres-good-and-evil/

177 *Correctional Populations   in the United States*, 2014 Kaeble, D. et al, U.S. Department of Justice: Office of Justice Programs Bureau of Justice Statistics BJS Bulletin December 2015, NCJ 249513

178 *Kesubos* 111a

179 *Kesubos* 111a-112b Rabbi Adin Steinsaltz, Orthodox Union website Retrieved on 24 April 2016 from www.ou.org/life/torah/masechet_ketubot_111112/

180 *Kesubos* 111a

181 *Zeal for Zion: Christians, Jews, & the Idea of the Promised Land* Goldman. S. (North Carolina: 2009) p. 272

182 Chief Rabbi Yehoshua Leib Diskin, Quoted on True Torah Jews Retrieved on 23 March 2016 from http://www.truetorahjews.org/diskin

183 *A Nazi Travels to Palestine* Boas, J. in *History Today* Vol. 30 Issue 1 January 1980 pp. 33-38

184 *The Years of Extermination: Nazi Germany and the Jews, 1939-1945* Friedländer, S. (New York: 2007) p. 304.

185 *The Holocaust Victims Accuse: Documents and Testimony on Jewish War Criminals* Shonfeld, M. (New York: 1977) p. 116

186 *Kesubos* 111a

187 *Pirates and Emperors, Old and New: International Terrorism in the Real World* Chomsky, N. (Cambridge MA: 2002) pp. 136-137

188 *The Terrorist Trap: America's Experience with Terrorism* Simon, J. D. (Indiana: 2001) p .45

189 *The Terrorist Trap: America's Experience with Terrorism* Simon, J. D. (Indiana: 2001) p .45

190 *Triumph of Military Zionism: Nationalism and the Origins of the Israeli Right* Shindler, C. (New York: 2010) pp. 217-218

191 Israeli Defense Force website, retrieved on 26 June 2016 from www.idf.il/1503-en/Dover.aspx

192 *IDF Orders West Bank Village Land Seized for Settler Road* Levinson, C. in *Ha-Aretz*, retrieved on 26 June 2016 from http://www.haaretz.com/israel-news/.premium-1.609313

193 Israeli Decorations Retrieved on 26 June 2016 from www.israelidecorations.net/MODServiceRibbons.htm

194 *The Controversy of Zion: Jewish Nationalism, the Jewish State, and the Unresolved Jewish Dilemma* Wheatcroft, G. (Addison Wesley: 1997)

195 Isaiah 11, *Kesubos* 111a

196 Neturei Karta, for example. www.nkusa.org

197 Isaiah 42:6

198 *Jihad: A Misunderstood Concept from Islam* The Islamic Supreme Council of America. Retrieved on 24 April 2016 from www.islamicsupremecouncil.org/understanding-islam/legal-rulings/5-jihad-a-misunderstood-concept-from-islam.html?start=9

199 Retrieved on 26 February 2016 from www.babycenter.com/baby-names-jihad-485965.htm

200 Ezekiel 20:25

201 *Record Number of New Laws made in 2010*, 7 May 2011, BBC News. Retrieved on 9 March 2015 from http://www.bbc.co.uk/news/uk-politics-13569604

Notes for chapter 15: Live and Let Leviticus.

1   Psalm 118:22

2   Genesis 3:5

3   Genesis 3:4-5

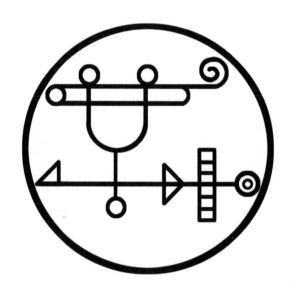